Estonians for Europe

National Activism for European Unification, 1922-1991

P.I.E. Peter Lang

Bruxelles • Bern • Berlin • Frankfurt am Main • New York • Oxford • Wien

Pauli Heikkilä

Estonians for Europe

National Activism for European Unification, 1922-1991

Multiple Europes
No. 54

Cover picture : © Google.

This publication has been peer-reviewed.

Éditions scientifiques internationales
Brussels, 2014
1 avenue Maurice, B-1050 Brussels, Belgium
www.peterlang.com; info@peterlang.com

Printed in Germany

ISSN 1376-0904
ISBN 978-2-87574-166-0
D/2014/5678/42

CIP available from the Library of Congress and the British Library, GB.

Bibliographic information published by "Die Deutsche Nationalbibliothek"

"Die Deutsche Nationalbibliothek" lists this publication in the "Deutsche Nationalbibliografie"; detailed bibliographic data is available on the Internet at <http://dnb.d-nb.de>.

Contents

Acknowledgements 9

INTRODUCTION. Expanding the History of European Integration 11

PART I
PANEUROPEAN DISCUSSION IN ESTONIA

CHAPTER 1. Paneuropean Union in Estonia 25

CHAPTER 2. Diplomatic Means 31

"This is the Aim of the Existing League of Nations" 31
Briand's Proposal of European Federation 34

CHAPTER 3. Economic Consequences 45

"Desire to Liberate Oneself from American Economic Hegemony" 45
Interlude of Regional Unions 51

CHAPTER 4. Cultural Premises 59

"It Demands a Common Spiritual Level for all Member Nations" 59
The Promise and Problem of the Baltic Region 66

CHAPTER 5. The Disintegrating 1930s 75

Tõnisson and Pusta in Geneva in September 1931 75
The Sunset of the Paneuropean Cross 77
The Rise of the Swastika 80

CHAPTER 6. Common Estonian Features in the Discussion 85

PART II
NAZI NEW EUROPE AND THE OCCUPIED ESTONIA

CHAPTER 1. Totalitarian Europe 91

Chapter 2. Aleksander Warma Consolidating Europe 97

Regional Unions of Small States 100
Peace as the Purpose of European Cooperation 103
Warma's Influence in Finland and in the United States 105

Chapter 3. Estonia in the New Europe 113

Part III
Estonian Emigrants in the European Movement

Chapter 1. The Estonian National Committee of the European Movement 117

Chapter 2. Creating Contacts and Joining 119

An Estonian at The Hague Congress 119
A Baltic Detour to Europe 124

Chapter 3. Inside the European Movement 133

The Central and Eastern European Commission 133
The Special Committee in the Council of Europe 140
European Culture and Anti-Communism 143
The Long Last Years in the European Movement 154

Chapter 4. The Outsider's View 167

Relations with American Organizations 167
Following the Economic Community 171

Chapter 5. Uniting the Divided Continent 179

Part IV
Conclusions

Estonians for European Union? 185

List of abbreviations 193

Bibliography 195

Indexes of places and persons 209

Acknowledgements

This monograph at hand is based on my doctoral thesis defended at the University of Turku in May 2011. The introduction with the list of articles is available here: [https://www.doria.fi/handle/10024/69598] (all the links presented in this book have been verified on August 4, 2013). The thesis consisted of six separate articles and they have been greatly modified, but not totally rewritten, for this publication. While articles represent condensed studies written on a certain question, this monograph allows greater elaboration for reasoning and presentation. Additional material has been used, especially when extending the original time frame of the thesis, which ended at 1957, to the whole period of the Cold War. This period now includes the Soviet occupation of Estonia in full.

I am grateful to the two official opponents of my original doctoral thesis, Docent Pertti Grönholm and Professor Andres Kasekamp, for their insightful comments and remarks, many of which improved the development of the project which was eventually finalized in this book.

Furthermore, the assistance and support provided by the following people: Timo Soikkanen, Vesa Saarikoski, Vesa Vares, Eero Medijainen, Hain Rebas, Heinz Duchhardt, Idesbald Goddeeris, Thijs Rommens, Kari Alenius, Anita Ziegerhofer-Prettenthaler, Toivo Nygård, Tuija Saresma, Jari Ojala, Juha Sihvola, Louis Clerc, Jan Hecker-Stamphel and Simo Klem deserves my acknowledgement as each one of these individuals was kindly on hand to help me with various issues on various occasions as this project was on its way to fruition. Additionally, as the dissertation writing process progressed, many editors and anonymous referees have commented on articles and thus contributed to its improvement and eventual publication. I am also grateful to Peter Lang and series editor, Hagen Schulz-Forberg, for accepting this book for publication within the series Europe plurielle/Multiple Europes.

The most significant portion of funding for my research came from Niilo Helanderin Säätiö, which provided two annual scholarships. Additionally, Turun Yliopistosäätiö, Suomen Akatemia and Alfred Kordelinin Säätiö provided travel grants. Both the scholarship at the Institute of European History in Mainz and my time as International Scholar at the KU Leuven were decisively important as I completed my doctoral thesis. With the thesis subsequently defended, I was to benefit from a month-long scholarship at the Herder-Institute in Marburg.

Briefly returning to this book's beginnings, my dissertation project started many years ago through the European Community Action Scheme for the Mobility of University Students at the University of Tartu. With my doctoral dissertation defended, I was to again return to Tartu to pursue a post-doctoral project on Estonian emigrant groups. Hence, the final phase of this research project was supported by the European Union through the European Social Fund (Mobilitas grant No. MJD259). It was Dr. Olaf Mertelsmann who invited me to apply for this post and it has been a pleasure to work under his supervision ever since.

This "European" research demanded a lot of travelling to visit archives which, in sum, consisted of six (seven) countries. Through the course of this research, I gave a total of ten presentations at international conferences in places ranging from Toronto to Sofia, in Paris as well as in Berlin. I had the privilege of staying – free of charge – in the apartments of many wonderful people.

Besides travelling to foreign places, this research project demanded the reading of material in several different languages (English, German, French, Swedish and Finnish); I even had to learn a new language, Estonian. This book also carries references to books in Polish and Lithuanian, but solely to their English summaries. I would especially like to thank all of my foreign language teachers, not only for their valuable tuition, but for also inspiring my further studies; learning one language does not impair the learning of another one. Rather than mentioning everyone, the most significant examples of this are as follows: Marja-Leena Hellemaa for English, Tuula Takala-Nurminen for Swedish and German (both at the Kiukaisten lukio) as well as Katrin Jänese and Tiia Ristolainen for Estonian (both at the University of Tartu).

Nevertheless, despite the fact that I studied various languages, the text of my thesis has been greatly improved by various proofreaders. To list all of them would be impossible.

Vanhempani ovat tukeneet parhaansa mukaan pyrkimyksiäni ja ovat jälleen kiitoksensa ansainneet.

In Tartu, 50 kilometres from the EU-Russia border but 400 kilometres from the geographical centre of Europe.

Expanding the History of European Integration

The well-known Estonian geographer, August Tammekann, once defined Europe not in terms of politics but described the continent from the perspective of his own field of study; "In Europe, the sea penetrates everywhere, it is omnipresent, as opposed to the immense distance of wide inner Asia from the sea. For most of the year, the marine effect prevails in the European climate."[1] For Tammekann, Europe was the land of the shore, between the soil and water.

Tammekann managed to avoid the question of nationalities in his concept of Europe. Europe, however, undeniably consists of nations. It is one question to ask which nations belong to Europe, and another – more difficult question – to ponder relations between Europe and its nations. The concept of Europe unites the nationalities of a wider Western civilization, and from another perspective, without nations Europe would be merely a dull and wide open sea.

The same metaphor of concurrence was used by another Estonian, writer Karl Ristikivi and, incidentally, a former student of geography: "*Meie ei tule kunagi tagasi siia randa. Aga nii kaua kui hingab meri, Sünnivad alati uued rannad*". (We shall never return to this shore, but as long as the sea breaths, new shores are born.)[2] It is impossible to address in a universally comprehensive way how the concept of nationality has met with the concept of (supranational) Europe, because the details are in constant flux. At the same time, this predicament has always remained fundamentally the same. The tides of time may demand a different emphasis and sometimes retreat far away from to shore – only to return again as a devastating tsunami, as happened during the 1990s.

The nature of these encounters depends foremost on the nationality at hand and hence this study looks at the Estonian discussion on European unification. When the Estonians were talking of or imagining Europe, they instinctively included Estonia within it. The time period of this study covers the heyday of nationalism and nation-states starting from the peace

1 Tammekann, 1942, pp. 199–211.

2 Ristikivi, 1972, p. 7.

settlements of World War I and ending with the confrontations of the Cold War. The programmes for European unification during this period include the Paneuropean Union, the Nazi New Europe and its resistance ideas, as well as the European Movement.

In the meantime, Estonia's national history witnessed independent statehood (1920–1940), both Nazi (1941–1944) and Soviet (1940–1941, 1944–1991) occupations, and the subsequent emigration resulting from these occupations. This extensive change of external environment provides an excellent opportunity to underline the stability of the concept of Europe in the Estonian context. Estonian emigrants relied on European unification as a method to restore national sovereignty, and although they retreated from this stand during the late 1950s, they kept contact with, or at least their eye on, the developments of the European Movement and the European (Economic) Community long after.

Estonia eventually joined the European Union with nine other countries in 2004 – and adopted the Euro currency in 2011. Although Europe is politically united, it desires a cultural unity, the creation of which would benefit from a common history. Thus, there is an evident danger of presenting the Estonians participating in the European discussion as pioneers of the present situation of a post-Eastern enlargement European Union. To avoid this, this research brings forth the opposition voices and alternative opinions on European unification in the public discussion and relates this topic to the wider national discussion. Despite the variety between the international context and the national situation, this research addresses one principal question for the entire period: what were the reasons for Estonians either supporting or opposing European unification?

Three Programmes for Unification

The history of European integration has developed into a sub-field of historical research. However, it has also been strongly associated with the evolution of the European Union; a trend Jost Dülffer calls "the Christmas story of European integration". Here the EU becomes complete in terms of both territory and depth, just as one candle is lit each week in December before full illumination is achieved on Christmas Day.[3] It is clear that, before their own state becomes a member of the expanding Union, a citizen from outside the original six founding members finds it very difficult to relate to such an analogy.

The aim of the present research is to go beyond such teleology and institutional situations. This justifies the study of the discussions on

---

3 Dülffer, 2009, pp. 22–23; also Lane, 2005, pp. 201–202.

European unification that took place before actual membership had even become possible. Examination of these discussions, as well as of failed attempts and proposals, may hopefully reveal reasons for the founding of European institutions and, furthermore, the meaning of Europe today – a meaning which is not wholly bound to the European Union. Even past meanings have relevance for us, since, as Alan Milward, one of the leading historians of European integration has put it, "systematic procedures and the way citizens choose within them are defined by history."[4]

Naturally, European unification has been a topic of discussion since the Middle Ages; these discussions have been documented in earlier research. The plans outlined then were mostly concerned with Central European matters and they gained only marginal interest by the north of the Baltic Sea.[5] This research starts in the heyday of nation states: the aftermath of World War I. The dynastic empires of Eastern Europe were replaced by several nation-states but, at the same time, various plans for restoring unity on the continent also emerged. These contrary phenomena highlighted the question: how should nation-states, the new core elements of political order, act towards each other and in a larger environment? Clashes were inevitable because the discourse of Europe mostly remained at the elitist level of civilizations but the materialization of the idea in the new democratic politics required the support of the masses. The focus of this research is not so much on the cooperation between states but rather on the ideas stressing the interdependence of nations. This question has faded over time but is still relevant today and, hopefully, examples from the period in which it was a paramount question might be useful when presenting new ideas for the current discussion.

Spatially, this research has two focuses. On the one hand, it concentrates on the programme of unification of the European centre and, on the other, the Estonian reactions to and discussions on this programme. Thus, the core of this research is actually on the national interpretations of these initiatives. This twofold approach attempts to offer both a new perspective of the history of these European ambitions and Estonia's national history. The front cover picture is a view of Europe from space but from a non-traditional perspective. One way to look at the picture is to see Estonia at the front and Central Europe behind her in the distance. We can also simultaneously interpret the picture with only two dimensions; when Europe is on the top and Estonia is below her. Gradually, like all optical

---

4 Milward, 1994, p. 201, also pp. 197–198.

5 For example, Delanty, 1995; Mikkeli, 1998; Schmale, 2001.

illusions, we become accustomed to the double meaning, and it's hard to return to a single explanation.

Why the choice of Estonia? The peripheral aspect was evident from the beginning: i.e. how is a programme from the European core interpreted in a European borderland? Estonia was a most promising case because it actually has a double peripheral nature: it is not only far from the core but it also borders a significant, partly European neighbour, Russia. This factor was assumed as playing a considerable role in Estonia's European discussion.

There were several further indicators showing that Estonia could be a fruitful case for enabling study of European discussion. The academic literature on European history contains a number of interesting references to Estonia. *Europe: A History* by Norman Davies is a comprehensive and renowned work on the history of Europe, both east and west. Davies includes several caption boxes and one of them is titled "*Eesti*", Estonia in the indigenous language. Allegedly, Otto von Habsburg, then president of the Paneuropean Union, reminded his audience of the small European nation: "Don't forget the Estonians!... they are the best of the Europeans." Davies himself is sure that small nations can cope in the Union and that, reciprocally, they benefit the Union.[6] In the actual research literature, Carl H. Pegg's *Evolution of the European Idea* thoroughly surveys the newspapers in several European countries, and also informs on the bold initiative in the League of Nations in 1931 by Estonians Jaan Tõnisson and Kaarel Robert Pusta to use governmental powers to enhance European, instead of national, thinking.[7]

The Paneuropean Union, led by Count Richard Coudenhove-Kalergi, was the most important promoter of the unification of Europe during the interwar period. Anita Ziegerhofer-Prettenthaler's *Botschafter Europas*[8] represents a comprehensive introduction to the Paneuropean Union but concentrates on the Viennese perspective. Its archives were confiscated by the Red Army in 1945 and they are presently located at the Russian State Military Archives (RGVA) in Moscow.[9] Some part of the original material has been copied to the Historical Archives of the European Union in Florence, Italy. The correspondence between the Estonians and the Viennese centre dealt mostly with daily matters and thus a list of Estonian members could not be found.

6 Davies, 1996, p. 944.

7 Pegg, 1983, p. 163.

8 Ziegerhofer-Prettenthaler, 2004.

9 [http://www.sonderarchiv.de/].

An initial glimpse at the primary sources gives indications of Estonian activity. The catalogue on Paneuropean Union in the Historical Archives of the EU includes two German-Estonian articles: "*Was bedeutet Pan-Europa für Estland*" (What Paneurope means for Estonia) by H.P. Lilienfeld-Toal in 1925 and "*Paneuropa, die Juden und Palästina*" (Paneurope, the Jews and Palestine) by P. Michelsohn, 1927.[10] Regarding the latter, an unfortunate, yet usual, omission occurred: Philipp Michelson was actually from Estonia's neighbouring country, Latvia. Hans-Paul Lilienfeld-Toal was a Baltic German, who had already left Estonia for studies in Germany. His short letter mainly supports the initiatives of Coudenhove-Kalergi and mostly ignores the Estonian situation.

Public sources have been more important for studying the Paneuropean Union, as Coudenhove-Kalergi himself underlined the importance of propagating his idea through the available mass media. In addition to his own publications, books, and journal (titled *Paneuropa*), he wrote effortlessly to national newspapers. Roughly a dozen writings by Coudenhove-Kalergi appeared in Estonian newspapers over the years[11] and many others introduced his ideas. Eventually Estonians were inspired to express their own opinions on the theme. As my method, I first consulted the catalogues of newspapers in the Estonian National Library in Tallinn and the Estonian Literature Museum in Tartu. Thus, I could locate the relevant events (European conferences, local speeches, etc.) while re-examining the newspapers from the relevant periods.[12]

Estonian historians have shed light on their previous European discussion, including the prospects for unification. It is worth mentioning Toomas

---

10 HAEU. PAN/EU 12: Book and printed material (extracts), on Paneurope [http://wwwarc.eui.eu/pdfinv/inv-pan-eu.pdf]; H.P. Lilientfeld-Toal, "Was bedeutet Pan-Europa für Estland?".

11 Coudenhove-Kalergi, "Ilu-eeetika," in *Agu* 1923:32, pp. 1031–1034; Coudenhove-Kalergi, "Paneuroopa," in *Päevaleht*, 7.10.1924, p. 2; Coudenhove-Kalergi, "Pan-Euroopa Locarno eest!" in *Päevaleht*, 4.9.1927, p. 2; "Kõik eurooplased on sugulased," in *Päevaleht*, 7.1.1928, p. 2; "Pan-Euroopa rahuprobleem," in *Päevaleht*, 7.1.1928, p. 3; Coudenhove-Kalergi, "Austria-Saksa ühinemine. ('Anschluss')," in *Postimees*, 12.9.1928, p. 3 and 13.9.1928, p. 3; Coudenhove-Kalergi, "Kas sõjaline või majanduslik julgeolek?" in *Päevaleht*, 4.4.1929, p. 2; Coudenhove-Kalergi, "Atlantis," in *Päevaleht*, 24.7.1930, p. 2; Coudenhove-Kalergi, "Kõigile eurooplastele!" in *Päevaleht*, 1.8.1930, p. 2; "Euroopa föderaalsed rigid," in *Päevaleht*, 3.5.1930, p. 3; Coudenhove-Kalergi, "Piits, nälg, preemia," in *Päevaleht*, 26.4.1931, p. 9; Coudenhove-Kalergi, "Euroopa võitlus vabaduse eest," in *Postimees*, 20.5.1931, p. 2; "Elu käsud," in *Vaba Maa*, 24.12.1931, p. 8; Coudenhove-Kalergi, "Kakskümmend aastat soda," in *Päevaleht*, 28.7.1934, p. 2; Coudenhove-Kalergi, "Euroopa ja Nõukogude-Vene," in *ERK* 1934:11/12, pp. 193–195; Coudenhove-Kalergi, "1935 – sõda või rahu?", in *Vaba Maa*, 1.1.1935, p. 2.

12 Newspapers are available online at [http://dea.nlib.ee/].

Karjahärm's project (with Väino Sirk) on Estonian cultural life from the dawn of nationalism during the 19th century onwards. In particular, the separate publication, *Unistus Euroopast* (A Dream of Europe), comprehensively introduces Estonian opinions on European culture. Here Karjahärm states that Paneuropean discussion did not reach a very fundamental level,[13] but he has limited his research to journals, whilst the actual discussion took place in newspapers with justifications placed both for and against. Perspectives applied to this issue ranged from those of human psychology to military security.

Coudenhove-Kalergi's Paneuropean Union was partly a reason for the French Prime Minister Aristide Briand making an official proposal for the study and establishment of a European Federation within the League of Nations in 1930. Here, official sources from the various foreign ministries become crucial. In order to study potential cooperation in drafting the national replies to Briand, I did not limit myself merely to the archives of the Estonian foreign ministry but also consulted the respective Finnish and Swedish archives. The anthology on the Briand Memorandum in 1998 has only one reference to Estonia – and completely ignores Sweden and Finland.[14]

Baltic collaboration had been vitally important in gaining independence immediately after World War I and a comparison between continental unification and international cooperation within a more limited area was also relevant in the public discussion afterwards. Preliminary quantitative analysis on Estonian newspapers indicated a strong negative correlation between the European and Baltic ideas. According to the catalogues of the Estonian National Library and the Literary Museum, interest in the Baltic states decreased considerably after 1927 and reached a low point in 1931.[15] At the same time, articles dealing with the question of Europe were at their most frequent.[16] The interest in the immediate neighbourhood seemed to

---

13 Karjahärm, 2003, p. 55.

14 Fleury and Jilek, 1998.

15 The catalogue of the Estonian Literary Museum in Tartu has a category 32(474), entitled "Balti riikide välispoliitiline olukord ja välispoliitika. Eesti suhted mõlema Baltiriikidega. Teiste riikide poliitika Baltimaade suhtes – Balti küsimus. Balti Liit" (Foreign policy situation and foreign policy of the Baltic states. Estonian relations with both of the Baltic states. Other countries' policies towards the Baltic states – Baltic question. Baltic Union); the National Library in Tallinn has a category 327 E:474 – "Eesti Baltimaade poliitilised suhted" (Estonian political relations with the Baltic states). The numbers of references in these categories by year are as follows: 1925, 75; 1926, 85; 1927, 75; 1928, 22; 1929, 27; 1930, 18; 1931, 11; 1932, 25; 1933, 58; 1934, ~130.

16 The newspaper sources for my research on the discussion on the European unification in Estonia during the same period consist of the following numbers of articles per year: 1925, 3; 1926, 5; 1927, 24; 1928, 6; 1929, 17; 1930, 31; 1931, 43; 1932, 16; 1933, 11; 1934, 5.

have reached the ultimate bottom in the late 1920s, when the discussion of European unification was at its peak. Although these catalogues cannot be considered as reliable indicators of actual publicity in newspapers, this preliminary exploration was enough to justify a closer look into the articles on Baltic and European imaginations.

The idea of European unification vanished soon after Briand's proposal and was resurrected as a counter-proposal for Nazi Germany's idea of New Europe. Like many exiled politicians from occupied Europe, Estonian Aleksander Warma pondered how to first restore his country's independence and then establish a more safe European system for all nations. In December 1942, he provided the U.S. State Department with a paper titled "Questions relating to the consolidation of peace in post-war Europe". The plan has been published in Warma's posthumous memoirs and his archives in the Baltic Archives at the Swedish National Archives in Stockholm include correspondence related to the plan. Curiously, previous research has ignored Warma's plan. Even in the Estonian literature the proposal for a Baltoscandian Federation made by Lithuanian Kazys Pakštas in the U.S. is more widely known than the European draft by Warma.[17] Like in any other European country, World War II has been extensively studied by Estonian scholars, but so far with only little emphasis on political resistance.

The chapter presents the main points of this plan and sets it into a context of similar plans for European unification drafted in Europe during World War II. The published source material on U.S. post-war planning (the so-called Notter File) reveals simultaneous thinking among the Western allies. Nevertheless, despite being written in isolation and, therefore being an original piece of thinking, Warma's plan is also an illustration as to how regional thinking was an essential element in post-war planning everywhere.

Generally speaking, my goal has been to overcome World War II as the ultimate point of departure for a new international order and, in this case, European integration. Estonian émigrés continued to emphasize their European connections during the Cold War. In Sweden, they were organized as the Estonian National Council. The archive of the Council has been brought to the Estonian National Library in Tallinn but the personal collections of the leaders are still in the Baltic Archives. The exile community rapidly established newspapers of which *Eesti Teataja* worked closely with the Estonian National Council and *Välis-Eesti* gave opposition voices

[17] Karjahärm, 2003, p. 58; Raig, 2008, p. 58.

a place for publication.[18] Both newspapers were nevertheless edited independently. There were, of course, other Estonian newspapers in Sweden, not to mention publishing activities elsewhere. The aforementioned were the largest of them and both present alternative opinions on European integration.

Historical research on the Estonian diaspora after the Soviet incorporation and World War II are taking shape only gradually. Two recent biographies of Estonian emigrants only briefly mentioned their connections to the idea of European unification.[19] *Tõotan üstavaks jääda...* (I swear to remain faithful...)[20] is an extensive collection of the history of the emigrant politics that barely mentions the foreign policy, an aspect that certainly merits more research. On the positive side, the book includes biographical data on exiled politicians. Regarding other personalities, information has been completed in, for example, contemporary encyclopedias and current reviews.[21]

In Europe, the Estonian National Council collaborated mostly with the European Movement (EM). It was a joint organization of six various groupings aiming for unification. Its correspondence is nowadays located in the Historical Archives of the European Union. When studying the promotion of national interests in international organizations, it is crucially important to look at the relationship between the sources of both parties in order to put national aspirations and influence within the context of the organization. Considering the magnitude of the organization, historical research has been minimal. There has been only one dissertation written on the EM, which nevertheless ignores the role of emigrant groups on the movement's agenda.[22]

Emigrants, and also in this case the Estonians, indeed had difficulties establishing relations with the EM. The primary achievement of the EM was the Congress of Europe in The Hague in May 1948. At the outset, the Estonians sent Arvo Horm as their delegate and he delivered a declaration with Lithuanian Juozas Lanskoronskis on behalf of the Movement for a Baltic Federation. However, the list of participants in the Congress

---

18 Valmas, 2003, pp. 32–37.

19 Tamman, 2011, p. 193; Ant, 2012, pp. 270–271.

20 Orav and Nõu, 2004.

21 For example *Eesti biograafiline leksikon* (1926–1929) and *Eesti entsüklopeedia* (1932–1934) on the former and Mulla, Triin *et al.* (eds.), *Eesti välisteenistus. Biograafiline leksikon 1918–1991*, Tallinn, Estonian Ministry of Foreign Affairs, 2006, on the latter.

22 Rebattet, 1962.

of Europe does not include either of them. It took a long year and a half before the Estonians became members of the EM in January 1950.

As Estonians were now participating enthusiastically in the EM, the organization itself set about searching for a role after the foundation of the Council of Europe and with even greater vigour related to the Coal and Steel Community when the real integration began to take shape. However, emigrants from Eastern Europe found themselves marginalized even within the EM and gradually Estonians started looking for alternative forums to promote their national cause; they nevertheless paid attention to various forms of European unification and kept attending European meetings, this research follows this gradual fading all the way until 1980s, when the post-CSCE effects started to show in the actual situation in Estonia and consequently also in Estonian emigrant attitudes. Warma declared publicly this change in their foreign policy in 1957, the year in which the narrative on European integration usually begins. I do not know what could better illustrate the contrasts and diversity in the history of European integration.

Three Dimensions of International Politics

The current European institutions and associations, such as the EU and the Council of Europe or even UEFA and the EBU, unintentionally give description to Europe. Earlier "Europe" was an idea, which had to be, or could be, defined ad hoc. To underline this difference, I primarily speak here about unification. The term integration was used rarely in my sources. This happened for the first time in 1957, but not in relation to the EEC. Heinrich Laretei visited a conference of the Assembly of Captured European Nations in Strasbourg and he considered its main focus on the liberation of Eastern Europe as being essential to "integration, i.e. to create some kind of United Europe".[23]

In addition to Alan Milward, René Girault was one of the founding historians of European integration. His project, "*La puissance en Europe*", was intended to look at the concept of power in four Western European countries over ten year intervals. Following the classical definition by Pierre Renouvin,[24] Girault divided power into six aspects: military, economic, colonial, political, public opinions, and decision-makers.[25] In my study, only three divisions are used: economic, diplomatic, and cultural.

23 Laretei, Heinrich, "EIRE konverentsi kokkuvõte," in *Välis-Eesti*, 12.5.1957, p. 2. On the development of European watchwords, see Stråth, 2000, p. 385.

24 Renouvin and Duroselle, 1967.

25 Dülffer, 2009, pp. 27–28. Dülffer probably instinctively uses the same tripartition.

These dimensions establish the disposition of this book. First, the book is chronologically divided according to three programmes and within these chapters the disposition runs along – more or less – the three dimensions with apparent emphasis on diplomacy; the federalist approach was without question the most prominent during this period.

This triangle defines the concept of unification. International cooperation takes place – or it can be imagined to take place – within these dimensions but to call such cooperation integration or unification, it has to contain all three dimensions. This is why Nordic cooperation does not qualify as unification. Although it has a strong cultural and even economic basis, it lacks a joint diplomatic institution: Nordic ministers meet regularly but make their decisions individually and independently.

Diplomacy refers to declarations and decisions by politicians on joint institutions, economic agreements, trade and other commercial actions. The third dimension is culture which includes the exchanges of immaterial goods, visions, hopes, and fears. This dimension largely defines the territorial borders of a unified area. Several approaches to unification can be found on the sides of the triangle. A federalist would stress diplomacy between the countries of a common culture, subsequently neglecting economic questions. The functionalists of the Coal and Steel Community presumed a cultural unity as a result of the primary economic cooperation. The approach of a strong political organization and economic interdependence with minor emphasis on common culture seems to reflect the attempts of the Fascist states within their idea of the New Europe.

The triangular definition was also used by Estonian contemporaries and the three corners were elementary also in Immanuel Kant's plan for "Eternal Peace" within a federation of sovereign states held together by preliminary articles. Enlightenment philosophers had faith in commerce for bringing nations together but their opinions of immaterial features varied. Kant himself spoke of the cosmopolitan right of universal hospitality and believed differing customs would eventually become similar. Others, such as Johann Gottfried Herder, took as granted the toleration and value of local customs.[26]

As my research considers the time before the formation of formal European institutions, it deals mostly with mental concepts: how should unification start; what should be the first step and how that step could affect – or spill over to –, other dimensions? For the same reason, actual

---

26 Pagden, 2002a, pp. 17–18; Tully, 2002, pp. 331–332, 343–344.

integration in social or military entities has to be excluded. In this context the years observed under this research were more about disintegration.

Clearly, the question of European or Estonian culture is a larger topic than can be discussed here. As part of my methodology, I have limited research to the articles and other sources that only deal with unification; articles dealing with cultural Europeanism are thus excluded. There may have been articles defining European culture without any reference to international cooperation at other levels but these were considered to be outside the area of research.

One interesting example of such cultural Europeanists would be Baltic German philosopher Hermann von Keyserling. He was born in Raikküla Manor, in what is today Central Estonia, but travelled frequently before settling permanently in Darmstadt in 1918. Thus, he had little connection to local Estonian discussion. Keyserling wrote the book *Das Spektrum Europas* in 1928, which underlined the multicultural aspect of European civilization and although he, for example, attended the conference on the future of Europe by the Institut International de Coopération Intellectuelle in Paris in 1933 and supported the Paneuropean Union, his text lacks any political proposals on how to manifest these ideas.[27]

Recently, a common European culture, public space or identity has been proposed as a cure for stagnation in economic and diplomatic integration. Elites have turned to citizens for the idea of Europe. However, declining turnout in European Parliamentary elections has been a matter of growing concern. There is a growing academic literature on this contemporary item of discussion and likewise on historical research of the older European idea. Although this increase is now – like it was in the 1950s – obviously connected to the institutionalization of the European Union, this literature usually nevertheless ignores the other two stressed dimensions of unification.[28]

---

27 Keyserling, 1928; "Rundfrage," in *Paneuropa* 1926:6/7, p. 41. The interest on Keyserling is kept on in Estonia mainly by Jaan Undusk (Undusk, 2003).

28 For example, Smith, 1992; Pagden, 2002b; Woolf, 2003; Duchhardt, 2005; Trunk, 2007; Loth, 2007; Lévy and Sicard, 2009.

Part I

Paneuropean Discussion in Estonia

Chapter 1

Paneuropean Union in Estonia

Estonia first emerged as an independent country out of the turmoil caused by World War I and the downfall of the Russian Empire after the War of Liberation against the Communist revolutionists and the German *Landeswehr*. The prospects of successful state consolidation were somewhat mixed. As a disadvantage, the new state had a small population, however, to its advantage, it was ethnically homogeneous, with the exception of a Russian minority concentrated close to the Eastern border. Estonians had traditionally resided in both the provinces of Estonia and Livonia before joining to form one administrative unit as late as the summer of 1917. Nonetheless, politicians and administrators had gained previous experience in Russia's imperial institutions. The constitution heavily emphasized the *riigikogu* (Parliament) while the governments remained weak. Nonetheless, the greatest danger to the democratic system came from abroad, the prime case of which being when local communists, backed by the Soviet Union, attempted a coup d'état in December 1924. In short, independence gave Estonia the opportunity to rapidly transform economically and culturally from a province ruled by Czarist Russia and to integrate itself more closely with Western Europe.[1]

Since Medieval times, ideas planning European unification had usually been devised in the aftermath of a calamitous war. The aftermath of World War I was no exception. On the other hand, the League of Nations was founded as an organization that would restrain the prospect of war, maintain peace and retain the status quo. Although the League represented a minor revolution in diplomacy, its duties were seriously undermined by constant national rivalries and the absence of both the U.S. and the Soviet Union.

However, the League was not enough for all and various calls for the unification of Europe emerged during the early 1920s. There were many movements for a united Europe, and some of them were known in Estonia. Prince Karl Anton Rohan of *Europäischer Kulturbund* visited

1 Raun, 1991, pp. 99–115; Hiden and Salmon, 1996, pp. 43–87; Smith, 2002, pp. 14–17; Elsuwege, 2008, pp. 11–28; Kasekamp, 2010, pp. 95–123.

Tallinn in spring 1927,[2] and *Päevaleht* also published an article about Herman Sörgel's *Atlantropa*.[3] Nevertheless, the Paneuropean Union of Richard Coudenhove-Kalergi was by far the most popular.

Multiple writings by Coudenhove-Kalergi appeared in the Estonian press over these years. His articles did not always deal strictly with European unification but also with his general philosophy. The Paneuropean Manifesto was published in *Päevaleht* in January 1924, only a year after it was first declared in 1923 in *Vossische Zeitung* and *Neue Wiener Presse*.[4] The introduction of the book *Paneuropa* was published in *Päevaleht* a few months later, notably with a misspelling of the author's undeniably peculiar name.[5] Three years later, the same journal published a rather uncritical review of the book's fourth edition.[6] Two leaflets, *Paneuroopa liit* (Paneuropean Union) and *Paneuroopa ABC* (Paneuropean ABC), were translated into Estonian, the latter was even distributed free of charge.[7]

As early as 1924, Coudenhove-Kalergi asked former Foreign Minister Kaarel Robert Pusta to initiate an Estonian section of the Paneuropean Union.[8] At that moment, the appeal proved unsuccessful but Pusta became a long-time advocate for Paneurope thereafter and joined the Council of the Paneuropean Union. Already a veteran diplomat, in 1919, Pusta belonged to the foreign delegation in Western Europe which demanded recognition of Estonian independence. Later, in 1920, he acted as Foreign Minister (but only for three days) and also between 1924 and 1925. Subsequently, Pusta's main posting was as Estonian envoy in Paris until 1932 before transfers first to Warsaw and subsequently to Stockholm.

Despite expectations, Coudenhove-Kalergi never came to Estonia; instead, economics expert of the Paneuropean Union, journalist Otto Deutsch, visited Tallinn and Tartu in June 1929 and gave a lecture on the topic of "the Baltic States and Pan-Europe".[9] At the Tallinn meeting, Ants

2 "Euroopa tulevik on vaimline problem," in *Päevaleht*, 22.4.1927, p. 5. See also Paul, 2005, pp. 21–45.

3 "Sajandi suurim project," in *Päevaleht*, 8.7.1931, p. 4. See also Spiering, 2002, pp. 177–199.

4 M.V., "Euroopa ja Saksamaa," in *Päevaleht*, 27.1.1924, p. 2 and 30.1.1924, p. 2.

5 Coudenhove-Kalergi, "Paneuroopa," in *Päevaleht*, 7.10.1924, p. 2.

6 "Pan-Euroopa," in *Päevaleht*, 31.5.1927, p. 5.

7 "'Pan-Euroopa päev' Tallinnas," in *Vaba Maa*, 16.5.1931, p. 2.

8 Pusta, 1992, pp. 116–117.

9 "Pan-Euroopa keskkomitee koos," in *Postimees*, 17.1.1928, p. 1; Deutsch, Otto, "Pan-Euroopa tähtis küsimus Balti riikidele," in *Päevaleht*, 8.6.1929, p. 4; "Eestis Pan-Euroopa komitee asutatud," in *Päevaleht*, 9.6.1929, p. 4; Deutsch, Otto, "Pan-Euroopa

Piip, Professor of International Law at the University of Tartu,[10] called supporters from the two cities to join and establish an Estonian Society of the Paneuropean Union. The call was accepted by some twenty people, but in addition to politicians, the organizers desired people from the fields of business, technology and engineering.[11]

This initiative ultimately proved to be an undoubted failure, and Pusta took over to establish the Estonian Society during his vacation. Two months later, on August 14, 1929, the "Committee to initiate Estonian Paneurope" organized a meeting at a community centre in Tallinn's Old Town. About 100 prospective members attended. According to *Vaba Maa*, the movement was both relatively new and somewhat unusual; thus the meeting attracted much attention. Piip and Pusta delivered the speeches. At the end of his speech, which was published the Estonian press,[12] Pusta foresaw the committee as the seed of an actual society, for which a preparatory council was formed by the meeting's end.

The society's leadership included Piip, Peeter Kann, Judge with the Supreme Court of Estonia, Businessman Joakim (Joachim) Puhk, and Märt Raud, Director of National Oil Shale Mining, who also became the secretary. The office of the mining company, situated within Tallinn's Old Town, was used as the postal address for the society. The leadership was later completed with the additions of Johannes Luikmil from National Oil Shale Mining and Artur Haman from the foreign ministry. The council of the society consisted of 30 members, which included among others, former Head of State Jaan Tõnisson, former Commander-in-Chief, Lieutenant General Johan Laidoner, Minister of Agriculture August Kerem, Major-General Juhan Tõrvand, Social-Democrat politician Karl Ast and public notary Jakob Kristelstein. Pusta was appointed as the Estonian representative for the Paneuropean Union's Central Council in Vienna.[13] Also folklorist and Estonian Minister in London, Oskar Kallas, joined the Paneuropean Union along with the Mayor of Haapsalu, Hans Alver.

ülesehitava jõuna," in *Postimees*, 9.6.1929, p. 2; *Paneuropa* 1929:6, p. 31; Ziegerhofer-Prettenthaler 2004, p. 277.

10 For more on Piip as professor of International Law, see Mälksoo, 2008, pp. 86–105.

11 "Eestis Pan-Euroopa komitee asutatud," in *Päevaleht*, 9.6.1929, p. 4.

12 "Euroopa kahes leeris," in *Kaja*, 16.8.1929, p. 3; Pusta, 1929a.

13 "Paneuroopa nurgakivi Eestis," in *Postimees*, 16.8.1929, p. 3; "Euroopa kahes leeris," in *Kaja*, 16.8.1929, p. 3; "Teel Pan-Euroopa poole," in *Vaba Maa*, 16.8.1929, p. 5; "Pan-Euroopa päev Tallinnas," in *Päevaleht*, 19.5.1931, p. 3; "Die Paneuropabewegung," in *Paneuropa* 1929:8, p. 40; Medijainen, Eero, "Eesti Pan-Euroopa ühingu ajaloost," in *Postimees*, 14.9.1991, p. 2. According to Palk, 1999, pp. 22–23, Jüri Jaakson from the Bank of Estonia was also on the council but I have not been able to locate him. Additionally, Davies, 1996, p. 944, dates the foundation far too early in 1923.

Baltic-German writer Louis Burlandt wrote several, more personal, letters to Coudenhove-Kalergi and Estonian esperantists wanted to have contact with him as well.[14] In sum, more than 100 persons joined the society in the beginning and in May 1931 it included 214 members in total.[15]

While membership of this club was small, it included the absolute cream of Estonian society. Notably, among Estonia's very top politicians of this era, only Konstantin Päts is missing. Although the Paneuropeans had managed to gain supporters among businessmen, the lack of support among cultural personalities is striking. The Young Estonia Movement spearheaded by Gustav Suits had declared Estonia part of Europe long before Estonian independence from the Russian Empire. According to their famous slogan "*Olgem eestlased, aga saagem ka eurooplasteks*" (Let's be Estonians, but let's also become Europeans) national development was crucially related to events in Europe.[16] Presumably, the political dimension of Europe did not interest them.

In 1931, Estonian society celebrated Paneurope Day with a seminar at the community centre. The guest speakers, Pēteris Berģis and Philipp Michelson from the Latvian society, discussed small states and the border issue. The same day, Piip spoke reciprocally in Riga about Paneurope and international peace.[17] This time *Vaba Maa* described the occasion in Tallinn as "quite silent and without attracting the attention of a wider audience". Approximately 50 listeners attended.[18]

Between 1924 and 1931 the theme of European unification recurred in the Estonian press.[19] The Estonians, among other nations, had to consider the place of their newly independent state in Europe. The first, and as it later appeared, the most comprehensive criticism of Paneurope was published in *Postimees* in February 1, 1927. The unknown author of "*Kõik-Euroopa pahed*" (The Flaws of Paneurope)[20] acknowledged the

---

14 RGVA 554-1-14, p. 218; 554-1-33, pp. 230–249; 554-1-43, pp. 273–288.

15 "'Pan-Euroopa päev' Tallinnas," in *Vaba Maa*, 16.5.1931, p. 2.

16 Karjahärm, 2003, p. 13; Karlsson, 2002, p. 178.

17 "'Pan-Euroopa päev' Tallinnas," in *Vaba Maa*, 16.5.1931, p. 2; "Paneuroopa päeva aktus," in *Kaja*, 17.5.1931, p. 8; "Paneuroopa päeva pidamine Tallinnas," in *Postimees*, 17.5.1931, p. 3; "Pan-Euroopa päev Tallinnas," in *Päevaleht*, 19.5.1931, p. 3; "Bericht über den Paneuropa-Tag. Estland und Lettland," in *Paneuropa* 1931:5, p. 156.

18 "Pan-Euroopa päev Tallinnas," in *Vaba Maa*, 19.5.1931, p. 3.

19 The discussion was more or less limited to four newspapers: *Vaba Maa* (published in Tallinn, affiliated with Labour Party), *Päevaleht* (Tallinn, independent but conservative), *Kaja* (Tallinn, Rural Union), and *Postimees* (Tartu, People's Party) (Hoyer *et al.*, 1993, pp. 130–132). Social-democratic *Rahva Sõna* publicized some news on Paneurope but refrained from commenting on them.

20 Occasionally Paneuropa was translated into *Üld-Euroopa* or *Kõik-Euroopa*.

benefits of unification, but clearly stated that flaws prevailed. The flaws included a threat to the League of Nations, economic antagonism against outsiders, and inadequate development of a national idea.[21] Apparently acting on instinct, the author divided international relations into the same three categories as subsequent research literature: politics (diplomacy), economics, and culture.

Although this article did not become a seminal text, which would be directly referred to, the three themes were separately repeated by opponents and subsequently responded to by advocates of unification. At the first meeting, Pusta ended his speech by saying: "When we are supporting Paneuropean Union, we are working for our own independence, economic success and the preservation of national culture."[22] It was no coincidence that both lists named the diplomatic dimension first as it was considered the most significant and therefore it is reasonable to here address it first also.

21 Ks., "Kõik-Euroopa pahed," in *Postimees*, 1.2.1927, p. 1. As the letter 'x' is missing in Estonian alphabet, 'ks' refers to an unknown subject.

22 Pusta, 1929a. Incidentally, also during the process of joining the EU the Estonian elite used the same triangular justification: "New European identity develops thus in the cooperation of politicians, businessmen, and cultural persons and on the basis of experience." (Ruutsoo, Rein, "Rahvusriik, identiteet ja Euroopa Liit", in *Eesti ja Euroopa Liit* 16 (October 2000).

Chapter 2

Diplomatic Means

"This is the Aim of the Existing League of Nations"

The article "Flaws of Paneurope" twice questioned the usefulness of European unification, as the League of Nations was already an international organization fostering universal peace. Furthermore, the text accused the Paneuropeans of arrogance, as they asked the League for assistance in unification, although their attitude towards the League was "far from crystal clear".[1]

The League of Nations, a cornerstone of official Estonian foreign policy, enjoyed strong popularity among the people as well.[2] Therefore, the advocates of Paneurope were eager to clarify the relation between the two organizations. They refused to see opposition between the Union and the League. On the contrary, they saw the former helping the latter to fulfill its European tasks in disarmament, minority issues, border disputes, and economic development. The Union would become a regional alliance within the League, which was permitted in its convention.[3]

Pusta made his stand clear in September 1925, when Britain withdrew from the negotiations for re-writing the convention, the Geneva protocol: "The future League of Nations could be divided into autonomous sections, individual continents." In his vision "the United States of Europe are one of the organizations, which could arrange all those countless questions of borders, tariffs, currencies, languages and nationalities." The good relations of the Paneuropean Union with the British Empire and the U.S. showed that United Europe did not have to be against the League of Nations.[4] Jaan Tõnisson agreed with Pusta on the need to reorganize the structure of the League as an assembly of continents. According to Tõnisson, this would not increase hostilities but, on the contrary, would

1 Ks., "Kõik-Euroopa pahed," in *Postimees*, 1.2.1927, p. 1.

2 For example, "Eesti ülesanded rahu korraldamisel," in *Vaba Maa*, 29.9.1925, p. 3; "Rahvasteliidu tööde kasutamine," in *Päevaleht*, 11.10.1930, p. 2.

3 Coudenhove-Kalergi, 1929, pp. 6–7; Coudenhove-Kalergi, 1931, pp. 10–11; Piip, 1932, p. 67; Kaasik, 1933, pp. 68–70; Ziegerhofer-Prettenthaler, 2004, pp. 452–474.

4 "Eesti ülesanded rahu korraldamisel," in *Vaba Maa*, 29.9.1925, p. 3.

provide the U.S. and the Soviet Union with a platform to enter international politics in a peaceful way.[5]

Johan Laidoner, despite being a council member of the Estonian Paneuropean Society, presented unification more clearly as the antithesis of the League, which had greatly promoted peace. The League's universal nature better guaranteed peace, especially at the Russian border. On the other hand, even Laidoner agreed that the risk of war would decrease with the creation of larger units, such as a united Europe.[6] There was also another article in *Päevaleht* in September 1927, which stressed the immaterial effects of the universal League of Nations. It would promote "constant progress and development in accordance with public legal convictions and political maturity."[7]

In addition to personal statements, *Postimees* promoted unification and sympathetic relations with the League. As an example, the paper announced a meeting of the Central Committee of the Paneuropean Union and presented its goal as promoting "political and economic union between European states within the framework of the League of Nations". At the same time, even Coudenhove-Kalergi recommended closer relations with the League and its non-governmental organizations. Later the Estonian Society for the League of Nations organized at least one meeting with the Estonian Paneuropean Society.[8]

Faith in the League was not, however, overwhelming nor illusory. Germany and France were praised as the biggest and most civilized countries in Europe, and their relationship was acknowledged as the starting point for unification of the whole continent. This was expressed in sentences like "when France and Germany are up in arms, European solidarity cannot be even discussed"[9] or "like before, Franco-German relations remain as the European focus".[10] Although some of these articles were clearly written by foreigners, Estonian newspapers agreed enough to publish them.

5 "Paneuroopa poolt ja vastu," in *Vaba Maa*, 25.10.1929, p. 10; "Pan-Euroopa kõneõhtu Tartus," in *Postimees*, 30.10.1929, p. 3; "Pan-Euroopa mõte laiemates hulkades," in *Päevaleht*, 1.11.1929, p. 2.

6 "Paneuroopa poolt ja vastu," in *Vaba Maa*, 25.10.1929, p. 10; "Kas rahuaade on teostav," in *Vaba Maa*, 29.11.1931, p. 5; "Ons maailmarahu teostav?" in *Päevaleht*, 29.11.1931, p. 3.

7 Ks., "Euroopa riikide liit," in *Päevaleht*, 6.9.1927, p. 2.

8 "Pan-Euroopa keskkomitee koos," in *Postimees*, 17.1.1928, p. 1; "Paneuroopa poolt ja vastu," in *Vaba Maa*, 25.10.1929, p. 10.

9 Ks., "Euroopa ühisvaimu valjavaated," in *Päevaleht*, 9.6.1927, p. 2.

10 "Euroopale taotakse uut saatust," in *Postimees*, 19.2.1933, p. 2; also for example: "Kesk- ja Pan-Euroopa," in *Päevaleht*, 7.4.1930, p. 2; "Kuidas teostuvad Euroopa ühisriigid," in *Postimees*, 24.4.1930, p. 2; S., "Euroopa peaprobleem," in *Päevaleht*, 13.8.1931, p. 2.

For example, journalist and writer K.A. Hindrey wrote under his own name in 1927 about the election of the French Aristide Briand as the honorary president of the Union, which was led by the German (sic) Coudenhove-Kalergi.[11] This was important also from the national point of view. Toomas Karjahärm defines Estonian Europeanness as finding inspiration from various directions in Europe, and thus suppressing the dominant Russian and German influences.[12]

Thus, when former Foreign Minister Hans Rebane wrote "We are too far from the great Europe" and questioned the Estonian ability to estimate French foreign policy,[13] he may have not been referring to geographical distance, but to magnitude. The relations of small and big states remained vital in the unification discourse during the entire period.

The article "Flaws of Paneurope" defined small nations as dependent on bigger ones. This dependency would increase in a European organization compared to the universal League of Nations. Therefore, the ideas of Paneurope "could be for us as a small state even more meaningful than for others."[14] This concern was repeated in subsequent discussions.[15]

Harald Tammer, who had been in sports and weightlifting – he won an Olympic bronze medal in heavyweight in Paris in 1924 – before entering journalism, defended the rights of the small and the weak in *Päevaleht*. He regarded the League as the best protector of small states and could also reverse the chain of deduction: it was in the common interest of small states to maintain the effect of the League and prevent the big states from destroying what was already a shaky system.[16] Additionally, Nikolai Kaasik's popular *Rahvasteliit* (League of Nations) showed how small states could increase their influence by joining in regional groups to reinforce the League.[17]

The League was important as a community of democratic nations. In the words of Tammer, "there cannot exist a separate domestic and foreign policy." For him, this meant maintaining the liberal democratic world vision between Fascism, Nazism, and Communism. This vision supported the League and underpinned his belief that it was effective.[18]

11 Hindrey, K.A., "Pan-Euroopa," in *Päevaleht*, 13.5.1927, p. 2.

12 Karjahärm, 2003, pp. 76, 101.

13 Rebane, Hans, "Briandi ühendriigid," in *Päevaleht*, 16.7.1930, p. 2.

14 Ks., "Kõik-Euroopa pahed," in *Postimees*, 1.2.1927, p. 1.

15 Ks., "Euroopa riikide liit," in *Päevaleht*, 6.9.1927, p. 2.

16 Tammer, Harald, "Väikeriikide osa," in *Päevaleht*, 28.10.1932, p. 2.

17 Kaasik, 1933, p. 40.

18 Tammer, Harald, "Käärimiste ajajärk," in *Päevaleht*, 17.12.1933, p. 2.

Estonian Paneuropeans connected the idea of democratic states to European unity. In his forewords in *Paneuroopa liit* (Paneuropean Union), Pusta stressed the democratic nature of Estonia and the movement. To publish the idea to a broader audience was to be in favour of both.[19] On the other hand, this was a national interpretation of paneuropeanism. Coudenhove-Kalergi himself was not known to have particularly democratic ideas. On the contrary, he was presented to support "the view that a democratic era is a period of transition between feudal nobility of blood and social nobility of spirit."[20]

Briand's Proposal of European Federation

Relations between the Paneuropean Union and the League of Nations became closer but also more complex when the French premier Aristide Briand proposed studying and establishing a European federation within the League in May 1930. There had been speculation concerning a serious attempt to foster European cooperation throughout the 1920s. Aristide Briand had been French Foreign Minister on multiple occasions and he was also a renowned advocate of peace and rapprochement between France and Germany, owing to his contribution to the Locarno Treaty of 1925. He was envisaged as the man able to take the next step. In July 1929, as the French Prime Minister, he officially informed the press and the Chamber of Deputies that a presentation would occur during the tenth session of the League Assembly in Geneva. There, on September 5, Briand raised the idea and it was further discussed at "the Banquet of Europe" four days later. It was agreed at this meeting that France would draft a memorandum, which would be studied by other European states. They would then transmit their views to the French, who would then write a further report for discussion and possible action at the next meeting of the Assembly.[21] The Memorandum for a System of European Federal Union was released on May 17, 1930. Consisting of about ten pages, it contained a blueprint for the organization, which resembled the League of Nations, and broad principles for the development of a positive European programme. Despite the title, the Memorandum was in fact mostly a part of French foreign policy and an effort to Europeanize French relations with Germany.[22]

Briand was the Honorary President of the Paneuropean Union and the concept of Paneurope was generally linked to his Memorandum

19 Pusta, 1929b, pp. 1–2; also Pusta, 1929a.

20 "Euroopa Ühisriigid," in *Kaja*, 5.10.1926, p. 5; Ziegerhofer-Prettenthaler, 2004, pp. 427–437.

21 Pegg, 1983, pp. 111, 119–121.

22 Pegg, 1983, pp. 140–142; Frank, 2002.

which was often spoken of under different titles, one such being; "Briand's Pan-European proposal". A fundamental problem emerged, however, as a result of the different agendas of the two projects. The Paneuropean plan did not include the Soviet Union or Britain and its relations with the League of Nations were ambiguous. Both these points were viewed as limitations by the Estonian government. In the Estonian foreign ministry, Assistant[23] August Schmidt[24] compared the Paneuropean idea with the Briand Memorandum, favouring the latter as a more realistic option.[25] This cursory and unfair comparison with Paneurope negatively created prejudices towards the Memorandum from the very beginning.

When the Ministries received the Memorandum from the French envoy, they usually made some form of immediate reply. The French Chargé d'Affaires in Tallinn, Henry Cosme, had visited Schmidt and they discussed the Memorandum. In general, Schmidt liked the Memorandum and considered it realistic. Although it did not promise a lot, he at least thought the method was practical: "Neither was Rome built in a day."[26]

With public discussion, little doubt was left in *Postimees*' commentary. After presenting the main aspects of the proposal, the paper almost testified: "The moment has never been more benevolent and there has never been as urgent a necessity to achieve something to reconstruct Europe". Union was presented as the requirement for the survival and advancement of the continent.[27] *Vaba Maa* was content with a short notification and published a larger commentary by a German Social-Democrat, who sympathized with Coudenhove-Kalergi's more radical ideas.[28] *Päevaleht* reported the matter in a much more negative manner and concentrated on the difficulties ahead.[29]

Despite the common goal, some differences were found between the Paneuropean Union and Briand's proposal. Even a Paneuropean like Pusta defended Briand as an elected leader, responsible to his parliament, something that "the prophet of Paneurope" lacked."[30] According to Tõnisson,

---

23 The dismissive title ("*abimees*") referred to the highest-ranking civil servant in the Estonian foreign ministry, who assisted the Foreign Minister.

24 Schmidt changed his name to Torma in May 1940; Medijainen, 1997, pp. 136, 199.

25 ERA 957-13-404. Tallinn, message to the envoy in Paris, 23.5.1930.

26 ERA 957-13-404. Tallinn, message to the envoy in Paris, 23.5.1930.

27 "Juhtmõtted tulevase Euroopa ülesehitamiseks," in *Postimees*, 21.5.1930, p. 4.

28 "Briandi märgukiri Euroopa liidu asjus," in *Vaba Maa*, 18.5.1930, p. 5; von Gerlach, Helmut, "Pan-Euroopa kavatsusi ja Rahvasteliit," in *Vaba Maa*, 20.5.1930, p. 4.

29 "Kuidas suhtub Eesti Pan-Euroopa unioonile?" in *Päevaleht*, 20.5.1930, p. 3.

30 Pusta, 1929a.

Briand transformed the old idea into a real political question.[31] In general, *Postimees* would later repeat the stances of these politicians. The paper criticized Coudenhove-Kalergi and the Paneurope-Union as a private organization that lacked the mandate of the people. However, the same article stressed how the replies from the governments were supported by common European opinions.[32] According to *Kaja*, the idea of European unification had "broken out from the realm of idealistic dreams" and had "become a problem of Europe's official politics".[33] *Vaba Maa* would later compare quite derisively Coudenhove-Kalergi, who had had to adjust his programme, to the more practical Briand.[34]

Harald Tammer considered the blueprints of Briand and Coudenhove-Kalergi as divergent methods for fulfilling the same idea. For him, the Paneuropean Union was an almost completely idealistic programme that aimed at "growing out of nationalism, being directed towards classless society, some kind of supra-nationalistic state-collective, which would be characterized only by geographical expedience." The unification of Europe by Briand meant first and foremost solving economic problems. He had brought the question into consideration and even taken the first steps towards Paneurope. Tammer did not have high hopes for the proposal, but instead focused on the convenient coordination of existing actions.[35]

After receiving the Memorandum, the first reaction of various foreign ministries across Europe was to find out what other states thought of the idea. This process depended on established diplomatic relations, which depended on the resources of the respective foreign ministries as well as their general foreign orientation. On May 24, the Estonians asked their envoys "to inform the foreign ministry, how the press in your posting has [...] reacted to Briand's Memorandum. In addition, it is desired to sound out the attitudes of respective governments to the Memorandum."[36]

Consequently, the idea of a European federation became a topic of discussion in all European embassies and legations.[37] A week after the visit

---

31 "Euroopa rahvad ühinemisteel," in *Päevaleht*, 25.10.1929, p. 5; "Pan-Euroopa kõneõhtu Tartus," in *Postimees*, 30.10.1929, p. 3.

32 "Eurooplase Briandi algatus," in *Postimees*, 21.5.1930, p. 4; also "Eurooplaste ühised mured," in *Postimees*, 16.1.1931, p. 3.

33 F.J., "Briand Euroopat ümber korraldamas," in *Kaja*, 23.5.1930, p. 2.

34 R.T., "Coudenhove-Kalergi Pan-Euroopa ja ametlik Pan-Euroopa," in *Vaba Maa*, 2.2.1931, p. 4.

35 Tammer, Harald, "Pan-Euroopa ja väikerahvad," in *Päevaleht*, 22.5.1930, p. 2.

36 ERA 957-13-441. Tallinn, note for all the envoys, 24.5.1930.

37 Pegg, 1983, pp. 140–142; Ziegerhofer-Prettenthaler, 2004, pp. 152–156.

of the French Chargé d'Affaires, the Finnish Envoy, Aarne Wuorimaa, visited Schmidt. By this time Schmidt was already questioning whether the Memorandum would ever come to fruition. Nevertheless, whilst Schmidt did not want to take a negative stand, he did not want to accept everything without criticism.[38] These occasional – and sometimes contradictory – talks between envoys and ministries reveal a desire for mutual cooperation. But since most of the drafting process took place inside foreign ministries, which are out of bounds for researchers, they are also informative regarding the domestic formation of the replies.

Estonia attempted to sound out its neighbour's attitude to the proposal. Valdis Bērziņš, who has written on the Latvian reply, briefly mentions how Latvia "learned of the position of Estonia, Lithuania and other countries". He has nothing to say, however, about the common reply of Estonia and Latvia.[39] Nevertheless, the Finnish envoy in Riga, P.J. Hynninen, reported on June 13, that Latvia desired an answer similar to what they had received from Estonia and that these governments had already started to negotiate how to adopt a common attitude.[40]

Hynninen added that the Latvians found it relatively hard to reply but in principle wanted to take a positive stand. The Estonian Envoy in Riga, Eduard Virgo, had already sent a similar message on May 26, stating that the Latvian foreign ministry was "quite sceptical, they don't believe in its realization, but nevertheless they want to take up a sympathetic and benign attitude towards the Memorandum in the official reply."[41]

Apparently scepticism prevailed as the Latvian reply was very reserved. Latvia had little interest in promoting the French desire for a status quo without Great Britain and the Soviet Union. The influence of smaller states would also decrease. Latvia's reply was finalized in mid-June and the Swedish Envoy, Carl Reutersvärd, enquired about cooperation with Estonia on this matter. According to the Latvians, there could not be a discussion before the Estonian Government had come to an internal understanding and this did not seem to be in sight. Neither had they asked the opinion of any other foreign government.[42]

Finland was another of Estonia's allies; in the end, the Estonian foreign ministry only made remarks to the replies of Latvia and Finland.[43]

38 UM 15 VII 35b. Report from Tallinn, 4.6.1930.
39 Bērziņš, 1998, p. 415.
40 UM 155 VII 35b. Report from Riga, 13.6.1930.
41 ERA 957-13-404. Report from Riga, 26.5.1930.
42 RA UD HP 1255 II. Report from Riga, 20.6.1930.
43 ERA 957-13-404. Replies by the states to the memorandum, undated.

Relations with these neighbours were not as good as had been hoped. In 1929, their proposal of a customs union with Latvia collapsed. During the debate on the Memorandum, a trade agreement with Finland advanced poorly: the Estonians wanted to establish at least a limited customs union, whilst the Finns wanted to protect their market from Estonian products. However, the Finns considered relations to be relatively good with Estonia. Yet, the Finns understood perfectly well that the Estonians were bitter at their reluctance to participate in official unions. The official Finnish stance of isolation was accepted by Estonian politicians, who usually refrained from suggesting otherwise. As negotiations continued, cracks also appeared when other issues were discussed.[44] The old dream of a Finno-Estonian federation was occasionally mentioned in Estonian newspapers. However, somewhat curiously, these references originated from Finland.[45]

The Finns and Schmidt were very much in harmony with regard to the value they placed on the importance of the League of Nations. Thus, Schmidt considered it "highly desirable that replies given by our countries would be as analogous as possible" and wanted to know the Finnish standpoint.[46] Reports by Envoy Alexander Hellat from Helsinki, however, showed that Finland did not share the same enthusiasm as the Estonians. On June 18, Hellat sent a brief response stating that the Memorandum evoked little interest in the Finnish press and "when it has had, their position had been negative".[47] In the monthly review this observation is elaborated upon and became a prickly commentary on the lack of a Paneuropean spirit in Finland. Foreign Minister Hjalmar Procopé was personally a Paneuropean and he had established the Finnish section of the Paneuropean Union. However, the section seemed to promote Finnish stately affairs rather than the European idea.[48]

The role of the League of Nations was vitally important for all the states of Northern Europe. Whilst the idea had been presented at the League, it remained under French auspices, and therefore the relationship between these two principles of cooperation was not clear. In hindsight, it seems inevitable, since the replies were almost unanimous regarding the placement of

---

44 UM 5 C 12:20. Especially Wuorimaa's reports No. 37 (19.3.1929); No. 46 (1.11.1929); No. 47 (4.11.1929); No. 76 (10.12.1930). See also "Eesti-Soome sild," in *Päevaleht*, 9.12.1929, (Kratt No. 49); Medijainen, 1997, pp. 98–101, 238–240.

45 "Eesti-Soome riikide union," in *Vaba Maa*, 29.2.1928, p. 3; "Soome-Eesti ühisriikideks?" in *Vaba Maa*, 22.1.1929, p. 2.

46 UM 15 VII 35b. Report from Tallinn, 4.6.1930.

47 ERA 957-13-404. Report from Helsinki, 18.6.1930.

48 ERA 957-13-406. Review of May 1930 II, 25.6.1930.

the European Federal Union within the League of Nations, especially among smaller countries.[49]

Also in Estonia, the League of Nations was perceived as an important institution and they could not participate in a process that would dilute the League's influence through the formation of opposing interest groups. Despite purportedly only briefly studying the Memorandum, Schmidt was pleased that it seemed to emphasize this aspect.[50] Yet, only a week later he expressed less confidant views in a discussion with Wuorimaa. To avoid any doubt, he stressed that it would take a long time before Briand's idea could threaten the League. In the end, both Schmidt and Wuorimaa primarily saw the Memorandum as a method to strengthen the League.[51]

The interest of maintaining the power of the League of Nations reflected opinions on the role of Britain, which was one of the permanent members of the League's Council. In almost every discussion between an envoy and a Foreign Minister the subject of Britain's mutual requirement was voiced. This sentiment was expressed for example by Estonian envoy Friedrich Akel in a conversation with Swedish Foreign Minister Fredrik Ramel in Stockholm in late June.[52]

Estonia soon took notice of the negative or careful attitude of Great Britain. Envoy Oskar Kallas wrote two dispatches in June about the British orientation away from the continent and towards its dominions. According to the British, a united Europe would irritate the United States and the Soviet Union. Furthermore, the Memorandum was said to have false foundations, as the League of Nations could not create political unity, but economic cooperation was natural. In its present form, it was merely considered a French tactic to maintain the status quo in Europe. Officially, the British had strong doubts vis-à-vis the real intentions lying behind the Memorandum, and therefore their reply was only of a temporary nature.[53]

This was the start of a series of alarming pieces of news from London. The British wanted to delay their reply until after a meeting on the dominions had taken place in the autumn.[54] Briand managed to avoid a delay by

49 Pegg, 1983, p. 152.

50 ERA 957-13-404. Tallinn, message to the envoy in Paris, 23.5.1930; Made, 1999.

51 UM 15 VII 35b. Report from Tallinn, 4.6.1930.

52 ERA 957-13-404. Report from Stockholm, 25.6.1930.

53 ERA 957-13-404. Reports from London, 5.6.1930 and 12.6.1930; ERA 957-24-404. Review of June 1930, undated.

54 RA UD HP 1255 II. Report from London, 27.6.1930.

explaining to the British envoy in Paris that such a scenario was out of the question, since he had been authorized by the European states. He expected the general reply to arrive in time; whilst the details could be negotiated at a later date. The British eventually replied a few days late and were highly critical. Britain's negative stand was anticipated as indirectly influencing the responses of the other countries from adapting their positions as the chances of the Memorandum succeeding seemed weak without British support.[55] This seemed especially the case with the Nordic countries; including Estonia, followed British opinion closely and they linked their participation with Britain. On the other hand, they were not aiming to undermine Briand or the League of Nations. The Nordic countries perceived Britain as part of Europe and it was also a great economic partner for all of them.

A measure of weight was attached to the German reaction. The Estonian foreign ministry made handwritten notes on two reports sent from Berlin. They were especially interested in the negative attitude of the German government. The Germans criticized two points: first the plan was unthinkable without the revision of borders and secondly they wanted to stress economic issues, contrary to the French. Although the German answer was firmly negative, it was written in a polite tone.[56]

After the necessary domestic and international consultations were made, it was time to officially ratify the reply. The Estonian Parliamentary Foreign Affairs Committee had already approved the reply by the time Schmidt, boasting that he had written it, presented the document to the Finnish Envoy Wuorimaa on July 5. Minister Jaan Lattik generally preferred domestic questions to foreign affairs and allowed Schmidt to play the more active role. The government would deal with it in a couple of days and potential changes would be "so trivial that they will not matter to the point of anything to speak of."[57] Estonia was ready to take part in European negotiations, provided that every appropriate state was included, the development of the League of Nations was not disturbed and that it did not conflict with its extra-European interests. Furthermore, Estonia stressed that economic factors preceded political questions. Consequently, Estonia was content to wait until a European conference in order to discuss what kinds of institutions were necessary. On July 10, Foreign Minister Lattik handed the Estonian reply to the French Chargé d'Affaires, Henry Cosme.[58]

---

55 Boyce, 1980, p. 39.

56 ERA 957-13-404. Reports from Berlin, 19.6.1930 and 2.7.1930.

57 UM 15 VII 35b. Report from Tallinn, 5.7.1930.

58 ERA 957-13-404. Reply, 11.7.1930; UD HP 1255 III. Report from Tallinn, 11.7.1930; for example, "Eesti vastus Briandi memorandumile," in *Rahva Sõna*, 11.7.1930, p. 2; "Estnische Note," in *Paneuropa* 1930:10, pp. 367–368.

The future of both the Memorandum and the idea of a European federation were laid-out in the replies of Britain, Germany and Italy. None of them were actually applauding the initiative. The French drafted the report on the basis of these replies and it was discussed in Geneva in September 1930. Schmidt was the Estonian representative at "the conference of European states considering European political and economic union", while Foreign Minister Lattik and Professor Piip attended the Assembly of the League the next day. Finland had included a proposal of further reflections on the subject and subsequently the Yugoslavian delegation accompanied by the Finns, proposed a commission to study the idea. The outcome was the establishment of the Commission of Inquiry for a European Union, headed by Briand, with Eric Drummond, the Secretary-General of the League of Nations, as secretary. The first meeting was ordered to convene in January 1931.[59]

These results must have been a disappointment to most Estonian newspapers, and direct comments were avoided. For example, *Postimees* let a foreigner applaud the Commission.[60] Most were content to publish the announcement by Foreign Minister Lattik, who described how Paneurope had, during the general meeting, "changed its own name and content."[61]

As an exception, *Päevaleht* celebrated the failure of Briand's proposal. It argued that the League succeeded in defending its fundamental idea of universalism. Remaining within the League, the European federation had a possibility to become true one day. Furthermore, the organization of Europe was now an issue for the whole world, not just for one country.[62]

Estonia sent envoy Aleksander Hellat from Helsinki to the first assembly of the Study Commission in January 1931.[63] *Vaba Maa* was wholeheartedly optimistic after the first meeting, although it recognized the gap between the ideals of Paneurope and the existing League of Nations. In May, during the second meeting on the issue, the paper considered the work of the Commission unproblematic.[64] *Postimees* maintained a positive stand as

---

59 ERA 957-13-401, Report from Geneva, 13.9.1930; Piip, 1932, pp. 68–70; Pegg, 1983, pp. 149–156.

60 "Eile algas esimene Euroopa konverents," in *Kaja*, 9.9.1930, p. 1; "Genfis luuakse Euroopa komitee," in *Kaja*, 17.9.1930, p. 3; "Briand Euroopa komisjoni esimeheks," in *Päevaleht*, 25.9.1930, p. 3; Felix, C., "Liigub siiski!" in *Postimees*, 27.9.1930, p. 2; "Rahvasteliidu 11. Täiskogu," in *Vaba Maa*, 21.9.1930, p. 4.

61 "Rahvasteliidus majandusküsimused esikohal," in *Vaba Maa*, 1.10.1930, p. 5; "Välisminister rahvasteliidu täöst," in *Kaja*, 1.10.1930, p. 7; "Eesti Rahvasteliidu täiskogul," in *Päevaleht*, 1.10.1930, p. 3.

62 Ks., "Euroopa organiseerimise saatus," in *Päevaleht*, 27.9.1930, p. 2.

63 ERA 957-13-401. Authorization, 13.1.1931.

64 R.T., "Coudenhove-Kalergi Pan-Euroopa ja ametlik Pan-Euroopa," in *Vaba Maa*, 2.2.1931, p. 4; "Melankoolne Briand Genfis," in *Vaba Maa*, 17.5.1931, p. 3.

well. European problems had to be solved among Europeans instead of through universal channels.[65]

However, disappointment within the Study Commission became evident at its first meeting. It was more likely that the plan would be blocked rather than actually implemented. Briand was forced to back down on many important questions.[66] The first Estonian comment on the initial failure of the Memorandum appeared as early as September 1930. This occurred in a report from Moscow, which may have been influenced by the local press. However, in December, before the Study Commission had convened for the first time, also Pusta had to admit in Paris that the Memorandum had not produced the desired atmosphere.[67]

Subsequent Commission meetings were reported in papers somewhat pessimistically.[68] After May 1931, only *Postimees* continued to assert that the Commission was not only the right but also the effective place to solve European problems.[69] Pusta kept on this work internationally. In sum, he wrote seven articles in German and French journals on the role of the Study Commission and defended it even against Coudenhove-Kalergi. According to him, the Commission had exceeded expectations by turning a utopian project into reality and at the same time it had enhanced the universal League of Nations.[70] His articles were occasionally referred to in Estonian newspapers.[71]

---

65 "Välisministrid ruttavad Genfi," in *Postimees*, 14.5.1931, p. 3.

66 M., "Genf jälle huvipunktiks," in *Kaja*, 22.1.1931, p. 2; Rebane, Hans, "Euroopa Ühendriigid," in *Päevaleht*, 23.1.1931, p. 2; "Prantsusmaa ja Eesti," in *Päevaleht*, 21.1.1931, p. 5.

67 ERA 957-13-406. Review of September 1930, undated, and Review of December 1930, undated.

68 For example, "Briand pöörab poliitikale selja," in *Kaja*, 17.5.1931, p. 3.

69 "Euroopa muutub jõuüksuseks," in *Postimees*, 17.9.1931, p. 3. News for example, "Kokkuvõte Euroopa liidu uurimiskomisjoni majanduslise koordinatsioonialamkomisjoni töödest," in *Postimees*, 11.9.1931, p. 4.

70 "Vers l'Union européenne. Etude des Principes du Memorandum français du 1er Mai 1930 et des Réponses des Gouvernements," in *Revue de Droit international* 1930:3; "L'Union Européenne devant la Société des Nations," in *Revue de Droit international* 1930:4; "L'idée de l'Union européenne devant les gouvernements et la Société des Nations," in *Revue de Droit international et de Législation comparée* 1930:1; "Europäische Union, Regierungen und Völkerbund," in *Baltisches Handbuch für das Jahr 1931*; "Fonctionnement et travaux de la Commission d'Etudes pour l'Union Européenne," in *Revue de droit international* 1931:4; "Die Europa-Kommission," in *Paneuropa* 1932:1; "L'Union Européenne et la S.d.N.," in *Les Cahiers de l'Union Européenne* 1932:1.

71 "Saadik Pusta Euroopa unionist," in *Päevaleht*, 30.7.1930, p. 3; "Euroopa Liidu otsesemaid ülesandeid," in *Postimees*, 15.10.1931, p. 2; Tammer, Harald, "K.R. Pusta kõne Diplomaatlikus Akadeemias," in *Päevaleht*, 27.10.1931, p. 5; "Paneuroopa miniatuuris," in *Postimees*, 27.11.1931, p. 2; "K.R. Pusta Paneuroopast," in *Vaba Maa*, 18.2.1932, p. 2.

Subsequently, the Commission did not provide any good news for its supporters (*Postimees*, *Kaja*, *Vaba Maa*), while opponents (*Päevaleht*) remained silent. Criticism only emerged later. For example, in Nikolai Kaasik's introductory work on the League of Nations in 1933; while Kaasik defended the Commission because the problems were so complex and wide, he accused the League of restricting its work.[72] A year earlier, Ants Piip in his *Nüüdne maailmapolitika ja Eesti* (Current World Politics and Estonia) could find only negative expressions on the Commission's work: it "has not actually been in specifics of great importance". He could not imagine the materialization of a European union in the foreseeable future and probably never.[73]

The diplomatic aspect in the Estonian discussion on Paneurope was essentially connected to the discussion on the League of Nations. The federation process was handed over to bureaucracy of the League of Nations and the Commission assembled only once after Briand's death in March 1932. The National Socialists had become one of the leading parties in Germany during this time, thus damaging the prospects of the League of Nations in general and European unification in particular.[74] The Estonian faith in both of them diminished rapidly during the early 1930s. One illuminating example comes in the form of two articles by Harald Tammer in *Päevaleht* produced during a half-year period. First, in September 1931 Tammer asked about the crisis of the League, and, after Japan invaded Manchuria in March 1932, the possible end of the League.[75] Two years later, for him, the League deteriorated into a French pawn. In hindsight, Briand's Memorandum seemed like a lost opportunity: "After the failed proposal for European union by Briand, we have no longer heard anything positive" from the League. Despite this, it remained a supporting pillar for small states.[76]

As late as 1936, *Eesti Entsüklopeedia* (the Estonian Encyclopedia) dealt with the issue of the Study Commission in Volume VI, with the search word "*Paneuroopa*". The entry did not deal so much with Coudenhove-Kalergi and his movement, but the focus was on Briand's proposal and the Study Commission, which "had produced relatively small results mainly in the economic field."[77] The transfer from the political field to

72 Kaasik, 1933, pp. 68–70.

73 Piip, 1932, pp. 70, 72, 74–75.

74 Pegg, 1983, pp. 149–156, 164.

75 Tammer, Harald, "Kas Rahvasteliidu kriis?" in *Päevaleht*, 7.9.1931, p. 2; Tammer, Harald, "Rahvasteliidu lõpp?" in *Päevaleht*, 1.3.1932, p. 2.

76 Tammer, Harald, "Ümbergrupeerumisi ja ümberorienteerumisi," in *Päevaleht*, 2.9.1933, p. 2.

77 "Paneuroopa," in *Eesti entsüklopeedia VI*, 1936, pp. 542–543. See also Piip, Ants, "Euroopa konverentsid," in *Eesti entsüklopeedia II* 1933, p. 1319.

the economic one had occurred first as a result of an evident dead-end in the former, and thus new methods were required. Additionally, the economic situation changed dramatically while the French were drafting the Memorandum due to the Wall Street stock exchange crash in October 1929, this also moved the focus to economic questions within European unification discussion.

Chapter 3

Economic Consequences

"Desire to Liberate Oneself from American Economic Hegemony"

During the interwar period, there were also plans, movements, and organizations promoting economic cooperation. The problem of tariffs was crucial. For example, international conversations on customs stabilization were occasionally presented by Estonian newspapers as part of Paneurope: "It is the first serious step by European states towards the creation of a European economic federation, Paneurope. The road is very long, perhaps thousands of steps must be undertaken, and if the pace does not increase considerably, only future generations will be able to see that federation."[1] However, economics was never that important for the Paneuropean Union. A customs union was never enough for Coudenhove-Kalergi. According to him, a customs union without political consolidation would be used to maintain the protectionist policies often used in the past.[2]

In 1925 Pusta had presented the idea that economic difficulties had always been the most important reason for clashes in foreign policy. He portrayed a dark image of Europe with decreasing productivity.[3] A year later, economic distrust and tensions again offered the strongest arguments for Paneurope.[4] Finally, in October 1929, Pusta justified Paneurope with a human desire to become rich. "That is a precondition for the re-creation of the continent." The satisfaction of basic needs would lead to cooperation at other levels.[5]

1 For example, "Kas Paneuroopa poole?" in *Kaja*, 12.3.1930, p. 2.

2 Coudenhove-Kalergi, 1929, p. 11; Coudenhove-Kalergi, 1931, pp. 12–13; also "Kõik-Euroopa," in *Päevaleht*, 10.10.1926, p. 2; Ziegerhofer-Prettenthaler, 2004, pp. 274–275.

3 "Eesti ülesanded rahu korraldamisel," in *Vaba Maa*, 29.9.1925, p. 3.

4 Pusta, Kaarel Robert, "Esimene Paneuroopa kongress," in *Vaba Maa*, 21.9.1926, p. 2; Pusta, Kaarel Robert, "Esimene Paneuroopa (Kõikeuroopa) kongress," in *Postimees*, 22.9.1926, p. 2.

5 "Pan-Euroopa mõte laiemates hulkades," in *Päevaleht*, 1.11.1929, p. 2; also Ks., "Euroopa riikide liit," in *Päevaleht*, 6.9.1927, p. 2.

Others, including Jaan Tõnisson[6] and Ants Piip,[7] brought economic difficulties and the debt owed to the U.S. as the main reasons for unification.

On the other hand, deteriorating economic conditions did not provide reasons to oppose unification during the 1920s. Even when economic difficulties really began, they were rarely cited. More as an exception to verify to rule, Hans Rebane commented in July 1930 that the major obstacles for unification were "economic conflicts between European states, which are escalating in accordance with rising tariff-walls."[8] Pusta's reaction to the emerging depression was that unification was needed more desperately. However, the U.S. ceased to be an example for a European union. Instead, the League of Nations gained more support.[9]

One of the flaws of Paneurope was the tendency to build continental economic areas. When the first Paneuropean Congress was held in Vienna in October 1926, the organ of the Estonian Socialist Workers' Party, *Ühendus*, argued that the movement was basically an attempt to save the present society; it did not abolish borders but built new, higher ones against the Soviet Union and Great Britain. Thus, the newspaper claimed it had revealed the capitalistic nature beyond the pacifistic appearance of the Paneuropean Union.[10]

The article "Flaws of Paneurope" also considered economic blocks dangerous, first because economic restrictions and borders would increase tensions in other fields as well. The text made particular reference to the U.S., which had become a creditor of Europe during World War I. Although the U.S. was not a member, this was another reason to stress the League of Nations as a forum to solve differences peacefully. Secondly, the article argued that economic borders were especially dangerous for Europe, which, with scarce natural resources, did not form an economic community.[11] Harald Tammer agreed later on both points.[12]

The discourse of blocks (economic restrictions leading to political contradictions) already shows that economics was mainly thought to be state economics, or macroeconomics. For example, after presenting the plan for a European Customs Union by the Austrian Chamber of

---

6 J., "E. Ü. R. – Euroopa Ühendatud Riigid," in *Päevaleht*, 20.9.1927, p. 2; "Euroopa rahvad ühinemisteel," in *Päevaleht*, 25.10.1929, p. 5.

7 "Pan-Euroopa kõneõhtu Tartus," in *Postimees*, 30.10.1929, p. 3.

8 Rebane, Hans, "Briandi ühendriigid," in *Päevaleht*, 16.7.1930, p. 2.

9 "Prantsusmaa ja Eesti," in *Päevaleht*, 21.2.1931, p. 5.

10 Orvusto, "Pan-Euroopa ja sotsialism," in *Ühendus*, 20.10.1926, p. 2.

11 Ks., "Kõik-Euroopa pahed," in *Postimees*, 1.2.1927, p. 1.

12 Tammer, Harald, "Pan-Euroopa ja väikerahvad," in *Päevaleht*, 22.5.1930, p. 2.

Commerce, Pusta expected the states to take action: "Governments will have the first word."[13]

This became even more evident during Briand's proposal. In diplomatic circles he was widely expected to tackle economic questions. In Estonia, *Kaja* emphasized economic problems and solutions when introducing the proposal.[14] Later, *Kaja* repeated this stance and blamed Germany and Italy for transforming the question into a political one. It grieved that "political and psychological conditions for the materialization of this grandiose plan were missing".[15] Apparently *Kaja* was implying that economic requirements did exist and should be the starting point.

The gulf between economic and political foundations became a dividing line in the Memorandum as well as in the replies. The question centred on whether economic problems depended on political conflict or vice versa. The perceived answer to this foundational question led to divergent plans of action. If economic issues were considered dominant, then European unification should begin by tentatively reducing customs at the expense of state sovereignty. On the other hand, a political solution demanded the declaration of a predestined programme and some kind of, even nominal, organization. Needless to say, those who benefited from maintaining the status quo favoured the latter option.[16]

The transformation from an economic foundation to a political footing formed the major change in the Memorandum compared to Briand's speech delivered in September 1929. The failure of the Custom Truce Conference in February-March 1930 most likely changed Briand's mind.[17] Additionally, in the meantime, the Wall Street stock exchange had collapsed and the beginning depression made economic questions particularly vital. As a political consequence there was the increase in right-wing radicalism especially in new democracies, such as *Vapsid* (Union of Participants in the Estonian War of Independence) in Estonia.

Nevertheless, the Estonian foreign ministry did not change course. In this matter, there was again great influence from the Paris by Envoy Kaarel Robert Pusta. On May 23, 1930 Pusta had a discussion with Alexis

---

13 "Euroopa tolliuniooni põhimõtted," in *Postimees*, 3.11.1929, p. 7.

14 "Euroopa liidu loomise poole," in *Kaja*, 21.5.1930, p. 2; F.J., "Briand Euroopat ümber korraldamas," in *Kaja*, 23.5.1930, p. 2.

15 "Euroopa konverents avati," in *Kaja*, 17.1.1931, p. 1; M., "Genf jälle huvipunktiks," in *Kaja*, 22.1.1931, p. 2.

16 This was also noticed by contemporaries. For instance, Pusta evaluated the arrived replies in early June. ERA 957-13-406. Review of June 1930, undated.

17 Pegg, 1983, pp. 137–138.

Léger, who was mainly responsible for the formulation of the Memorandum.[18] Most of the report consists of a review of what Léger had said, and it is therefore hard to tell which opinions are his and which are Pusta's. Nonetheless, two aspects had an influence on the Estonian reply. Firstly, although Léger hesitated greatly on whether to favour economic or political issues, Pusta was clearly on the side of the former. Secondly, the then present situation in Europe did not offer especially bright prospects for the future of small states, and thus Estonia had to take a positive stand.[19]

Hans Rebane summarized: "Politics and economics, how much their ways of thinking have in common, yet how much they are different. However, economics seems to bear more and more preference. That is the knot which first waits untying."[20]

Examples dealing with tourism, trade, finance, etc. were rare, and the most interesting case was an article on the cooperation of European banks by Peeter Ruubel in 1929. Unfortunately, the article introduced mainly dated German plans, and the promise by the editors to study the issue more closely was never fulfilled.[21]

Promoters of Paneurope attempted to clarify future European relations to other units. According to Pusta, European unification would not go against the U.S. Rather; the U.S. could be instrumental in organizing Paneurope. The increased purchasing power of a united Europe would eventually benefit the Americans as well.[22]

In his original plan, Coudenhove-Kalergi excluded Great Britain from Paneurope.[23] This met with wide-spread opposition in Estonia for obvious reasons, since Britain was a major trading partner.[24] Johan Laidoner asked whether Estonian should exclude herself for economic reasons as well. Others also wondered about the same thing.[25]

Neither could Harald Tammer accept the exclusion of Great Britain. Coudenhove-Kalergi justified the exclusion because of Britain's large

---

18 *Ibid.*, p. 140.

19 ERA 957-13-404. Report from Paris, 23.5.1930.

20 Rebane, Hans, "Euroopa Ühendriigid," in *Päevaleht*, 23.1.1931, p. 2.

21 Ruubel, 1929.

22 Pusta, 1929a; "Eesti ülesanded rahu korraldamisel," in *Vaba Maa*, 29.9.1925, p. 3; Pusta, Kaarel Robert, "Esimene Paneuroopa kongress," in *Vaba Maa*, 21.9.1926, p. 2; also Coudenhove-Kalergi, 1929, p. 6; Coudenhove-Kalergi, 1931, pp. 11–12; "Kõik-Euroopa," in *Päevaleht*, 10.11.1926, p. 2.

23 Coudenhove-Kalergi, 1929, p. 6; Coudenhove-Kalergi, 1931, pp. 8–9.

24 Pihlamägi, 2004, pp. 218–225.

25 For example, M…i., "Euroopa Ühisriigid," in *Vaba Maa*, 12.8.1926, p. 2; "Paneuroopa poolt ja vastu," in *Vaba Maa*, 25.10.1929, p. 10.

empire. While Laidoner had accepted this argument, Tammer found it irrelevant, since other European states had territories and colonies outside Europe as well.[26] Afterwards Coudenhove-Kalergi changed his opinion on the British case.[27] During a public meeting held in August 1929, Jaan Tõnisson asked Pusta about relations with Great Britain, and Pusta seized the opportunity to state that a customs union was now preferred by both parties.[28]

For Coudenhove-Kalergi, the Russian Empire was a territory too big to be a part of Paneurope, and European agriculture should be protected from Russian products. Furthermore, by transforming into the Soviet Union, Russia had renounced European culture. Communism as such presented an imminent threat to Europe. United Europe could prevent Russia from interfering in European politics; reciprocally, Europe would not interfere in Russian politics.[29]

Joakim Puhk, the chairman of the Estonian Chamber of Commerce, repeated Coudenhove-Kalergi's ideas and proposed in the journal *Paneuropa* how a united Europe could be used against the rising Eastern power. In Puhk's opinion, the Soviet Union was aggressive both economically and politically and, as such, was the greatest threat against Europe. The Soviet Union had already abandoned the rules of capitalism by adopting state monopolization of foreign trade, which then subordinated economic questions in favour of political purposes: it made Western states and traders compete with each other. Europe could respond likewise and create a joint organization for Russian trade.[30] In 1938, Puhk would later write the foreword for the Estonian translation of Coudenhove-Kalergi's *Totaler Mensch – Totaler Staat*. In this piece, Puhk stressed Coudenhove-Kalergi's anti-communism, moreover, the book preached against any kind of totalitarian state systems.[31]

Quite a different approach was proposed in Estonia by Russian-born Mikhail Kurchinskii, Professor of Statistics at the University of Tartu. He published his own ideas on European unification first in newspapers[32]

---

26 Tammer, Harald, "Pan-Euroopa muutub sõjakaks?" in *Päevaleht*, 6.10.1932, p. 2.

27 R.T., "Coudenhove-Kalergi Pan-Euroopa ja ametlik Pan-Euroopa," in *Vaba Maa*, 2.2.1931, p. 4.

28 "Teel Pan-Euroopa poole," in *Vaba Maa*, 16.8.1929, p. 5.

29 Coudenhove-Kalergi, 1929, p. 6; Coudenhove-Kalergi, 1931, pp. 6–8; Ziegerhofer-Prettenthaler, 2004, pp. 372–386.

30 Puhk, Joakim, "Vorschlag zur Regelung des Wirtschaftsverkehrs mit der UdSSR," in *Paneuropa*, 1931:3, pp. 83–91.

31 Coudenhove-Kalergi, 1938.

32 Kurchinskii, Mikhail, "Euroopa kaos," in *Postimees*, 9.7.1925, p. 2, 10.7.1925, p. 4, 12.7.1925, p. 2, 14.7.1925, p. 2, 15.7.1925, p. 2, 16.7.1925, p. 2, and 18.7.1925, p. 2.

and eventually his book *Соединенные Штаты Европы* (United States of Europe)[33] came out in 1930. The book got good reviews in *Päevaleht*.[34] When Briand floated his proposal, Kurchinskii lectured on the issue in Tartu, Riga, and Kaunas.[35] Kurchinskii agreed with Coudenhove-Kalergi on many issues, however there were major disagreements over Russia. Unlike Coudenhove-Kalergi, Kurchinskii did not identify Russia with the Soviet Union and anticipated the end of the communist regime. After this, his vision saw Russia as economically integrated with Europe, especially as a producer of oil (liquid fuel) and agricultural products. Since Coudenhove-Kalergi had shown flexibility in the case of Great Britain, Kurchinskii proposed similar changes in relation to Russia. With the contemporary regime this was obviously impossible. However, a united Europe would hamper Soviet foreign trade and hasten its downfall. Subsequently, a customs union would be useful for Europe and Russia both economically and culturally in preference to polarization between the two entities.[36]

In the official reply to the Briand Memorandum, relations with the Soviet Union were also important, but for the opposite reason. According to Walter Lipgens, the German envoys in the Baltic states reported the positive attitude of the local governments and they stressed the perceived threat of the Soviet Union as a primary factor in the conceptual idea of a European union.[37] Their evaluation may have been oversimplified given the different nature of responses from the three states. On the other hand, finding military or political guarantees against the Soviet Union was the general goal of Estonian foreign policy, and the Memorandum seemed to give opportunities to increase them while using oblique terms. The Treaty of Locarno dealing with Germany's western border was not as such mentioned in the Memorandum but it referred to the politics of international guarantees initiated in Locarno. This was enough for Pusta, who took it for granted that the Memorandum would lead to similar permanent agreements of borders and obligations across the whole of Europe.[38] The extension of the Treaty of Locarno was a delicate matter for many countries, especially in Germany, so it could not be mentioned directly.

33 *Соединенные Штаты Европы. Экономические и политические перспективы этой идеи*. Derpt, Tartu, 1930.

34 E.P., "Euroopa Ühendriigid," in *Päevaleht*, 25.8.1930, p. 2 and 26.8.1930, p. 2.

35 "Tartu teated," in *Postimees*, 4.4.1930, p. 6.

36 E.P., "Euroopa Ühendriigid," in *Päevaleht*, 25.8.1930, p. 2 and 26.8.1930, p. 2; Smith, 1999.

37 Lipgens, 1966, p. 325.

38 ERA 957-13-404. Report from Paris, 23.5.1930.

Interlude of Regional Unions

In June 1930, with Briand's proposal under the consideration of European governments, the idea of European unification was at its peak. As the first symptom of a turn for the worse, Poland simultaneously proposed a different initiative for closer cooperation in the field of agriculture among the countries of Central and Eastern Europe.[39] This Polish initiative was a consequence of the economic depression, which had started half a year earlier in the U.S.

The first conference was held in Warsaw, August 28–30, 1930, and the list of participants succeeded in covering a wide territory, when even Hungary and Finland, states pursuing passive foreign policies, participated as observers – only Lithuania refused to attend. Estonia was represented by Minister of Agriculture August Kerem and local envoy Karl Tofer.[40] Naturally, the Agrarian *Kaja* paid much attention to the conference and to the creation of an 'agrarian bloc'. It stressed relieving the difficulties of basic agriculture, which should bypass the contemporary political dispute. Although *Kaja* was delighted by the attention the conference had received in the rest of Europe, it did not present it as model for further European unification. Instead, the development of European agriculture was presented as a complementary response to the cheap American wheat.[41] The next conference was held soon after in October of the same year, in Bucharest.[42] But the question faded away shortly thereafter, for various reasons. For one thing, the Balts disliked the Slavonic majority, and there were conflicts in other areas as well. Most importantly, every state was concerned to protect its own agriculture.[43]

Concurrently to the meeting in Bucharest, six Balkan countries held their own conference in Athens, which seemed to promise a full federation. Agreement was arrived at only as to subsequent regular meetings, but eventually none of them took place. Both conferences were embarrassing for Estonia and the Baltic states as the 'uncivilized' Balkans had appeared

39 "Ida- ja Lõuna-Euroopa põllumajanduslik liit," in *Kaja*, 19.7.1930, p. 3; "Põllumajandusliit Donau kallastelt Balti mereni," in *Päevaleht*, 19.7.1930, p. 4.

40 "Varssavi konverents algab home," in *Kaja*, 27.8.1930, p. 3; Piip, 1932, p. 109.

41 "Põllumajanduse huvide kaitseks," in *Kaja*, 16.8.1930, p. 2; "Põllumajanduse huvide kaitseks," in *Kaja*, 17.8.1930, p. 2; "Põllutööministerite konverents Varssavis," in *Kaja*, 28.8.1930, p. 2; "Varssavi agraarkonverentsi avamine," in *Kaja*, 30.8.1930, p. 7; "Varssavi konverents lopes," in *Kaja*, 2.9.1930, p. 7; "Varssavi konverentsi tulemusi," in *Kaja*, 4.9.1930, p. 2.

42 ERA 957-13 fonds 430–432. Agrarian conferences in Warsaw and Bucharest; "Bukaresti konverents lopes," in *Kaja*, 23.10.1930, p. 5.

43 Pegg, 1983, pp. 157–158; Karjahärm, 2003, p. 48.

to have overcome the problems which had prevented a Baltic union. The title of a 'northern Balkan', and any resemblance of South-East Europe, had earlier been eagerly denied in Estonian discussions.[44]

Although these conferences did not yet challenge the idea of a Paneuropean federation proposed by Briand, they exposed the difficulties of Baltic cooperation, which previously could be ignored in view of the fact that other regions had even less cooperation. Furthermore, they were the first regional conferences particularly in the field of agriculture, which became popular in subsequent years. For example Vienna hosted a series of such meetings in March 1931, where even industrial Germany participated.[45]

A more serious blow for Briand and European unification came in March 1931, when Germany and Austria took Europe by surprise and announced a customs union to relieve their economic emergency. The treaty was actually meant to be declared on March 21, but the information was leaked two days earlier. The information gave rise to protests in France, which claimed that the treaty violated the Peace Treaty of St. Germain. In other words, it threatened Austrian independence, which was under French protection. As a provisional solution, the treaty was sent to the General Assembly of the League of Nations and the International Court of Justice in The Hague. The latter found the treaty illegal in September, but Austria and Germany cancelled the treaty before the verdict to guarantee foreign credit to Vienna.[46]

From the beginning, both the Germans and the Austrians had announced the treaty as a step towards the economic unification of Europe under the principles of Paneurope. Additionally, the treaty stole the attention at a meeting of Briand's European Study Commission a few weeks later.[47] When the whole Commission met in May, German Foreign Minister Julius Curtius recalled the failure of the universal Customs

44 -s., "Balkan Baltist ette jõudnud," in *Päevaleht*, 23.10.1930, p. 2; also "Ida-Euroopa ja Balti liit," in *Postimees*, 23.9.1927, p. 2; "Esimene Balkani konverents Ateenas," in *Kaja*, 15.10.1930, p. 5.

45 "Kesk-Euroopa majanduskonverents," in *Kaja*, 25.3.1931, p. 9.

46 For example, "Saksa-Austria tolliliit äratab umbusku," in *Päevaleht*, 23.3.1931, pp. 1–2; "Saksa-Austria tolliuniooni nurgakivi," in *Postimees*, 23.3.1931, p. 1; "Euroopa kardab Saksa-Austria liitu," in *Vaba Maa*, 25.3.1931, p. 3; "Saksamaa ja Austria liitumas," in *Kaja*, 26.3.1931, p. 2; "Curtiuse vastus Briand'i süüdistusele," in *Päevaleht*, 2.4.1931, p. 3; "Saksa-Austria tolliuniooni küsimused Genfis," in *Päevaleht*, 4.9.1931, p. 5; "Austria peab jäämä rippumatuks," in *Postimees*, 7.9.1931, p. 1.

47 "Saksa-Austria tolliliit äratab umbusku," in *Päevaleht*, 23.3.1931, pp. 1–2; "Euroopa majandusliidu poole," in *Postimees*, 25.3.1931, p. 3; "Curtiuse vastus Briand'i süüdistusele," in *Päevaleht*, 2.4.1931, p. 3; "Saksa ja Austria loobuvad tolliliidust," in *Postimees*, 4.9.1931, p. 1.

Truce Conference three months earlier. While economies were worsening rapidly, it was appropriate to focus on more limited customs unions.[48]

The customs union treaty was unpleasant for the rest of Europe for two reasons. In Estonia, *Postimees* worried about how the treaty had first increased distrust between France and Germany and secondly how it would affect the Study Commission. The positive side was that Briand and France were forced to concentrate on economic aspects of his proposal and of the Study Commission.[49]

Kaja made some accurate conclusions about the "turning-point period" of European macroeconomics in 1931. It discerned two methods: the Germans and the Austrians had agreed on the condensation of economic relations between the two states. On the other hand, the French offered credit and agricultural banks promoting European cooperation. *Kaja* nevertheless mistook the Austro-German treaty as a turn from isolation to unification, seeing the treaty as a step towards Paneurope.[50]

On the contrary, subsequent studies have regarded the treaty as moving away from the proposals for a common federation to regional solutions.[51] Pseudonymous *Majandusmees* (Economist) in *Päevaleht* recognized this in March 1931: "Europe is not yet ready for general economic agreements. That has become ever clearer. [...] Therefore it is surely wise to endorse regional agreements." The article correctly calculated that European customs barriers would in fact rise when the higher tariff of Germany or Austria expanded.[52] *Päevaleht*, which had doubted the Paneuropean idea, welcomed the new side-track. On the other hand, it also kept in mind the long-term aim: "This would be a realistic opportunity and in the current situation a practical path towards the United States of Europe."[53]

But Harald Tammer, who had opposed Briand's continental plan, opposed the Austro-German customs union as well. His analyses focused on relations between small and big states. It seemed that a large industrial country was swallowing up a small agricultural one. Although he had

48 "Saksa soov pääsis Genfis võidule," in *Päevaleht*, 18.5.1931, p. 1.

49 "Välisministrid ruttavad Genfi," in *Postimees*, 14.5.1931, p. 3; also "Briand'i vastuaktsioon Saksa-Austria tolliunioonile," in *Päevaleht*, 4.4.1931, p. 4; "Kas Euroopa tolliliit toeks saamas?" in *Vaba Maa*, 4.4.1931, p. 3.

50 "Kas pöördeaeg Euroopa majanduspoliitikas?" in *Kaja*, 26.6.1931, p. 2; also Tupits, A., "'Anschlussi' esimene vaatus nurjus," in *Kaja*, 6.9.1931, p. 2.

51 Pegg, 1983, pp. 160–161; Ziegerhofer-Prettenthaler, 2004, pp. 201–202.

52 Majandusmees, "Uus ajajärk Euroopa kaubalepingute poliitikas," in *Päevaleht*, 24.3.1931, p. 2.

53 M., "Kolm välisministrid on rääkinud," in *Päevaleht*, 10.4.1931, p. 2.

opposed the Briand proposal, he now preferred a Paneuropean arrangement of centralizing agricultural trade; the industrial Western Europe should buy their bread from Eastern Europe rather than from America. This arrangement would grant the same results as regional customs treaties. As such, the treaty had worsened European relations in his opinion as well as provoking even greater distrust between Germany and France.[54]

Nor did *Kaja* understand Germany's bid for regional customs unions; like Tammer, it preferred continental cooperation. In fact, Europe was already unified in many ways and this unofficial development continued to go on. Thus, the treaty was a step backwards and diplomatic work in the League of Nations was preferable, even though it was a long and winding road: "Of course such a movement is not easy to materialize, and perhaps we, like many other generations will die before European unification becomes reality".[55]

The French counterproposal was eventually published on March 1, 1932. The short-lived Tardieu plan for a Danube Federation included Austria and Hungary in addition to the Little Entente of Romania, Yugoslavia and Czechoslovakia. This too was presented as a first step towards the economic reconstruction of Europe. The plan was discussed in London among representatives of Germany, Italy, France and Great Britain. The meeting as such placed the smaller countries in the position of passive objects; this was noticed in the Estonian newspapers. However, this did not concern them as long as Estonia was not particularly mentioned. The papers primarily wrote about saving and helping Eastern Europe.[56]

Tammer had in the meantime moved to Paris and frequently mentioned the Tardieu plan in his reports. Although he considered the plan impractical, more importantly he recognized a clear change in the European policy of both France and Britain: the continental Briand proposal was ultimately rejected, and plans limited in territory but with greater impact were promoted. The great powers had bigger interests in the Balkans, but in addition the earlier Balkan cooperation had attracted

54 Tammer, Harald, "Saksa-Austria tolliunioon ja Euroopa majanduslik tervenemine," in *Päevaleht*, 13.5.1931, p. 2; Tammer, Harald, "Saksa-Austria tolliunioon," in *Päevaleht*, 29.7.1931, p. 2; Tammer, Harald, "Tolliunioon tumestab endiselt Saksa-Prantsuse suhteid," in *Päevaleht*, 10.9.1931, p. 2.

55 Tupits, A., "'Anschlussi' esimene vaatus nurjus," in *Kaja*, 6.9.1931, p. 2.

56 For example, "Donau-riikide majandusliit," in *Postimees*, 10.3.1932, p. 2; H.L., "Donau riikide föderatsioon," in *Päevaleht*, 2.4.1932, p. 2; "Kuidas Donau-riike aidata," in *Kaja*, 6.4.1932, p. 3; A.M., "Tükk Euroopa saatust," in *Postimees*, 7.4.1932, p. 2; "Neljariigi konverents läks lõhki," in *Vaba Maa*, 10.4.1932, p. 1.

them. Consequently, Tammer advised greater Baltic cooperation to turn the British and French focus to the Baltic Sea.[57]

In addition to these European, theoretical considerations, not directly involving Estonia, the Austro-German customs treaty immediately evoked conclusions related to the unsuccessful Baltic customs union. *Vaba Maa* pointed out that the Germans of two countries had managed in few months to come to a resolution, while the Balts had been trying in vain for the last ten years.[58] This was a deliberate provocation, as the German upper class was the significant 'other' in the Estonian national narrative. *Postimees* explicitly hoped that the Baltic states would follow and bring their economies closer together. Although the position of pioneer in constructing regional cooperation was lost, the last place had to be avoided. *Päevaleht* expressed similar aspirations.[59] *Postimees* also gave space to a humorous column which maliciously prophesied blessings for Germany and Austria on the basis of Baltic experience. It also criticized the newspaper itself and other Europeanists, who rejected the regional attempt at their general goal.[60]

The initial Latvian response to the Estonians appeared in *Brīva Zeme*. According to the newspaper, comparison of the two treaties was unfair, since the Germans had agreed on many more reduced clauses. Nevertheless the treaty was a good model for the Baltic states, especially since it included some ideas which Latvia had earlier proposed to Estonia.[61]

In the next two years there were many attempts for deeper cooperation between the Baltic states. Diplomats had practiced some cooperation in their international missions and within the League of Nations. This was probably at its most intensive during the general meeting of 1930; however, not because of the Briand Memorandum but due to a vacant seat in the Council of the League. An unofficial rotating system of seats had evolved in the League and the diplomats wanted the Northern European seat previously occupied by Finland to go to one of the Baltic states. Nevertheless their cooperation was eventually futile, when the seat was ultimately

57 Tammer, Harald, "Donau probleem ja meie," *Päevaleht*, 13.4.1932, p. 2; Tammer, Harald, "Uus poliitiline suurjõud Euroopas," in *Päevaleht*, 21.2.1933, p. 2; Tammer, Harald, "Vilno, Balti liit ja väikeriikide ühisrinne," in *Päevaleht*, 28.3.1933, p. 2.

58 "Saksa-Austria tolliunioon hakkab maksma tulevast aastast," in *Vaba Maa*, 25.3.1931, p. 5.

59 "Balti merest kuni Brennerini," in *Postimees*, 24.3.1931, p. 2; Majandusmees, "Uus ajajärk Euroopa kaubalepingute poliitikas," in *Päevaleht*, 24.3.1931, p. 2; "Üks unenägu tõeks saamas?" in *Päevaleht*, 26.3.1931, p. 5.

60 K., "Austria-Saksa 'kolhoos,'" in *Postimees*, 4.4.1931, p. 4.

61 "Lätlased tolliliidust Eestiga," in *Postimees*, 28.3.1931, p. 4.

inherited by Norway.[62] In January 1931 the legations of the five Baltic Sea states in Paris started to have monthly 'Baltic lunches' to advance their joint problems with the French government. The first such lunch was held at the Estonian embassy.[63] The monthly schedule was later given up; subsequent lunches were organized in March by Latvia and in June by Poland.[64]

There were also suggestions for more frequent conferences, a Baltic study commission to follow in Briand's footsteps, and the unification of legations for instance in the Baltic Sea region. The cultural Pan-Baltic idea and other expressions of a common destiny also gained more popularity in this period: "Without further explanations it is undoubtedly clear that these states stand and fall *together*. If one of them would disappear for reasons of foreign policy, the *others* will be finished as well." The turn of the year 1931/1932 was the most active time for such proposals, and private representatives of the Latvian foreign ministry also spoke publicly of such ideas.[65]

In Estonia, it was *Vaba Maa* that was the most receptive. With *Jaunākās Ziņas* of Riga, it launched an inquiry among leading Baltic businessmen in the three states concerning economic cooperation, with the idea of making it closer. *Päevaleht* commented with an assurance of Estonian innocence in the imbalance of trade with Latvia; on the contrary, it accused Latvia of misusing the transition trade.[66] Likewise *Postimees* replied bitterly to Latvian proposals, ignoring charges that Estonia had ruined the mutual customs union. It did not bother even to mention where the problems and difficulties had originated: it was common knowledge they came from Latvia. Despite this, *Postimees* did not want to remain in the past but hoped the customs union would come true, on Estonian terms of course.[67] Also Pusta denied Estonian guiltiness and hinted to opposite direction.[68]

Estonians naturally followed developments in their neighbourhood. Norway, Sweden, Denmark, the Netherlands, Belgium and Luxembourg

---

62 "Välisminister rahvasteliidu tööst," in *Kaja*, 1.10.1930, p. 7. The same on the Latvian side: "Eesti ja Läti koostöö rahvasteliidus," in *Kaja*, 25.9.1930, p. 5.

63 "Esimene 'Balti eine' Pariisis," in *Kaja*, 14.1.1931, p. 7; "'Balti eine' Pariisis," in *Postimees*, 15.1.1931, p. 2; "'Balti lõunad' Pariisis," in *Kaja* 18.1.1931, p. 3.

64 "Kolmas 'Balti eine' Pariisis," in *Vaba Maa*, 28.3.1931, p. 7; "Balti eine Pariisis," in *Kaja*, 28.3.1931, p. 1; "'Balti eine' Pariisis Poola auks," in *Kaja*, 14.6.1931, p. 5.

65 K., "Kõik-Balti mõte," in *Päevaleht*, 5.2.1932, p. 2; also "Balti riikide koostöö," in *Postimees*, 29.10.1931, p. 4; "Pan-Baltoonia Läti lehtedes," in *Päevaleht*, 8.1.1932, p. 5; "Läti tahab Pan-Balti uniooni," in *Päevaleht*, 29.1.1932, p. 1.

66 "Eesti, Läti ja Leedu majanduslik koostöö," in *Vaba Maa*, 25.10.1931, p. 2; 27.10.1931, p. 2; 29.10.1931, p. 2; "Balti majandusblokk," in *Päevaleht*, 31.10.1931, p. 2.

67 "Balti riikide koostöö," in *Postimees*, 29.10.1931, p. 4.

68 Pusta, 1929a.

signed the Treaty on Convention of Economic Rapprochement in Oslo in December 1930; Finland joined this Oslo group in 1933. There appears to be no Estonian desire to join this loose treaty, but it served as a model for *Postimees* to propose similar agreement with Latvia to refrain from elevating mutual tariffs in February 1932. After three months, when nothing had happened, the frustrated newspaper returned to the issue once again.[69] Both countries, like most of Europe, had continued to affirm their protectionist economic policies.

69 "Balti tollirahu," in *Postimees*, 24.2.1932, p. 3; "Mis saab Balti riikide tollirahust?" in *Postimees*, 22.5.1932, p. 2.

Chapter 4

Cultural Premises

"It Demands a Common Spiritual Level for all Member Nations"

The debate as to whether to use political or economic methods in the attempt to gain European unity during the interwar period was accompanied with a constant discussion on European culture as the foundation for any practical solutions. Almost from the beginning, religious vocabulary, from prophecy to confession, was related to the Paneuropean idea.[1] An article in *Päevaleht* in September 1927 claimed that Paneurope was so far not widely comprehended and preached only by the devoted. Furthermore, the same article ignored the political initiatives of the programme and instead treated it as an outline for a new world vision (next to conservatism, socialism, and pacifism). As soon as the blueprint gained sufficient popularity, its goal, a European federation, would come true.[2]

In September 1927, there were still reasons to be optimistic despite the great problems and lack of results. The Paneuropean idea had so far gained only slim popularity and outside the movement the influence was mainly "platonic". However, eventually courageous plans would reach the ears of politicians as long as the greater public would keep them on the agenda. "The idea of federation of European states is on the move, it has come to its novice stage." The great problems included disputes between nations, states and races both at the economic and cultural levels. Europeans had nevertheless more in common than things keeping them apart. The greatest reason and justification for unification was "the natural need for people and nations to socialize with the similar ones".[3]

Coudenhove-Kalergi's political vision was based on a European "cultural community", which was divided into several languages, races, and religions. Europeans shared social practices and norms, economic interests and also

1 For example, N.A., "Euroopa tolliunioon ja Kõik-Euroopa liikumine," in *Postimees*, 31.1.1926, p. 3.

2 J., "E. Ü. R. – Euroopa Ühendatud Riigid," in *Päevaleht*, 20.9.1927, p. 2.

3 Ks., "Euroopa riikide liit," in *Päevaleht*, 6.9.1927, p. 2.

important historical ideas such as Christianization, humanism, enlightenment, nationalism, and socialism. Additionally, a European community complemented European nations.[4]

According to Pusta, Paneurope was not merely a political or economic programme, but also a spiritual one. After all, politicians and diplomats often moved to new positions. Therefore, there was a need to give birth to "conscious European solidarity, European 'patriotism' in every class, especially among the young." The Paneuropean Congresses and national societies were organized for this purpose.[5]

Also Tõnisson stressed that Coudenhove-Kalergi spoke of "European cultural solidarity" as the basis for unification. On the other hand, European "individual spirit" formed a barrier for unification at all levels. English was proposed as the common language to improve the situation. According to Tõnisson, the Paneuropean Union would hopefully increase knowledge of the spiritual variety among European nations and thus give birth to European culture, which would then consequently unify Europe as a state.[6] Several days later, Tõnisson mentioned that "undoubtedly when we evaluate the real circumstances we must also pay attention to the intellectual life of European nations, which is currently characterized by highly evolved national feelings, the idea of sovereignty and cultural individuality."[7]

Laidoner agreed on a common European culture. However, that culture had expanded elsewhere; thus to draw European borders was impossible. Laidoner's solution was simple: "it's nice to be a European citizen, but it would be even nicer – a global citizen." Tõnisson replied that both restrictions and establishing borders were natural elements of human nature.[8]

The eastern border of Europe was crucial in the Estonian debate. Coudenhove-Kalergi made a historical analogy between how a centralized and half-civilized Macedonia could conquer the superior but divided Greece. The book review in *Päevaleht* emphasized this.[9] Piip was another to

---

4 Coudenhove-Kalergi, 1931, pp. 13–15.

5 Pusta, Kaarel Robert, "Esimene Paneuroopa kongress," in *Vaba Maa*, 21.9.1926, p. 2; Pusta, Kaarel Robert, "Esimene Paneuroopa (Kõikeuroopa) kongress," in *Postimees*, 22.9.1926, p. 2.

6 "Paneuroopa poolt ja vastu," in *Vaba Maa*, 25.10.1929, p. 10; also "Euroopa rahvad ühinemisteel," in *Päevaleht*, 25.10.1929, p. 5; "Pan-Euroopa kõneõhtu Tartus," in *Postimees*, 30.10.1929, p. 3; "Pan-Euroopa mõte laiemates hulkades," in *Päevaleht*, 1.11.1929, p. 2.

7 "Pan-Euroopa mõte laiemates hulkades," in *Päevaleht*, 1.11.1929, p. 2.

8 "Paneuroopa poolt ja vastu," in *Vaba Maa*, 25.10.1929, p. 10.

9 "Pan-Euroopa," in *Päevaleht*, 31.5.1927, p. 5.

repeat Coudenhove-Kalergi's point of view. Furthermore, he was convinced that Paneurope would be strong enough to "oppose every attempt, which Russia could mastermind to defeat the Western civilization."[10] Pusta saw that Russia had isolated herself from Europe. In addition, he presented the opinion of Fyodor Dostoevsky who argued that Russia's destiny was to be that of a mediator between Europe and Asia. Pusta did not, however, expect a sudden attack from Russia and did not want a united Europe to escalate tensions.[11] Tõnisson agreed that Europe should become stronger to defend itself from possible Russian attacks.[12] According to Harald Tammer, Russia by size alone and "with Asian traditions" did not belong to Europe.[13] As late as 1935, August Tammekann, Professor of Geography, replied to Coudenhove-Kalergi's inquiry concerning the eastern border of Europe. Although Tammekann denied the existence of absolute geographical borders, he argued that, politically, Russia had evolved into its own community and did not belong to "actual Europe".[14]

Although Estonians agreed on the danger of both the Soviet Union and Communism, there was no need to underline this opposition. Coudenhove-Kalergi asked the secretary of the Estonian Paneuropean Society, Märt Raud, for anti-communist organizations in Estonia. Raud assured "Estonia to be practically immune to Communism." According to Raud, due to an attempted coup d'état, communists were officially enemies of the state and regular news from across the border kept the citizens alert. All private collectives were against Communism in one way or another.[15]

As the Soviet Union was perceived as an entity of its own, outside Europe, its invitation to the Study Commission was suspected by Pusta and others. The country did not even belong to the League and was fundamentally hostile to the unification of 'bourgeois' Europe.[16] Something similar was alluded to in the commentary in *Päevaleht*, which noted "the invitation of Russia to the fellowship of European states. Thus, the

---

10 Piip, 1932, pp. 25–26, 65–66, 97–101.

11 Pusta, Kaarel Robert, "Esimene Paneuroopa kongress," in *Vaba Maa*, 21.9.1926, p. 2; "Balti liit – Pan Euroopa eelkäija," in *Päevaleht*, 10.8.1927, p. 3; Pusta, 1929a.

12 "Euroopa rahvad ühinemisteel," in *Päevaleht*, 25.10.1929, p. 5.

13 Tammer, Harald, "Pan-Euroopa muutub sõjakaks?" in *Päevaleht*, 6.10.1932, p. 2.

14 HAEU, PAN/EU 30. Tammekann to Coudenhove-Kalergi, 27.10.1935; "Wo liegt die Ostgrenze Europas?" in *Paneuropa* 1935:10, pp. 318–322; Ziegerhofer-Prettenthaler, 2004, pp. 337–338.

15 RGVA 554-1-43, pp. 294–295. Raud to Paneuropa-Verlag, 7.4.1933.

16 M., "Genf jälle huvipunktiks," in *Kaja*, 22.1.1931, p. 2; "Vene kutsutakse osa võtma Euroopa liidu uurimiskomisjoni töödest," in *Vaba Maa*, 21.1.1931, p. 3; H.R., "Euroopa Ühendriigid," in *Päevaleht*, 23.1.1931, p. 2; Pusta, Kaarel Robert, "Sõnadelt tegudele," in *Postimees*, 1.2.1931, p. 4.

European states are not now alone deciding on the organization of their own continent."[17] The issue was not addressed as an economic question, but as a cultural one.

In general, the Russophobia of Coudenhove-Kalergi applied to the Estonians only with some modifications. While it was vital for the Estonians to distinguish themselves from Russia, they also wanted to present themselves as a bridge between the West and the East. These contradictory objectives could not be realized.[18]

Alternative views touched upon European history. For example, Ants Piip started his presentation with a thorough review of former plans for unification.[19] Tõnisson discussed how the unification of Europe had been an ideal goal for a long time, but only Napoleon had tried achieve it, albeit unilaterally and violently; the conquest of Europe was not the same as unification. However, Tõnisson's interpretation of the crusades as the manifestation of European unanimity based on common religion[20] is strange not only because it presents Europe as an aggressive opposite to the general pacifist nature of Paneurope, but also because the Baltic region has always been a border territory for two, maybe even three Christian churches. Napoleon was a point of reference also to others, but Laidoner instead compared the Holy Alliance to the current League of Nations.[21]

Pusta focused upon the unifications of Italy and Germany. Additionally, he wrote about technological progress, which had shrunk the world theoretically. However, in practice, it took as much time to cross the same distance due to border controls, etc.[22] Tammer disputed similarities to the unifications of the previous century because the latter were promoted by "realistic people of action, like Cavour and Bismarck" instead of "hypocritical men of cabinets". According to Tammer, despite the 20th century idealism represented by Paneurope, the world was still ruled by the materialism of the nineteenth – or of any – century.[23] Additionally, Tammer

17 Ks., "Euroopa organiseerimise saatus," in *Päevaleht*, 27.9.1930, p. 2; also, K., "Austria-Saksa 'kolhoos'," in *Postimees*, 4.4.1931, p. 4.

18 Piip, 1932, pp. 96, 111–112; Karjahärm, 2003, pp. 49–51, 67, 96–100, Karlsson, 2003, p. 175.

19 Piip, 1932, pp. 52–61.

20 "Euroopa rahvad ühinemisteel," in *Päevaleht*, 25.10.1929, p. 5; also "Paneuroopa poolt ja vastu," in *Vaba Maa*, 25.10.1929, p. 10; "Pan-Euroopa kõneõhtu Tartus," in *Postimees*, 30.10.1929, p. 3; "Pan-Euroopa mõte laiemates hulkades," in *Päevaleht*, 1.11.1929, p. 2; Napoleon was mentioned by others as well: Konik, Konstantin, "Ühendatud Euroopa," in *Vaba Maa*, 17.9.1929, p. 4.

21 "Kas rahuaade on teostav," in *Vaba Maa*, 29.11.1931, p. 5.

22 Pusta, Kaarel Robert, "Esimene Paneuroopa kongress," in *Vaba Maa*, 21.9.1926, p. 2.

23 Tammer, Harald, "Euroopa partei kava," in *Päevaleht*, 8.10.1932, p. 2.

came up with a brilliant historical analogy of the idealized example of Switzerland as the model for European unification, while in reality the bitter quarrels and endless compromises might result in something like Austria-Hungary.[24]

A different kind of history was presented in *Päevaleht* in September 1927. Accordingly, "Europe has indeed never existed as a unity". On the contrary, segregation and divisions were characteristic of its past. Napoleon and Germany during the World War (Friedrich Naumann's *Mitteleuropa*) only had deceptive programmes to rule Europe. Instead, only the balance of power of Europe of the 19th century was presented as an equivalent to Paneurope.[25] Earlier, *Päevaleht* had doubted the possibility of European unification because history did not have similar examples; "It must be found only now and then reconciled to life." Furthermore "historically evolved units – current states" had created their own customs and coherence.[26] As seen, this was recognized as a problem by the advocates as well.

The article "Flaws of Paneurope" presented another vision of history and pointed out the inadequate historical development of the national idea. According to the text, a nation is born by distinction from others and in its initial stages develops by emphasizing its particular characteristics. Only later, at a higher level of development, does a nation become more open to cooperation. At that moment, the initial stage seemed to continue strongly. The emergence of new nation-states after the war and subsequent minority movements were cited as supporting evidence. On the other hand, the text required a common spiritual level among member nations, "a great European feeling of unity" for diminishing national hatred and extending peaceful cooperation.[27]

Harald Tammer later repeated this view. He clarified the definition of small states: "Small nations, have suffered under the pressure of great ones for centuries". These nations were ready to reduce their living standards if they could maintain their independence, for which they had fought for decades, even centuries. Due to their fresh status, such nations were instinctively timid and careful about committing to political "combinations". "A member of a small nation cannot feel yet as a European, as a Paneuropean." Although Tammer had a firm opinion, he nevertheless left the door open for further development.[28]

24 Tammer, Harald, "Pan-Euroopa ja väikerahvad," in *Päevaleht*, 22.5.1930, p. 2.

25 J., "E. Ü. R. – Euroopa Ühendatud Riigid," in *Päevaleht*, 20.9.1927, p. 2.

26 Ks., "Euroopa riikide liit," in *Päevaleht*, 6.9.1927, p. 2.

27 Ks., "Kõik-Euroopa pahed," in *Postimees*, 1.2.1927, p. 1.

28 Tammer, Harald, "Pan-Euroopa ja väikerahvad," in *Päevaleht*, 22.5.1930, p. 2.

Pusta drew a dissimilar conclusion from the same premises. He considered the freedom of small states both the reason and a result of World War I. Therefore, small states had a special moral duty to consolidate international politics, despite the presence of bigger and older states. "Estonian and other states brought about after World War I are feasible only in a peacefully organized, strong and unanimous Europe. Everything, which strengthens European togetherness, fortifies also our national sovereignty." While the rest of Europe suffered from the loss of being an economic and cultural centre, new countries enjoyed and felt empowered by their independence.[29]

At least *Postimees* did not consider the smallness of states a problem – quite the opposite. European unification meant summoning common forces against other strengthening continents, and small states would benefit more than others. Recognizing this, as Estonians did, did not mean that "we insult our own national identity" when bigger nations were just reaching the same level.[30]

The development toward unification was not exclusively positive. Professor August Tammekann pessimistically predicted great difficulties in maintaining both education and culture in the Estonian language. He presented the alternatives, whether to assimilate voluntarily to a greater nation or deliberately remain on a lower cultural level. His view did not please everyone and one of his publishers, the student council of the University of Tartu, demanded the removal of this remark from Tammekann's forthcoming work.[31] Tammekann was also pessimistic about the political means to prevent assimilation, because "such isolation brings along only economic and cultural stagnation", especially for small states. While there were serious difficulties in cooperation on a smaller scale between neighbours, "Paneurope, i.e. the idea of United States of Europe, seems at least at the moment completely utopian."[32]

Tammer, too, recognized a slippery slope from economic dependency to cultural stagnation. Although a federation or customs union could be established on the basis of administrative equality, economically larger members would subjugate the smaller ones first economically and inevitably, culturally, making them ethnographic peculiarities. Therefore, "while recognizing the necessity of the Paneuropean idea from a European point

29 Pusta, 1929a.

30 "Eurooplase Briandi algatus," in *Postimees*, 21.5.1930, p. 4.

31 "Eesti ülikooli prof. A. Tammekann Eesti iseseisvuse võimalust eitamas," in *Sõdur*, 1933:9/10, p. 357.

32 Tammekann, 1932, p. 1676.

of view; from an Estonian perspective, there is no reason to accelerate the process."[33] Philipp Kaljot, the Estonian consul in Copenhagen, expressed the fear that small states would assimilate into Paneurope without tariff walls. Tõnisson replied that the fear was justified, but rejected the proposition: the state borders could not stop the development, if the people could not take care of themselves without them.[34]

It was not far from comparing Paneurope to the U.S., and occasionally the aim of the Paneuropean Union was mentioned as "united Europe by the example of the United States of America",[35] although Coudenhove-Kalergi clearly denounced this.[36] Nevertheless, Tammer made a comparison to the United States, where the population had already developed into "a hypernational nation – into Yankees". However, in Europe the diversity of nations, cultures, and languages hindered even the beginning of cooperation. Although Tammer saw unification in some form as necessary for the future, he stated that, "concerning this issue, European federative states will perhaps never appear as an entity such as the United States of America." Therefore, Paneurope was not an agreeable goal but sustaining the League of Nations was worth trying. "Of course, it is a long way from Briand's European fraction in the League of Nations to Yankeefied Europeans." The same argument was also repeated later.[37]

Possible national policy for the unified Europe could be based on existing minority politics. Partly due to the exemplary minority legislation of Estonia,[38] Pusta was to become the expert on questions of minority nationalities within the Paneuropean Union in 1927 and wrote the article in the movement's journal. Pusta acknowledged that the question was old and difficult. His modest proposal focused on providing better information on the rights and duties of minorities. Rights were to be instituted simultaneously in neighbouring countries; with the possibility of doing this best seen as within Paneurope.[39]

---

33 Tammer, Harald, "Pan-Euroopa ja väikerahvad," in *Päevaleht*, 22.5.1930, p. 2.

34 "Paneuroopa poolt ja vastu," in *Vaba Maa*, 25.10.1929, p. 10; "Euroopa rahvad ühinemisteel," in *Päevaleht*, 25.10.1929, p. 5.

35 "Pan-Euroopa looja," in *Vaba Maa*, 6.10.1926, p. 8; also Täht, Herman, "Saagu teoks Paneuroopa idee," in *Kaja*, 22.1.1929, p. 2.

36 Coudenhove-Kalergi, 1931, p. 11.

37 Tammer, Harald, "Pan-Euroopa ja väikerahvad," in *Päevaleht*, 22.5.1930, p. 2; also, K., "Kõik-Balti mõte," in *Päevaleht*, 5.2.1932, p. 2.

38 Alenius, 2003.

39 Pusta, Kaarel Robert, "Das Minoritätenstatut und die Rolle der Minderheiten in Paneuropa," in *Paneuropa* 1927:7, pp. 6–15; also, "Eeltööd Kõik-Euroopa kongressiks," in *Postimees*, 12.5.1927, p. 3; Hindrey, K.A., "Pan-Euroopa," in *Päevaleht*, 13.5.1927, p. 2.

Two years later, in a public event, Peeter Kann asked Pusta about the role of minorities in the Paneuropean movement. Based on his article on *Paneuropa*, Pusta identified minorities as reasons for disputes in international relations. If the minorities joined the movement, they could instead become a binding element and important factor in European unification.[40]

Coudenhove-Kalergi later included the protection of national and religious minorities as an essential element of Paneurope. The problem could be solved only via European unification.[41] Later, when the International Paneuropean Party was established, section 6.b of the programme promoted "the protection of all European minorities by the example of Switzerland and Estonia". Tammer, who commented on the programme in *Päevaleht*, expressed thanks for the compliment, but possibly not in a totally sincere manner.[42]

It is perhaps a case of the irony of history that Estonia was among the most ethnically homogeneous states in Europe during the interwar period, when it could establish the most liberal minority policy, which was then hailed as a model for others in the discussion of European unification. During the Soviet occupation the share of the titular nation within the Estonian Soviet Socialist Republic decreased from 88% to 61% due to mostly Russian immigration. Once again, the contemporary has brought up the issue of minorities in Estonia within discussion of European unification, but this time in a negative context. During the process of membership negotiations to European Union, the rights of the Russian minority were the sole controversial issue in the Estonian application. Eventually Estonia complied with the demands of the OSCE and consequently the EU. However, relations between the ethnic groups are minimal and tensions arising from this sparked the notorious riots of April 2007, the largest in Estonia since the restoration of independence.[43]

The Promise and Problem of the Baltic Region

Likewise individuals belong simultaneously to several groups, groups strive for various references, for divergent reasons and with changing levels of commitment. Estonia, for example, is part – among its other

40 "Teel Pan-Euroopa poole," in *Vaba Maa*, 16.8.1929, p. 5. The attitude by the minorities' movement was not as positive, see Hiden, 2004, pp. 172–175.

41 Coudenhove-Kalergi, 1929, p. 9; Coudenhove-Kalergi, 1931, p. 18; Ziegerhofer-Prettenthaler, 2004, pp. 477–481.

42 Tammer, Harald, "Euroopa partei kava," in *Päevaleht*, 8.10.1932, p. 2.

43 Karlsson, 2003; Raik, 2003, pp. 54–55; Crols, 2005; Elsuwege, 2008, pp. 21, 37–39, 108–110, 240–244, 269–288, 421–449; Kasekamp, 2010, pp. 154–155, 184–186.

affiliations – of the West, of Europe, of the Baltic Sea Region and of the Baltic states. Rather than treating regionalism and Europeanism as opposites, I understand the latter as an example of the former: Europe too is a region.[44] The interests of these regions can sometimes be contradictory and can be used against each other. In the following, I explore the relationship between the concepts of Baltic and Europe in the Paneuropean discussion.

Baltic cooperation had started already under the Russian Empire as a way to establish the independence of the three states. Between the declarations of independence in 1918 and de jure recognition by the greater powers during the early 1920s, the usefulness of cooperation in reaching these goals was acknowledged already by contemporaries. The most extensive conference was held in Bulduri, near Riga, in August 1920. After that cooperation faded out and when other countries dropped out of the plans, the defence union between Estonia and Latvia in 1923 remained the culminating point; talks and meetings of foreign ministers, however, continued until 1925.[45]

Meetings continued at a lower level and led to the signing of a customs treaty between Estonia and Latvia in autumn 1926, which, however, was never ratified. At the same time the first Paneuropean Congress took place in Vienna. This led to what was probably the clearest relationship between Europe and a region: they were treated as opposite and mutually exclusive. *Päevaleht* demanded "less Europe, more Baltic" in Estonian foreign policy. At that moment this policy was aiming at too high an ideal; thus "hands and feet would grow too big at the expense of head and stomach". Accordingly, diplomatic efforts in the League of Nations and the major western capitals could not replace intimate relations with close neighbours: "All help does not indeed come from Europe." A common Baltic foreign policy was possible and desirable because of the common enemy. "The Baltic states form a separate wall between West and East, a barrier between two such distinct worlds."[46] Soon afterwards the socialist *Ühendus* also criticized the Paneuropean idea as the latest capitalist defence union; it preferred a truly Pan-European project on socialist terms. This seemed to be too far into the future; until when it recommended "facilitating relations between individual states".[47]

44 Neumann, 1999, p. 113; Passerini, 2004, p. 58.

45 Piip, 1932, pp. 102–108; Carlgren, 1993, p. 19; Lehti, 1999; Karjahärm, 2003, pp. 70–74; Pihlamägi, 2004, pp. 78–86.

46 Rba, "Kus on meie välipoliitika raskuspunkt?" in *Päevaleht*, 2.10.1926, p. 2.

47 Orvusto, "Pan-Euroopa ja sotsialism," in *Ühendus*, 20.10.1926, p. 2.

Such juxtaposition was avoided in Kaarel Robert Pusta's writings. According to him, different regions were not mutually exclusive alternatives but complementary entities. Each nation and state ought to primarily help itself but at the same time improve the general conditions for peace. Consequently, cooperation with neighbours did not prevent action towards national sovereignty. Later Pusta presented the Baltic League, in combination with the League of Nations, as the cornerstone of Estonian foreign policy.[48]

On the other hand, regional cooperation did not narrow Pusta's perspective to merely the country's immediate neighbours, as the coalition with Latvia was open to other Baltic Sea Region states (Lithuania, Poland and Finland were mentioned): "the more distant, the more European our aim is, the more certainly and rapidly we will achieve something in a narrower sphere."[49] At the same time, Pusta denied any kind of universal citizenship or limitless humanism: "As global citizens we consider ourselves first as Europeans."[50]

At the first Paneuropean Congress, Pusta advocated regionalism, giving a presentation "on the blueprints of a Baltic Union, aimed at assembling one part of European nations within a narrower regional area."[51] Soon afterwards he presented Baltic cooperation as an example for other new European countries, instead of waging economic wars against each other. In addition, as he said, "I am confident that it can be regarded and hailed as a pioneer of a forthcoming Paneurope".[52] While founding the Estonian Society of Paneuropean Union in August 1929, Pusta suggested that the Bulduri protocols of 1920 would easily "construct a blueprint of a small European federation". He claimed that these conferences and talks had aroused lively interest in Europe, and were seen as a model and prototype for cooperation on a larger scale.[53] This seems to have been followed by years of silence, however as late as 1933, Pusta once again stated that Baltic consolidation and a common declaration of peace would contribute to a genuine European peace.[54]

---

48 Pusta, 1929a.

49 "Eesti ülesanded rahu korraldamisel," in *Vaba Maa*, 29.9.1925, p. 3; also Pusta, 1929b; Pusta, Kaarel Robert, "Die Baltenstaaten in europäischen Staatenbund," in *Baltisches Handbuch für das Jahr 1930*, pp. 102–104.

50 "Eesti ülesanded rahu korraldamisel," in *Vaba Maa*, 29.9.1925, p. 3.

51 Pusta, 1929a; also, "Pildikesi Pan-Euroopa kongressilt," in *Kaja*, 10.10.1926, p. 5.

52 "Balti liit – Pan Euroopa eelkäija," in *Päevaleht*, 10.8.1927, p. 3.

53 Pusta, 1929a; also "Die Paneuropa-Bewegungen. Paneuropäische Union in Estland und Lettland," in *Paneuropa* 1927:3, p. 29.

54 "Balti merele eri statuut," in *Postimees*, 9.1.1934, p. 4. Pusta's article was published in *Les Cahiers de l'Union Européenne*, which included also other texts on Baltic issues.

Pusta lived up to his words of Baltic cooperation in the Paneuropean Union. Together with Aleksander Skrzyński, the former Polish Prime Minister, he managed already in 1927 to include collaboration among agricultural states in feeding Europe in the programme of the union.[55] A striking instance of Baltic cooperation within Paneurope took place on Paneurope Day May 17, 1931: Pēteris Berģis and Philipp Michelson arrived from Riga to talk about small states and borders in Tallinn, while Ants Piip travelled to Riga to talk about international peace.[56]

The elusiveness of membership was a distraction for the Baltic states. There was never an agreement of the nations, which should be included in the Baltic cooperation. Needless to say, it was hard to create a region on this basis.[57] Finland and Poland had participated in the Bulduri conference of 1920 and as late as 1932 Ants Piip wanted to also include them in the concept of Baltic. Despite the diversity of these countries, Piip defined the area in terms of a common culture, derived from Western civilization, and location between greater neighbours. Surprisingly, he could also use the term in an even broader sense, encompassing all the states bordering on the Baltic Sea, including Germany and Russia.[58] At the first Baltic lunch, Pusta also wanted to also include Sweden, Denmark and Norway in this group.[59]

These mutual relationships also affected relations between other states. Estonian relations with Poland were traditionally warm, but Lithuania and Poland quarreled during the whole interwar period over border issues and especially over Vilnius, which was annexed to Poland in 1922. Estonian relations with Lithuania were therefore bad as well, and deteriorated further when the Elder of State Otto Strandman visited Vilnius on his way back from Warsaw. This led to anti-Estonian demonstrations in Kaunas consisting of allegedly no fewer than a thousand participants.[60] This relationship later improved, and an Estonian-Lithuanian Friendship Society was established a year later.[61] Despite the polite rhetoric of Baltic friendship, destiny and common space, practical cooperation was easily hampered by nationalistic claims.

---

55 "Eeltööd Kõik-Euroopa kongressiks," in *Postimees*, 12.5.1927, p. 3.

56 "'Pan-Euroopa päev' Tallinnas," in *Vaba Maa*, 16.5.1931, p. 2; "Paneuroopa päeva pidamine Tallinnas," in *Postimees*, 17.5.1931, p. 3; "Paneuroopa päeva aktus," in *Kaja*, 17.5.1931, p. 8; "Pan-Euroopa päev Tallinnas," in *Päevaleht*, 19.5.1931, p. 3.

57 Neumann, 1999, p. 162; Karjahärm, 2003, pp. 60, 70–73.

58 Piip, 1932, pp. 96–97.

59 "'Balti eine' Pariisis," in *Postimees*, 15.1.1931, p. 2.

60 "Eestivastane meeleavaldus Kaunases," in *Kaja*, 15.2.1930, p. 1.

61 "Asutati Eesti-Leedu ühing," in *Kaja*, 18.2.1931, p. 5.

A preliminary statistical analysis implies a negative correlation between European and Baltic issues. According to the catalogues of the Estonian National Library and the Literary Museum, interest in the Baltic states decreased considerably after 1927 and reached a low point in 1931. At the same time articles dealing with the question of Europe were at their most frequent. After this, interest in Europe seems to have declined rapidly and the Baltic states recovered their previous popularity.[62] It would be oversimplifying matters, however, to claim a direct correlation between European and Baltic issues.

There is no denying that at the turn of the 1930s interest in the Baltics decreased to a point close to zero. Even articles such as Ants Piip's review on Independence Day in 1928 referred to the Baltic League in the past tense, although Piip acknowledged that the problem remained unanswered.[63] In similar fashion the idea of a customs union was kept alive,[64] but in practice Estonia had difficulties even in extending commercial treaties toward both the south and the north. Contemporaries connected these issues. For example, when reporting on the troublesome negotiations, *Päevaleht* announced abruptly in October 1930 that "the idea of an Estonian and Latvian customs union has at the moment been definitely abandoned." This was most regrettable, since "the customs union would not only have had an economic, but a much broader and deeper, meaning in every field." The negotiations for the commercial treaty advanced poorly and the negotiators were losing faith in reaching a satisfying outcome.[65]

Practical difficulties became an easy target for Euro-sceptics. K.A. Hindrey was the first to compare the setbacks in Estonian and Latvian relations with regard to European unification, thus demonstrating the magnitude and expected difficulties in the latter.[66] At a public meeting on October 23, 1929, General Johan Laidoner referred to the worsening relations with Latvia as an example of how hard it was for states to enter into alliances.[67] Harald Tammer followed this thinking and described the new, small nation-states as instinctively timid and cautious when it came to engaging in alliances with each other, as the example of the Latvian customs union showed.[68]

62 See introduction.

63 Piip, Ants, "Balti liit," in *Postimees*, 24.2.1928, p. 8; also, "Tolliunioon ja Eesti-Läti suhted," in *Postimees*, 22.3.1928, p. 3.

64 Piip, 1932, p. 108; Pihlamägi, 2004, p. 85.

65 -s., "Balkan Baltist ette jõudnud," in *Päevaleht*, 23.10.1930, p. 2.

66 Hindrey, K.A., "Pan-Euroopa," in *Päevaleht*, 13.5.1927, p. 2.

67 "Paneuroopa poolt ja vastu," in *Vaba Maa*, 25.10.1929, p. 10.

68 Tammer, Harald, "Pan-Euroopa ja väikerahvad," in *Päevaleht*, 22.5.1930, p. 2.

Coudenhove-Kalergi contacted other Estonian politicians and wrote a letter to another former Foreign Minister, Friedrich Akel, in late 1928. Unlike Pusta, however, Akel was not enthusiastic about Paneurope and, as an excuse, referred to the unhappy situation between Estonia and Latvia in order to point out the practical difficulty on the way towards the idealistic goal. Although due to historical, political and economic similarities they could be called "twin-states", their actual cooperation had not improved for the past five years up until that point.[69]

The promoters of European unification were also naturally aware of the problems in Baltic cooperation. For example, in 1926 Pusta almost apologized that the wreck of the Baltic League had also done harm to the fulfilment of the Paneuropean idea. The two regions remained in interaction: "It is not possible to completely arrange one part of Europe independently of the rest of Europe [...] On the other hand; a Paneurope is not feasible without these (Baltic) states." Pusta went as far as linking their national sovereignty to some kind of continental organization: "Outside Europe, Estonia and other Baltic states are not independent politically, not to mention economically."[70]

Likewise in his opening speech at the meeting of the Estonian Society of the Paneuropean Union, Pusta had to acknowledge that "we retreated from the realization of the Baltic Union [...] Even now the idea has not been abandoned, but has been laid aside, waiting for its opportunity." Nevertheless these problems could not be used as excuses for turning away from Europe.[71]

An economic expert of the Paneuropean Union, Otto Deutsch, who visited Tallinn in June 1929, was also aware of problems in regional cooperation. However, he did not become disillusioned but attempted to turn the situation in the favour of Paneurope. According to him, the Estonian-Latvian customs union was basically a political agreement, and this was the key to problems. Within Paneurope, economic experts alone would solve economic questions. Problems in smaller circles could be solved when they were brought into a larger context.[72]

As a foreigner Deutsch differed from Estonian Euro-enthusiasts, above all Pusta, who did not have such preferences: the two regions were in

69 HAEU. PAN/EU 30. Akel to Coudenhove-Kalergi, 10.12.1928.

70 Pusta, Kaarel Robert, "Esimene Paneuroopa kongress," in *Vaba Maa*, 21.9.1926, p. 2; also Pusta, Kaarel Robert, "Esimene Paneuroopa (Kõikeuroopa) kongress," in *Postimees*, 22.9.1926, p. 2.

71 Pusta, 1929a.

72 "Eestis Pan-Euroopa komitee asutatud," in *Päevaleht*, 9.6.1929, p. 4.

constant interaction and thus there was no need to focus on either region. On the other hand, the Eurosceptics of the time had preferences – but opposite ones. They doubted the prospects of continental unification, considering the problems experienced with immediate neighbours. At that moment, in the late 1920s, closer regional cooperation was not proposed as an alternative but implicitly the road to Europe would have to be taken by way of the next door neighbours.

As mentioned, Pusta stressed that European unification had diplomatic, economic and cultural dimensions. Similarly, cooperation between Estonia and Latvia had more than one dimension. A customs union was intended to accompany the defence union. In 1927, Pusta referred to two roads of negotiations for future plans: "a general political road, with many diplomatic agreements, and an economic-political road, which has started with the Estonian-Latvian customs union."[73]

During the interwar period there was considerable expression of Baltic and also practical cultural cooperation, at various levels.[74] Even the military journal *Sõdur* wrote about this new dimension of international politics. Treaties were no longer entered into between emperors but between nations and peoples. Political agreements therefore had to be supported by immaterial friendship between the parties. As a small state, Estonia required alliances and the struggle shared with Latvia during the liberation war established the necessary basis for a Baltic Defence Union: "The defence forces and nations of both member states are bound with friendship and esteem".[75] Furthermore, the Chambers of Commerce of the three states started to hold conferences, which dealt with plainly commercial issues but also with economic policies and the need to bring them closer to each other.[76] When director Joakim Puhk visited Kaunas in 1927, he gave a report to *Päevaleht*, which used a bold and quite irrelevant headline: "The idea of Pan-Baltic is materializing".[77]

The concept of the Pan-Baltic, "*Kõik-Balti mõte*", in fact became popular only in the early 1930s. According to the advocates this idea had to have mass support among the people in order to work, and thus Estonians, Latvians, and Lithuanians needed to be educated about their neighbouring nations. This required a common language; and rather than

73 "Balti liit – Pan Euroopa eelkäija," in *Päevaleht*, 10.8.1927, p. 3.

74 Karjahärm, 2003, pp. 70–73; for example, "Balti vendluse mõtte edendamine," in *Kaja*, 3.6.1930, p. 7.

75 Miles, "Riikidevahelised liidud," in *Sõdur*, 1927:12, pp. 294–295.

76 Pihlamägi, 2004, pp. 86–89.

77 "Pan-Baltikumi idee teostumas," in *Päevaleht*, 26.3.1927, p. 3.

choosing one out of three, a foreign language had a better chance. Even this was not easy: Russian was no longer acceptable, nor was German (or not yet), and English thus seemed to prevail, partly due to Scandinavian expectations.[78] The need for a common language became evident on the above-mentioned Paneurope Day, May 17, 1931, when Berģis spoke in Russian and Michelson in German.[79] The question of a common language for the Baltic or even Europe has faded due to the triumph of the English – despite the several official languages of European Union. It is evident also from this study, and not merely on the surface as the language of this text, but also in the sources; French gradually disappears in correspondence at the expense of English. The use of German ceases completely after World War II.

[78] K., "Kõik-Balti mõte," in *Päevaleht*, 5.2.1932, p. 2; R., "Skandinaavia-Balti liit," in *Päevaleht*, 15.3.1932, p. 2.

[79] "Pan-Euroopa päev Tallinnas," in *Vaba Maa*, 19.5.1931, p. 3.

Chapter 5

The Disintegrating 1930s

Tõnisson and Pusta in Geneva in September 1931

The Estonian discussion on European unification may have been triggered by contemporary events but it touched the fundamental elements regarding the issue of nation-building. Furthermore, this discussion of a cultural dimension (meaning of borders, history, relations between nations) was expanded from the ideological discussion to a practical method aimed at promoting unification in the League of Nations. When the Study Commission met in September 1931, Estonian Foreign Minister Jaan Tõnisson detached the question of European unification from political and economic issues onto "the basis of comprehensions and convictions", to use the expression of *Postimees*.[1]

First of all, Tõnisson was not going to hide the enormous challenges of this undertaking. He discerned two sides in European unification and economic consolidation had advanced recently since the worst of depression. "The adjustment of the economic interests of Europe" was nevertheless insufficient on its own but required support from the ideological sphere "to restore complete harmony between the various nations". Due to an outdated "notion of an absolute and exclusive sovereignty", economic sanctions were considered a bigger threat to national ideals than to material income. This, according to Tõnisson, formed the greatest burden for international development.[2]

Tõnisson wanted "to bring about an evolution of theoretical notions" and promote "the advent of a new form of public law which will be really European". To achieve this goal, he proposed that the Commission would

---

1 "Rajatagu teed uuele rahvusvahelisele õigusele," in *Postimees*, 11.9.1931, p. 2; "Välisminister J. Tõnissoni algatus," in *Vaba Maa*, 12.9.1931, p. 2; "Välisminister J. Tõnissoni kõne Euroopa uurimiskomisjonis," in *Kaja*, 12.9.1931, p. 4. Foreign minister Tõnisson granted interviews after returning to Estonia: "Välisminister J. Tõnisson Rahvasteliidu tööst," in *Postimees*, 27.9.1931, p. 5; "Välisminister Rahvasteliidu tööst," in *Päevaleht*, 3.10.1931, p. 3; "J. Tõnisson rahvasteliidu konverentsist," in *Vaba Maa*, 3.10.1931, p. 3; "Välisminister andis seletusi," in *Postimees*, 3.10.1931, p. 3. Pegg, 1983, p. 163; Made, 1999, p. 267.

2 Commission 1931.

invite European governments to "the spread of the European idea among the general public" by all means available. He particularly mentioned the press, school textbooks, film and radio.

Five days later, September 8, Pusta, who was accredited as an envoy both in Paris and at the League, followed Tõnisson in the general meeting of the League of Nations, which was going to vote on the continuation of the Commission. Pusta first declined the need for such decision, because the Commission was given the task but not a deadline; its mandate would be permanent. He then criticized the Commission for focusing too much on economic problems and urged it to take the next step or return to its primary functions to study the conditions and organization needed for federation. As a result, the Commission was permitted to continue with the Estonian reminder of the eventual goal, development of a plan for a European union.[3]

Both speeches aroused much attention, largely positive during the meeting.[4] Moreover, Estonian newspapers followed the event closely, but a longer comment was produced only in an editorial of *Vaba Maa* by Eduard Laaman. He praised the initiative, because eloquent words were not enough to guarantee peace, especially during an economic depression.[5] Later, Professor Ants Piip appreciated the initiative, since it publicized the work of the Commission to a wider audience.[6]

Vaba Maa also published less complimentary comments from Geneva and Paris.[7] Domestic criticism was absent, since the topic was not relevant any more. Aboard, envoy Friedrich Akel in Stockholm asked for instructions on how to answer ironic questions concerning Pusta's speech and why "the Estonian delegation regards this question as the most important". It seems he was embarrassed, but August Schmidt proudly dispersed any suspicions. Pusta had spoken with the permission of the foreign minister, the leader of the delegation, and his speech was in line with general foreign policy. Any reaction on Estonian policy was welcome and irony

---

3 ERA 957-13-571. Foreign minister's account on XII general meeting, 7-29.9.1931; ERA 957-13-571. Kaarel Robert Pusta's account on XII general meeting, 30.9.-26.10.1931.

4 "Kiirustatagu Euroopa liidu ehitamist," in *Postimees*, 10.9.1931, p. 5; "Eesti propageerib Pan-Euroopat," in *Vaba Maa*, 10.9.1931, p. 3; "Rahvasteliidu koosolek avati," in *Kaja*, 10.9.1931, p. 1; "Kõnesid ja vaidlusi Genfis," in *Päevaleht*, 10.9.1931, p. 4; "Ühine häda sunnib koostööle," *Rahva Sõna*, 10.9.1931, p. 1.

5 Laaman, Eduard, "Rahu allkirjad ja tegelikud raskused rahu teel," in *Vaba Maa*, 29.11.1931, p. 4.

6 Piip, 1932, p. 70.

7 "Prantsuse lehed Eesti delegaatide kõnedest," in *Vaba Maa*, 18.9.1931, p. 5; "Briand ja meie Pusta," in *Vaba Maa*, 19.9.1931, p. 1.

was merely born out of envy. "It is renowned that a European Union (*Euroopa Unioon*) is evident, the question can only be – when, whether in five or one hundred and fifty years. And what is a century compared to eternity?" These surprisingly idealistic words by the factual leader of the Estonian foreign ministry were backed with the faith that Pusta had in mind when he envisaged the pursuit of a more positive and long-term foreign policy rather than the seeking of more short-term advantages. "If someone won't understand this, there's nothing to do, history will surely one day appreciate it."[8]

The Sunset of the Paneuropean Cross

During the heyday of Paneuropean thought in early 1931, *Postimees* published two articles on its hopes and fears for international politics that portrayed Europe in general as devastated, gloomy, and miserable. One of the few glimpses of light, the Briand proposal presented an "important moral victory". By the Study Commission, which was going to convene shortly, European governments had themselves confessed to be aware of their common destiny while lacking both economic and political unity. Final solutions even for domestic problems were possible only by common European efforts.[9] The same slight optimism was shared by Foreign Minister Tõnisson.[10]

Nevertheless, after September 1931, the proposal was funneled into another committee within the League and lost diplomatic interest and relevance. In the shadow of the economic depression, the Paneuropean movement lost its bearing. The correspondence between the centre in Vienna and the society in Tallinn had, even before this, focused on technical matters. Paneurope Day 1932 was not celebrated in Estonia at all and the society led a quiet life at least until 1934.

Coudenhove-Kalergi was disappointed but not defeated. In the following years, he gained publicity (also in Estonia) with bold and imaginary initiatives of building a tunnel under the Polish Corridor or organizing a joint referendum in Europe as a whole.[11] His greatest effort to re-launch the unification process was the third Paneuropean Congress in Basel in

---

8 ERA 1587-1-53. Akel to Schmidt, 22.9.1931 and Schmidt to Akel, 25.9.1931. Nowadays European Union is in Estonian "Euroopa liit".

9 "Euroopa lootused algavad aastal," in *Postimees*, 6.1.1931, p. 4. The second article was "Euroopa kartused uue aasta lävel," in *Postimees*, 4.1.1931, p. 4.

10 Tõnisson, Jaan, "Mis toob uus aasta?" in *Postimees*, 2.1.1931, p. 2; "Eurooplaste ühised mured," in *Postimees*, 16.1.1931, p. 3.

11 "Tunnel Poola koridori alla," in *Päevaleht*, 20.8.1931, p. 4; "Veel üks rahvahääletus!" in *Kaja*, 19.2.1933, p. 4.

October 1932. Kaarel Robert Pusta participated in this conference as well. At the conference, the League of Nations was criticized directly for living in the illusions of its own resolutions. The line of action was sharpened by the founding of the international Paneuropean party. The red cross on the golden sun had been, from the beginning, the symbol of Paneurope but now the use of symbols was intensified, for example with the introduction of blue uniforms. The party aspired to achieve full employment, equality of genders, monetary union, and corporative councils.[12]

Harald Tammer, who was then the only journalist in Estonia paying attention to the Paneuropean Union, reported on the conference in *Päevaleht*. He saw the aims partly contradictory and too idealistic to be feasible. Furthermore, as the Paneuropean Party required the existence of a European union to function, its plan of action did not address the questions of the day. In conclusion, Tammer expected the same poor success for Paneurope as before. He made it specifically clear that he did not want to appear as a supporter of the Union.[13]

Tammer turned out to be right. But Coudenhove-Kalergi kept looking for new alternatives to promote his cause and next he turned to economic issues. The Paneuropean Economic Centre was founded in Vienna in 1935. It was supposed to study problems of finance and trade within the continental context. Coudenhove-Kalergi gathered their members from each European country, Estonia was represented by Joakim Puhk, who had already published in their journal. His membership was rather passive and, the following year, he declined to travel to the conference of the centre. Instead, Voldemar Johanson, director of the commercial Landbank, represented Estonia in the Agricultural Conference held in September 1936. In 1935, in the fourth Paneuropean Congress, Estonia had kept low profile and the country was represented by a local honorary consul and merely as an observant.[14]

After the Anschluss, Coudenhove-Kalergi escaped to Switzerland and later to New York. He returned to Europe after World War II and founded the European Parliamentary Union to pursue unification. Pusta joined him

---

12 Ziegerhofer-Prettenthaler, 2004, pp. 210–217. The first congress was held in Vienna, October 1926, and the second one in Berlin, May 1930.

13 Tammer, Harald, "Pan-Euroopa muutub sõjakaks?" in *Päevaleht*, 6.10.1932, p. 2; Tammer, Harald, "Euroopa partei kava," in *Päevaleht*, 8.10.1932, p. 2; Tammer, Harald, "Rahvusvaheline sinisärkide armee," in *Päevaleht*, 13.10.1932, p. 6.

14 RGVA 554-1-51, pp. 116–139, especially p. 122. Puhk to Coudenhove-Kalergi, 15.1.1936; HAEU. PAN/EU 16. Liste der prominenten Teilnehmer am IV Paneuropa-Kongress; Johanson, Voldemar, "Ueber die Finanzierungsänderungen der Landwirtschaft," in *Paneuropa* 1936:7/8, pp. 58–59.

again at conferences and declarations until his death in 1964. Pusta never showed any doubt in the progress of European unity. For example, he attended the meeting of the Central Council in Paris in December 1957, reminding of the half of Europe being denied of European solidarity. Two years later he was among other veteran diplomats commemorating the 30th anniversary of the Briand Memorandum, when he reminded that World War I resulted in the collection of European nations together at the League of Nations but that World War II divided Europe into two halves.[15]

After Coudenhove-Kalergi's death in 1972, new chairman Otto von Habsburg revitalized the union for the next years. On behalf of the Estonians, Arvo Horm attended their conference in Strasbourg and Kehl in 1975 and also the jubilee conference a year later; the latter event was accompanied with a folk festival, where a group of Estonian dancers also performed. The dancers also performed during the conference in 1977 but there is no mention of an Estonian delegation. Four years later, when the German section of the Paneuropean Union organized their meeting by the Baltic Sea in Kiel, Heinrich Mark represented the Estonians.[16]

This activity faded once again for a couple of years, until the Estonian Society of Paneuropean Union was established for the second time in exile on February 2, 1988 and Mark became the chairman. The aims of the association were rather paradoxical since it aspired to "cooperation with all European nations and states in order to achieve unified Europe" and at the same time "implementation of right for stately self-determination […] to the Estonian nation occupied by the Soviet Union". Tallinn was named as the hometown of the organization but during the occupation it was de facto Stockholm. The establishment was followed by participation in the Paneuropean conference in Karlsruhe during the next summer and Mark saw membership as something important linking Estonians to Europe.[17]

---

15 Pusta, Kaarel Robert, "Lühidalt suurtest üritustest," in *Teataja*, 8.2.1958, p. 5; "Paneuroopa Uniooni Kesknõukogu koosolek," in *Teataja*, 16.10.1958, p. 1; "Paneuroopa Uniooni kesknõukogu," in *Välis-Eesti*, 9.11.1958, p. 1; "Millal teostub Euroopa Unioon?" in *Teataja*, 10.10.1959, p. 3; Pekomäe, Vello, "Näeme ühendatud Euroopa sündi," in *Välis-Eesti*, 3.3.1962, p. 4. Le centre d'archives européennes at the L'Institut européen de l'Université de Genève in Coppet, Switzerland, contains the personal files of Coudenhove-Kalergi after World War II and they include correspondence with Kaarel Robert Pusta but it involves mostly practical matters.

16 "Nõuti Euroopa sõjalise liidu loomist," in *Teataja* 24.5.1975, p. 1; "Leo Tindemani Euroopa-uniooni projekt tuleb kiiresti teostada," in *Teataja*, 29.5.1976, p. 3; "Pan-Euroopa Uniooni aastakongress Saarbrückenis," in *Teataja*, 21.5.1977, p. 7; "Paneuroopa Uniooni Euroopapäevad Kiilis," in *Teataja* 18.4.1981, p. 5; "Baltikum peab saama vabaks!" in *Teataja* 16.5.1981, p. 5.

17 ERA 4969-1-87. The statute of the Society of Paneuropean Union; Mark, Aksel, "Eesti PAN Euroopasse," in *Teataja* 27.2.1988, p. 2; Mathiesen, Mihkel, "Ka Baltikum peab

Further actions were planned but, for obvious reasons, the emigrant organization had to be closed down a few years later.

The third time the Estonian Society of the Paneuropean Union was founded was in Soviet Estonia, in Tartu, in October 1990. Enn Tarto, one of the most prominent dissidents, became the chairman but Orientalist Linnart Mäll succeeded him shortly. The society invited Otto von Habsburg to Estonia and during his visit in March 1992 he was presented with the brass plate of the first society as a symbol of Estonia's long-held aspirations in European unification.[18]

The Rise of the Swastika

Back in the international politics of the 1930s, outside the Paneuropean Union, Adolf Hitler's ascension to power in Germany in early 1933 created shock waves. This became evident in March, when Mussolini proposed to France, Germany, and Britain an agreement on the consolidation of peace and economic recovery, thus decreasing the role of the League of Nations. At the same time, Britain proposed new restrictions on armaments. Both proposals were unanimously rejected in Estonia. The proposals were compared to the Concert of Europe, the Holy Alliance, and a "European upper chamber".[19] They seemed to render small states into passive bystanders. The attitude had considerably changed in a year, when during the Tardieu Plan, similar plans were perceived as being of assistance to Eastern Europe.

The new situation also increased appeals for regional cooperation. As a prelude, Ants Piip had written his popular work on world politics in 1932, where he stressed the new beginning of Baltic relations and rapprochement between Lithuania and her neighbours. He trusted that regional cooperation would come to life almost by itself. These plans had

---

kuuluma Ühendatud Euroopasse," in *Teataja* 2.6.1988, p. 4; "Eesti Rahvusnõukogu tegevus jätkub," in *Teataja* 26.11.1988, p. 4.

18 Karelsohn, Kristi, "Eesti noored lülituvad Paneuroopa liikumisse," in *Postimees* 22.11.1991, p. 2; Vilgats, Kalev, "Pan-Euroopa liikumine toetab Balti riike endiselt," in *Postimees* 4.6.1992, p. 11; Vilgats, Kalev, "Otto von Habsburg: 'Ärge minge läbirääkimistele Venemaaga üksi!'" in *Postimees* 21.3.1992, p. 1; Davies, 1996, p. 944; Heinz Valk, who coined the term "Singing Revolution", is another example of europeanism among former dissidents [http://arvamus.postimees.ee/1188640/heinz-valk-euroopa-foderatsioon-kaitseks-eestit-putini-eest].

19 "Euroopa ülemkoda?" in *Postimees*, 21.3.1933, p. 5; "Rahu kümneks aastaks," in *Vaba Maa*, 22.3.1933, p. 1; Tammer, Harald, "Macdonaldi desarmeerimiskava hädaoht Eestile," in *Päevaleht*, 22.3.1933, p. 2; "Tagasi Euroopa kontserdi juure?" in *Postimees*, 25.3.1933, p. 2; "'Euroopa kontserd' jalule?" in *Kaja*, 25.3.1933, p. 2; Ziegerhofer-Prettenthaler, 2004, pp. 222–223.

failed with the Warsaw Protocol in 1924, but that disappointment had since vanished. Although an alliance was not possible between states, attitudes among the people had grown warm.[20]

The discussion in the Baltic states was initiated by *Lietuvos Žinios* of Kaunas in March 1933, but it soon ended in the same deadlock as before. Estonia and Latvia were, in principle, ready for an alliance but wished to stay out of the Lithuanian border dispute with Poland over Vilnius, which on the other hand, was primary for Lithuania. In addition, Lithuanian goals were considered too pro-German.[21]

At the same time the idea of a 'Baltoscandia', as an entity between East and West combining Baltic and Scandinavian regions, emerged in the lectures of Professor Edgar Kant,[22] and Carl Lindhagen, former Chief Magistrate of Stockholm, introduced his initiative on cooperation across the whole Baltic Sea Region. Lindhagen included the Vilnius question: since it could not be resolved bilaterally, it should be discussed among a larger group.[23]

The chief editor of *Kaja*, Hans Oiderman, had already a week earlier anticipated and dismissed such broad, "fantastic" plans. His advice was to focus on practical cooperation in the economic field. A relationship did already exist; it was only necessary to organize it properly. As if to confirm this claim, the next day's front page anticipated a customs union between Estonia and Latvia in the steel industry.[24] *Päevaleht* followed along similar lines. Despite problems, the three countries should strive first towards to a union of their own. This was not nevertheless enough: "The final aim should nevertheless be at Scandinavia-Baltic cooperation. But the road to that destination appears to be very long and take via other stations."[25]

Postimees recognized that Yugoslavia, Czechoslovakia and Romania had already reacted to the Nazi ascension by increasing their cooperation. Without fear of exaggeration, it focused on an even brighter future: "The new confederation does not merely possess greater weight in the family

---

20 Piip, 1932, pp. 109–110.

21 For example, "Balti liit tuleb sõlmida," in *Postimees*, 17.3.1933, p. 2; "Balti riikide liit peab olema täiesti iseseisev," in *Päevaleht*, 19.3.1933, p. 3; "Eesti Poolaga sõtta!" in *Vaba Maa*, 25.3.1933, p. 3; "Leedu seisukohti Balti liidu asjus," in *Kaja*, 26.3.1933, p. 3; "Kuhu lähed, Leedu?" in *Postimees*, 29.3.1933, p. 3.

22 "Baltoskandia – kõige põhjapoolsem kultuurmaa," in *Päevaleht*, 23.3.1933, p. 2.

23 "Rootslase arvamine Balti liidust," in *Kaja*, 28.3.1933, p. 5; "Väikeriikide kontsert", in *Vaba Maa*, 30.3.1933, p. 2.

24 Oiderman, Hans, "Praktiline Balti poliitika," in *Kaja*, 17.3.1933, p. 2; "Tolliunioon Lätiga kõigepealt metallitööstuse alal," in *Kaja*, 18.3.1933, p. 1.

25 R., "Skandinaavia-Balti liit," in *Päevaleht*, 15.3.1933, p. 2.

of nations, but in the hands of capable diplomacy it could easily develop into the nucleus of an even larger union." To make sure that the Estonian foreign ministry understood the hint, the editorial concluded: "We will do well, when we follow developing events carefully."[26]

Already at the time of the Tardieu Plan, Tammer had stressed that the countries' own activity toward increased regional cooperation would make the great powers interested in supporting individual countries. Although preliminary action was needed to avoid being relegated to a passive position, the great powers were necessary as guarantors. Similar hope of activity was expressed in *Vaba Maa*.[27] Tammer's concern increased after Hitler gained power. Neutrality was no longer an option, and the Western powers could no longer offer their assistance in establishing a Baltic union.[28] Instead, Tammer looked for model groups and found them in Scandinavia and Central Europe. The three Baltic states were too small and thus far had not managed to form an alliance. Tammer's solution was to use the Baltic as a mediator between these groups; instead of the traditional east-west bridge, it meant opening doors in a north-south direction. This would bring about the creation of adequate economic and political unity. As a sign of desperation, Tammer appealed to the communication routes of the Viking era as the basis for such an alliance.[29]

The rising political power in Estonia, Vapsid, did not pay a lot attention to foreign issues or look into influences from abroad. Like a typical right-wing movement of the time, they emphasized autarchy in social and economic policy. Neighbouring Latvia presents an exception of regional imagination, as the local *Pêrkonkrust* (Thunder Cross) openly endorsed a political, economic and military Baltic union.[30] As the geographic centre, Latvia would have obviously dominated the prospective Baltic union.

Eventually, Estonia plunged into authoritarian politics, when Konstantin Päts seized power in spring 1934.[31] Three months later, in *Päevaleht*, pen name Balticus returned to the fifteen-year-old question of Joseph Caillaux, "*Quo vadis, Europe*". Previous promises on the abolition of wars,

26 "Euroopale taotakse uut saatust," in *Postimees*, 19.2.1933, p. 2.

27 Tammer, Harald, "Donau probleem ja meie," in *Päevaleht*, 13.4.1932, p. 2; also, Tammer, Harald, "Uus politiline suurjõud Euroopas," in *Päevaleht*, 21.2.1933, p. 2; Tammer, Harald, "Vilno, Balti liit ja väikeriikide ühisrinne," in *Päevaleht*, 28.3.1933, p. 2; "Neljariigi konverents läks lõhki," in *Vaba Maa*, 10.4.1932, p. 1.

28 Tammer, Harald, "Uus poliitiline konstellatsioon," in *Päevaleht*, 25.3.1933, p. 2.

29 Tammer, Harald, "Ümbergrupeerumisi ja ümberorienteerumisi," in *Päevaleht*, 2.9.1933, p. 2.

30 Kasekamp, 2000, pp. 77, 145.

31 Raun, 1991, pp. 115–123; Hiden and Salmon, 1996, pp. 51–58; Smith, 2002, pp. 17–23; Elsuwege, 2008, pp. 26–28; Kasekamp, 2010, pp. 109–112.

democratization, economic community, and restoring European hegemony in the world had failed. On the other hand, no one prophesied any more class war or the total disappearance of statehoods, which gave hope for the future. More recently, the League of Nations had failed to become a general universal organization but Europe had witnessed a new, seemingly firm, balance of international relations. Balticus' advice for the next fifteen years was to concentrate on building the future of each nationality.[32] European unification or even regional unions, as an intermediate objective, or "upper chambers" were not even worth rejecting. The discussion on European unification had come to an end.

Estonian foreign policy diminished its focus to the regional unions, but with little enthusiasm. They seemed the only option. *Sõdur* returned to the theme in the summer of 1934. It was disappointed both in the League of Nations, for its failure to create a general peaceful atmosphere, and in Sweden and Finland as potential allies. Everyone was looking for an ally for national security, and this was especially vital for a small state like Estonia. This was not, however, to refrain from an active defence policy. In the end it was proposed to "create closer cooperation among the three purely Baltic states and at the same time to finally dismiss those moral obstacles which, to some extent, hamper the good concord of Baltic nations."[33]

In September 1934, after Poland had entered into non-aggression pacts with Germany and the Soviet Union, the three Baltic states were decisively left without partners except themselves. Thus, the Treaty of Better Understanding and Collaboration, shortly the Baltic Entente, was signed in Geneva during the General Assembly meeting of the League of Nations. The treaty was consultative in nature, without mutual guarantees, and therefore could not become a basis for defence.[34] The treaty allowed other states to join in later; this was intended primarily for Poland and Finland. This may have been wished in Estonia but it was unsurprisingly denied by the Lithuanian press.[35] The 'silent era' of the Päts regime had already begun, and the four major newspapers published, without comment, the

---

32 Balticus, "Kuhu tüürib Euroopa?" in *Päevaleht*, 21.6.1934, p. 2. The same pen name had already previously stressed that the cooperation of Baltic Sea region must respect autonomous, national particularities: Balticus, "Rahu koostöö kaudu," in *Päevaleht*, 20.3.1933, p. 2.

33 Ho., "Euroopa politilised vastolud ja Eesti julgeolu," in *Sõdur*, 1934:27/28, pp. 723–725; also Ho., "Meie riikliku julgeoleku alused," in *Sõdur*, 1933:14/15, pp. 460–462.

34 "Balti lepingu tekst," in *Kaja*, 14.9.1934, p. 3; "Eesti-Läti-Leedu lepingu sisu," in *Päevaleht*, 14.9.1934, p. 3; Arumäe, 1983, pp. 70–92.

35 "Soomel ja Poolal võimalus ühineda Balti liiduga," in *Vaba Maa*, 15.9.1934, p. 1.

same news of the interest in the event shown by international journalists located at the League of Nations.[36] Only *Päevaleht* interviewed Heinrich Laretei of the Estonian foreign ministry, who considered the treaty to foster the international position of the three countries and potentially to deepen peace in Eastern Europe. Above all, however, it was "proof of our endeavours to consolidate our independence and peace."[37]

36 "Balti leping kirjutati Genfis alla," in *Kaja*, 13.9.1934, p. 3; "Kolm riiki, üks sõprus," in *Postimees*, 13.9.1934, p. 1; "Eesti-Läti-Leedu leping kirjutati alla," in *Päevaleht*, 13.9.1934, p. 3; "Balti sõprusleping kirjutati alla," in *Vaba Maa*, 13.9.1934, p. 1.

37 "Eesti-Läti-Leedu leping kirjutati alla," in *Päevaleht*, 13.9.1934, p. 3.

Chapter 6

Common Estonian Features in the Discussion

The "evolution of the European idea" in Estonia followed the trends of continental Europe. After a steady growth of interest, the first Paneuropean Congress in October 1926 experienced a peak of success followed by a rapid downfall.[1] This was also evident in Estonia, where the discussion restarted only after a visit by Otto Deutsch in June 1929. The sudden collapse of the European idea and instead the increase in region-building was experienced due to the Austro-German customs union treaty in spring 1931.

In addition to the article "Flaws of Paneurope" and the speech by Pusta, there were very few texts that referred directly to all three (diplomatic, economic and cultural) dimensions of unification. However, many included two dimensions. This happened also with opposition viewpoints; authors either gave a better alternative or implied increasing difficulties in other spheres of activity if unification could potentially be seen as starting with one particular aspect. Different people may have come to opposite conclusions from the same premises (economic hardships or recently gained independence), but the adopted reasoning remained the same, even the external programme or proposal changed. European unification was not discussed on an ad hoc basis but perceived from established political points of view. For example, for the Paneuropeans, Tõnisson and Pusta, common European culture was the prerequisite for political and economic unification. The political lines could be perhaps expanded also to newspapers in general: *Kaja* stressed economic issues throughout the whole period; *Postimees* defended the Study Commission against regional solutions; and *Päevaleht* presented the League of Nations as the best protector of small states.

Since, in the discussion, European issues were integrated with Estonian domestic politics (they were seen as affecting and benefiting each other), Estonians became eager to influence the Paneuropean movement. Although this participation was limited more or less to two men, Pusta and Tõnisson, their initiative in the League of Nations clearly echoed the domestic discussion.

---

1 Pegg, 1983, pp. 23–95.

Despite lively discussion and clear opposing lines, common – Estonian – features could be found. Most importantly, Estonia was identified as a small state, and what was best for this group of reference was identified. Often this group was specified as the newly independent states in East Central Europe. The unifiers saw this recent status as an obligation to act; the opponents, at least for that moment, considered this status a handicap. The perceived relations between small and bigger states were crucial throughout the whole period.

Secondly, the League of Nations, whether in the present form or re-organized, was appreciated as the foundational organization of the international system. Partly because such a political organization already existed, economic questions were generally considered more vital in European unification. On the other hand, they were admittedly more difficult to solve.

Additionally, the League was cherished as a community of democratic nations. The emphasis on democracy was the third common Estonian feature. To enhance democratic procedures at all levels was to oppose other forms of government, mainly Fascism and Communism, which were dangerous for small states. This is a clear difference from Coudenhove-Kalergi and his aristocratic views. There is also a slight difference from the Viennese centre in relation to Russia. Although Estonians wanted to separate from the former ruling state, their attitude did not include presenting Russia as an imminent threat to Europe. Rather, they tried to ignore the East and flatter the West.

The public discussion concerned Estonia's place in Europe also with respect to more limited cooperation among neighbours. Although Baltic cooperation was practised and was represented as vital for national independence, its popularity faded rapidly. During the tranquil 1920s it remained an ideal picture, which could be seen as a first step towards Europe – as an example of cooperation on a broader scale. At the same time there was no need to take action towards these miscellaneous visions.

Even the economic depression as such did not intensify talk about regionalism; this happened only after the external programme started to prefer regional unions and the tide shifted from the continental Briand proposal to customs unions between Austria and Germany. As a result, the poor state of Baltic cooperation was revealed, but Estonia could still support it within the European framework. Nevertheless, even these initiatives were held back by mutual complaints. The sceptics of European unification had earlier cited the Baltic case as an example of the futility of practical measures in international cooperation; but the new situation did not increase receptivity to regional solutions. Instead, the European dimension diminished as the perspective of future allies and prospective influence waned: such plans were mentioned less often and in more limited forms.

Within three years the scope for relations among neighbours had shrunk, first from a continental European plan to the Baltic Sea Region and subsequently to the Baltic states alone. In the end, the Baltic Entente was the last resort and served almost entirely national interests. It was a regional treaty without regionalism. On the eve of an unprecedented economic depression, and situated between two rising great powers, the pleasant words of solidarity and brotherhood were easily dismissed and a commitment was made to narrow, short-sighted national interests: not just in Estonia but in other Baltic – and European – states as well.

The discussion of European unification during the same period showed a remarkable sustainability of preferences at the economic, diplomatic and cultural levels. In contrast, opinions regarding regionalism were very elusive. This was due above all to the elusiveness of the concept of the Baltic. One problem was the lack of definition of the countries belonging to it. Secondly, its role as a mediator was emphasized; thus it was defined by non-members rather than actual members. Although this clearly implicates the exclusion of Russia, there were only a few articles specifically mentioning the threat of the Soviet Union as a reason for Baltic cooperation or even referring to any kind of defence union.

Occasional references to psychology or human nature do not reveal so much about the Estonian national ideal, but more about how collectives are always based on individuals and their aspirations. In a similar fashion, references to the discussion today on European integration can be easily found. For example, Johan Laidoner's question in October 1929 of global versus European citizenship was also pondered by Montesquieu in the 18th century, who regarded politics criminal, if it was "useful to my country" but "detrimental to Europe". More recently, during the spring of 2003, Jürgen Habermas (and Jacques Derrida), while condemning the U.S. invasion in Iraq, also speculated on European peculiarities, as European culture is nowadays shared globally.[2] The discussion on European community deals with the timeless question of the relationship between an individual and the community. Furthermore, it has expanded into the relationship between communities of different magnitude (nations versus Europe). In issues like these, there are no definitive answers.

---

2 Montesquieu, 1949, p. 981; Habermas and Derrida, 2003.

Part II

Nazi New Europe and the Occupied Estonia

Chapter 1

Totalitarian Europe

Europe was escalating towards another war, as the great powers expanded their military forces. Smaller nations were left as either bystanders or victims. Germany under Hitler annexed Austria and the western part of Czechoslovakia, and his last prey by diplomacy was the taking of Memel/Klaipėda from Lithuania. The Molotov-Ribbentrop Pact, signed in Moscow August 23, 1939, divided Central and Eastern Europe into spheres of influence shared between Germany and the Soviet Union. Subsequently, Estonia was forced to sign a treaty with the Soviet Union giving Moscow naval bases on Estonian soil, this treaty would lead to the incorporation of Estonia into the Soviet Union the following summer.[1]

This gloomy prospect also affected Estonian views on Europe. The pessimism was evident in an article by Leonhard Vahter in December 1940. Europe had become the victim of its success. The ideas of the Enlightenment had taken Europe to conquer the world but the same liberalism had given room for disintegrating ideas to develop. Now this nationalistic, "caesarian private person" was threatening the fundamental concept of freedom and essence of Europe. Europe did not even have cultural unity any longer.[2]

But the European dream still lived in the minds of some Estonians. In his last published article, Jaan Tõnisson speculated on the idea of a European federation in December 1940 as a means to restore peace in Europe. His article is, frankly, mostly a review of the long history of the idea of unification. Tõnisson, however, did not want to fall into pessimism in front of such a long list of failures. On the contrary, for him, this list proved the strength and vividness of the idea, which had remained alive for such a long time.[3] Tõnisson was soon arrested by the Soviet authorities and his fate remains unknown. The Soviets arrested, convicted, and executed most of the Estonian national elite. For example, only four of

1 Raun, 1991, pp. 139–156; Hiden and Salmon, 1996, pp. 105–115; Smith, 2002, pp. 23–29; Elsuwege, 2008, pp. 29–32; Kasekamp, 2010, pp. 124–131.

2 Vahter, Leonhard, "Kuhu lähed, Euroopa?" in *Uus Eesti*, 17.12.1939, p. 4.

3 Tõnisson 1940.

twelve men in the council of the Estonian Paneuropean Society suffered a natural death: these were Jakob Kristelstein, Johannes Luikmil, Karl Ast, and Kaarel Robert Pusta, the latter three in exile. Thus, only one of this group of twelve died in his home country.

The Estonian experience describes a clear case of getting out of the frying pan and into the fire, when Germany launched its attack on the Soviet Union in June 1941. Just few weeks before, the Soviets had deported roughly 10,000 Estonians to Russia and with other ominous experiences of the first year in the Soviet Union, advancing German forces were not significantly opposed neither during the few months of the invasion or the subsequent three years of occupation. Related to this, the Nazis implemented their concept of New Europe in the occupied territories. Although the slogan of a New Europe was an important part of Nazi propaganda, there never was a consistent German plan for European unification. Instead, the party offices, the army, the SS, and the state fought among themselves to define the contours of a possible unified Europe. The Minister of Eastern Areas, Alfred Rosenberg, who was born in Tallinn, insisted on giving the Eastern nationalities some autonomy to win their support. On the other hand, like all Nazi plans, this would be carried out under strict German leadership, and in any case, Rosenberg had only little influence on the Nazi hierarchy.[4]

This did not matter to collaborators in the occupied Europe. In Estonia, Hjalmar Mäe, was appointed as the leader of the self-administration (*omavalitsus* in Estonian, *Selbstverwaltung* in German), although "to call it a 'puppet government' would be an exaggeration of its powers", as Andres Kasekamp candidly formulates. Mäe had even prior to the war, in May 1938, requested Germany to take Estonia under its protection. As *Landesdirektor* he publicly expressed faith and confidence in the Nazi project from an Estonian point of view.[5] For example, his speech during the celebration of Estonian Independence Day or Freedom Day, February 24, 1942, prophesied "real freedom for all European nations" after the defeat of the Soviet Union and the Estonians "can begin reconstruction in the middle of New Europe, which is based on mutual trust and respect." The Germans were the only support in the Estonian struggle against the Soviet Union as they attempted to overcome the difficulties being experienced at the time.[6]

---

4 Mazover, 1999, pp. 156–160; Kletzin, 2000.

5 Oras, 1958, pp. 219–221; Myllyniemi, 1973, pp. 30–31, 107–110; Arumäe, 1983, p. 18; Kasekamp, 2010, pp. 132–139.

6 "Sajandeiks õnnelik tulevik Eesti rahvale," in *Eesti Sõna*, 26.2.1942, pp. 1–2.

According to Ants Oras, locals were assured that Germany would make Estonia "a successful member in the new community of European nations". At the same it was obvious for everyone that the deeds and the explanations were not in accordance with each other. The Nazis justified their cruel behaviour on account of the Russian threat but their actions increasingly resembled the same style as that taken by the former Soviet overlords.[7]

After the war Mäe escaped to Austria, where he had studied both physics and law in his youth. He attended the Nuremberg Trials, not as accused, but as a witness; only six decades later the Estonian International Commission for investigation of Crimes Against Humanity would prosecute and, ultimately, find him guilty. Since the 1950s, Mäe worked as an attorney and journalist, and he published articles annually in *Der Europäische Osten*. The journal, like Mäe's articles, was essentially anti-communist aiming at revealing the situation in Eastern Europe that lay behind Soviet claims. Occasionally, Mäe dealt with the process of Western integration and hailed its progress: "A concentration of power always works like a magnet." According to Mäe, the advancement of the EEC was closely followed behind the Iron Curtain as it could foster resistance to the Soviet regime.[8]

The Estonian attempts to retain remnants of national independence gathered around former Prime Minister Jüri Uluots. He came together with, for example former chairman of the Second Chamber of the Estonian Parliament, Alfred Maurer, and Professors Edgar Kant and Nikolai Kaasik, as soon as the Soviets left the country. The Germans allowed their activities to a certain extent, because they as well disparaged Mäe's administration. Uluots, on the other hand, had credibility in the eyes of the Estonian people and could be used to convey messages and appeals. In March 1944 they formed *Eesti Vabariigi Rahvuskomitee* (the National Committee of the Republic of Estonia), which on September 18, 1944, when the Germans left Tallinn, declared the legitimate Estonian government as restored. The Soviets invaded Tallinn on September 22, and arrested nearly all the members of the government.[9]

As the prospects for Estonian independence within the confines of German occupation proved to be wishful thinking, Admiral Johan Pitka

---

7 Oras, 1958, pp. 210–211, 222.

8 Mäe, Hjalmar, "Eine Neue Europa-Politik," in *Der Europäische Osten* 1962 September (90), pp. 323–330; also Mäe, Hjalmar, "Gemeinsame Europa-Politik," in *Der Europäische Osten* 1960 February (64), pp. 75–79.

9 Klesment, 1959; Mälksoo, 2006.

wrote to Finnish President Risto Ryti about the situation in Estonia in November 1941. He proposed a union of states ("*valtioyhdistys*") between the two countries to guarantee their security, economy and culture for a brighter future. The union would be decided by (Estonian) referendum and it would contain a common head of state, a common foreign policy, and a common commander-in-chief would lead the joint army forces. Furthermore, it would entail a "unified economic life with common monetary system, which as such, would also take place in the new European economic system". Curiously enough, Pitka sent two copies to Ryti and the last sentence only appears in one.[10]

Moreover, President Konstantin Päts, who had isolated the country, had tried a similar method of union roughly a year earlier under Soviet pressure. In his last day in office on July 30, 1940 he gave his so-called political testament, which proposed a Finno-Estonian personal union and federation. It was intended to take place in a larger context of European reconstruction after the war. Only if the winning nations would promote guaranteeing the security of the Baltic states would the proposed union be comprehensible. Also Päts had a wider reorganization of European politics in mind, as the last, tenth, point in his proposal alluded to the union of Latvia and Lithuania with Poland to foster their security and provide Poland with harbours.[11]

While the German occupation was relatively lenient in Estonia and it was accepted after the experience with the Soviets. The resistance movement emerged gradually in Estonia and it provided information via Finland to the Estonian political centres abroad for publication. *Vaba Eesti Võitlusrinne* (the Free Estonia Front), led by Juhan Reigo and Endel Inglist, who were eventually executed by the Soviet authorities, published in sum 14 issues of the journal *Vaba Eesti*. The aim was to inform the rest of the world that despite public promises, the Germans were not planning to hand over any kind of state autonomy to Estonia or any other invaded country. *Vaba Eesti* attacked the concept of New Europe early 1943, showing inequality and distrust between Estonians and Germans in various domains. Everything labelled as European was going to benefit only the Germans. "Estonian people do not want to belong in such a New Europe! [...] We want to be the leaders in our own country!"[12]

---

10 KA. Ryti Y4061, Pitka to Ryti, 29.11.1941.

11 Warma, 1971, pp. 188–189.

12 "Adolf Hitleri Uus Euroopa," in *Vaba Eesti. Võitlusrinde häälekandja*, No. 4 (Reprinted in *Akadeemia* 2000:9, pp. 1888–1891); Lauk, 1993, pp. 169–170, 173; Warma, Aleksander, "Eesti Vabariigi Välisdelegatsioon ja Vabariikliku Rahvuskomitee loomine," in *Teataja*, 17.11.1962, p. 3; Warma, 1971, pp. 171–174; Pihlau, 2001; Paavle, 2009, pp. 377–378.

Professor of English Language, Ants Oras was also involved in this kind of action and he named journalist Jaan Ots and Director of the National Museum, Eerik Laid, as his partners.[13] He escaped to Sweden in 1943, where he recorded his experiences in *The Baltic Eclipse*. The book included a positive definition of Europe, which "meant a Europe for Estonians, culture on the best European level, but resting on a firm national basis."[14] The author may or may not be the same as above, but it nevertheless reflects the complete disagreement in the concept of Europe by the Germans and the Estonians.

Another source of criticism was written by Professor Edgar Kant, almost at the same time, in December 1942. His article "The Future of Europe" differed in many ways from the Nazi conception. Most significantly he rejected the idea of an external threat as the element of collective solidarity among Europeans. Nevertheless, he also discerned Europeanism from the international or general-humanistic cosmopolitan idea: Europe should have some kind of borders and it should be discernible from its neighbours. Kant paid much more attention to coherence among Europeans. Political unity in a certain "geopolitical space" required the discernment of a supranational identity, which "does not betray the nationality, or opt out of love towards one's homeland, but lifts one morally to a higher level". Kant found an allegory of how national identities had previously grown from tribal solidarities and that this could take place in the wider extent as well. According to Kant, this was "achieving unity in diversity".[15]

Moreover in Kant's view, the future of Europe "depends on solidarity, whether cultural, spiritual or the connection of fate". According to him, only the first one existed sufficiently and significantly: "there are hardly any other areas on the planet, other cultural domains, where it occurs to a greater extent and more closely". Spiritual solidarity did exist, but it had to be fostered. Kant's last sentence first reveals the interaction between the dimensions and, secondly, the repeated call for action: Europe would not unite by itself (even with a common culture) but it had to be united by its people. Kant promised to continue these themes in a forthcoming book, which was never published. Most likely it was not due to probable actions by the Germans but because of Kant's increasing duties in the course of the war.

13 Oras, 1958, pp. 229–231, 262–265.

14 *Ibid.*, p. 17.

15 Kant, 1942.

Chapter 2

Aleksander Warma Consolidating Europe

The Nazi plans of New Europe were nothing more than propaganda promises. Nevertheless, they worried the Western allies, who did not have anything equivalent to show for the resistance movements or exiled politicians. The Nazi plans gave an impetus to them to draft and present their visions of the future Europe.[1]

Aleksander Warma assumed this task among Estonians. He was born on June 22, 1890 in a coastal village in Northern Estonia. Specializing in international maritime law during his studies, he became an officer in the Estonian navy. Established in a career with the foreign ministry, he had worked at the Estonian consulate in Leningrad when he arrived in Helsinki, just a day before the outbreak of the Winter War on November 29, 1939. Warma was one of those who rejected the Soviet annexation: on September 24, 1940 in Stockholm, together with August Rei and Heinrich Laretei, he founded the Estonian Foreign Delegation for the government in exile. Warma stayed in Helsinki until September 1944.

This topic was discussed in Helsinki between Warma and the American Ambassador, H.F. Arthur Schoenfeld. Inspired by their talks, Warma drafted his own proposal and on December 13, 1942, he finished *Rahu konsolideerimise probleemist sõjajärgses Euroopas*, in English *Questions relating to the consolidation of peace in post-war Europe*. The plan was sent to the U.S. Secretary of State, Cordell Hull, via Chargé d'Affaires Robert McClintock.[2] Warma included it in his memoirs, *Diplomaadi Kroonika*.[3]

Warma's plan consisted of four main points and their attending remarks and comments. The first two are both the most important and somewhat are also contradictory to each other: the decentralization of Great powers into quasi-federations, and the inclusion of the smaller entities born out of this process into larger, European-sized confederations.

---

1 For example, Łaptos and Misztal, 2002, p. 19.

2 BA. Warma 2. "Rahu konsolideerimise probleemist pärastsõjaaegses Euroopas" with Finnish and English translations.

3 Warma, 1971, pp. 182–187.

In the first point of his plan, Warma deals with the partitioning of Great Powers into quasi-federations. Like smaller states, the new entities born of these partitions would perform their "political functions independently" while observing the limits of their constitutions and the principle of equality. In his confidential letter to the U.S. Secretary of State, McClintock also pointed out the need for a "strict juridical equality for small nations".[4]

Warma's idea that states should have equal resources so that there would be no interest in starting wars can be traced back to Plato, yet his considerations on the nature of small states owe much to his Estonian background. In fact, considerations about small states emerged at the same time all across Eastern Europe, in an effort to find solutions to the region's economic and political instability during the interwar years.[5] As the citizen of a small state invaded during the war, both by the Soviet Union and Nazi Germany, Warma stressed the smaller states' right to sovereignty and to independent existence. According to him, the emergence of small states after 1918 had been totally in accordance with "natural law". It was due to a "natural reaction of the human instinct of self-preservation". Warma stated that "all the small States have strived for the consolidation of peace, and have in their international actions worked to avoid the war." Consequently, it was absurd for Great Powers to consider small states as threatening. Warma also mentioned to Schoenfeld how small states had constantly supported plans for international cooperation during the interwar period.[6]

Roughly a third of Warma's plan is taken up answering various allegations ranging from the European small states' obsolescence to their weakness or inability to defend themselves. Recalling the yearbooks of the International Labour Office, Warma reminded his readers that social status and the level of education were higher and national debt per capita was lower in smaller countries than in either Germany or Russia. He had discussed the topic with Italian Ambassador Vincenzo Cicconardi who, as a representative of the fascist state, considered military strength as the only indicator of the state power.[7] Going against this vision, he criticized the claim that smaller countries were incapable of defending themselves, calling it "superficial and purposely assumed [...] grotesque". Using France

---

4 BA. Warma 2. Confidential letter to the Secretary of State by Chargé d'Affaires Robert McClintock.

5 Gross and Dziewanovski, 1986; Łaptos and Misztal, 2002, pp. 15–18.

6 Warma, 1971, p. 182.

7 *Ibid.*, pp. 176–178.

as an example, he emphasized the suffering and misfortunes of some large European countries in the war, and posited that size was not a relevant basis for assessing the solidity of a state. Warma finally refuted the lack of spiritual creativity on the part of small states by referring to the English history professor Herbert Fisher and the German economist and sociologist Wilhelm Röpke's *Die Gesellschaftkrisis der Gegenwart*. He emphasized with them that everything valuable and lasting was born in small places: Shakespeare in Elizabethan England, the Bible in Israel, the Renaissance in Florence etc.

Although the Battle of Stalingrad had already started, the German rule in Europe was still at its peak in 1942. Nevertheless, Warma envisaged Germany's defeat when drawing his plan for a disbandment of Great Powers: when the war is over, he states, "there will be no Great Continental European Power which can boast of having been strong enough to defend itself." In a private letter that same month, Warma envisioned a new 1918, with Germany collapsing internally and occupied areas being left without a ruler. At any rate, according to Warma, the Estonian government had to be ready for action whenever the opportunity would arise.[8]

In many respects, the part of Warma's plan related to small states resembles the draft written by the Belgian Hervé de Gruben (under the pen name Ajax) in January 1942. Despite fundamental similarities, de Gruben emphasized less than Warma the democratic form of government and did not present small states as advocates of peace but as "apples of discord and objects of undue temptation".[9] Warma on the contrary presented centralized power as a symptom and federations of small states as the cure. For example, he stated "the nearer to absolute centralization a government has been or is, the greater have been the resulting catastrophes [...] to Europe". Warma also stressed this issue when handing his plan to McClintock.

In line with his decentralizing idea, Warma made no demands about state intervention in economics. He was swimming against the stream because increased intervention was a fundamental change in economical thinking during the war and was carried out after the war in Western European countries.[10] Warma accidentally referred to Wilhelm Röpke, a German economist who had gone to exile first to Turkey and later to Switzerland, who supported such state intervention in the German economy. Yet the importance of Röpke to Warma was more political than economic: Röpke was one of the few supporters of European unification among German

8 BA. Warma 1. Warma to Klesment, before 6.12.1942.

9 Ajax (Baron Hervé de Gruben), 1942.

10 Mazover, 1999.

emigrants. Furthermore, he also proposed regional unions: his Europe was a "true worldwide community of nations, which can only take form of a genuine federation, which means that it must be composed of regional and continental sub-groups".[11] Röpke's writing, together with the Päts' testament, have both to be recognized as the most important influences behind Warma's plan.

Naturally, if small states were considered as a positive force, all the blame is put by Warma on larger ones, namely Germany and Russia, referred to in roundabout ways as "two great aggressive European States" or "the great European powers, where government power was centralized to the highest degree". Probably due to what he saw as a Soviet policy of false promises and ever-increasing demands in Estonia, Warma repeatedly stressed the fact that actions "must take place both formally and, above all, in practice". However, Warma identified the centralized state largely with a machinery of submission, stating that the most important component of decentralizing power was to give the state's military, police, justice and political powers to the decentralized level. Warma would allow cooperation in defence and other specific duties to be listed in a convention. There would also be no centralized religion.

Regional Unions of Small States

While asking for the dismantlement of Great Powers into smaller states, Warma considered nonetheless that a form of larger union was vital for the prosperity of these small entities. Warma's second point dealt thus with "the need of coordination in the functions of the small European states", this being the formation of small and mid-sized regional unions out of the small entities born of the Great Powers' dismantlement. A federation and a regional union would both have a similar "permanent collective central organ". The difference between a federation and a regional union would not be in their functionality but only in how they were created.

Warma's ideas can be tied to other exiled politicians' proposals to promote small steps towards European unification for the post-war period. This was especially true in Central Eastern Europe, where the idea of federalism had previous examples like the Polish Commonwealth, and independent states had emerged in the form of federations during and immediately after World War I. Estonia had also promoted the policy of the Baltic League in the early 1920s. The relations between continental and regional union were discussed in most exiled circles,

11 Röpke, 1942, p. 378; Voigt, 1986, pp. 578, 620.

especially among federalists from Central Eastern Europe.[12] Regional solutions were also a starting point for wider cooperation amongst exiles from Holland and Belgium.[13]

Here again, Warma's plan bears striking similarities with de Gruben's plan, who also proposed a policy of dividing the big and uniting the small into "groups, which will be roughly of the same size". Most likely, Warma and de Gruben were unaware of each other, as keeping contact with the West from Helsinki or Stockholm was hard during the war.[14] Although he was only 80 kilometres from Tallinn, Warma was also an exile, not only isolated from his home country but also from the main federalist centres formed by exiled politicians from Central Eastern Europe in London and New York.[15] Warma can also be set in the context of the intellectual activity of exiled governments from Denmark and Norway, who made only a few blueprints for the unification of Europe. Additionally, these did not consider a Nordic union as a prerequisite despite the tradition of Scandinavism. On the contrary, wartime meant expansion to stress Atlantic cooperation. There was also an interesting division between Norwegian exiles depending on their location: those in Stockholm relied on Nordic cooperation, while those in London promoted Atlantic relations.[16]

Although Warma did not specify the exact nature of the regional unions he hoped for, he posited that such unions should have economic, ethnic, cultural and historical ties. The federalists from Central Eastern Europe also emphasized cultural ties among the peoples of the region as well as political and economic interdependence with the main problem for them being also the question of how to address the questions of international security and economic rebuilding.[17] Needless to say, the criteria for building functioning unions of small states were hard to meet, and Warma refrained from naming any regional unions. In a private letter written in late 1942, he expressed doubts that a Baltic bloc of three states or a combined Finland and Estonia would be large enough. He favoured integrating Estonia with Scandinavia, and Lithuania and Latvia with Poland.[18]

Similarly, the discussions among federalists from Central and Eastern Europe did not deal with the Baltic as a region but occasionally included

[12] Gross and Dziewanovski, 1986.

[13] Gotovich, 1986, pp. 414–417; Mans, 1986, pp. 451–456.

[14] Warma, 1971, for example p. 148.

[15] Gross and Dziewanovski, 1986, pp. 356–359; Łaptos and Misztal, 2002, pp. 19–20.

[16] Hecker-Stampehl, 2007, pp. 136–139; Nielsen, 1986, pp. 476–479.

[17] Gross and Dziewanovski, 1986, p. 360.

[18] BA. Warma 1. Warma to Klesment, before 6.12.1942.

Lithuania with Poland, with Latvia and Estonia being left unmentioned.[19] The Lithuanian geographer Kazys Pakštas was an exception when he envisioned Scandinavian and Baltic unions, but he even proposed a combination of them within a Balto-Scandinavian federation while in the U.S. in 1942.[20] The Finn, who commented on Warma's plan, Väinö Voionmaa, also added that "the pacification of the Baltic Sea would be a main project, which could unify the Baltic and Nordic federations and perhaps even a wider territory."[21]

The Baltic states were not considered as an entity of three states in the U.S. post-war planning either. A draft, written on June 15, 1943, hoped that the unification of Estonia and Latvia would satisfy the needs of the Soviet Union and that Lithuania would unite with Poland. Whether the Baltic states included two or three states, they would be too small and would form a federation, probably placed "under Soviet influence, in which they would have autonomy in their domestic affairs."[22]

One reason for these ambiguities and unwillingness to define clearly the contours of eventual federations can be found within the exile governments themselves. Individual states did not want to melt into federations and lose their independence again. Polish or Czech exiles were willing to establish a union encompassing the entire Baltic-Danube-Balkan region, partly because they could not agree on a more limited union. Although there was cooperation between the exiled Polish and Czech governments in London, mutual ground was harder to find as the war waged on and political attitudes towards the advancing Soviets created discord. There was some support for larger federations among resistance movements and even an exchange of ideas between centres of exiled governments and occupied areas, but most of the Eastern European resistance was nationalist, not pro-European.[23]

Considering this problem of federations of small states, and although Warma's national background explains some features in his plan, it might be exaggerating to define him and his plan as the expression of a general Estonian opinion. Like de Gruben had caused confusion within the Belgian exile community, Warma seems to be the only Estonian who referred to federations in post-war planning. Joint resolutions where Warma was involved,

19 Łaptos and Misztal, 2002, pp. 40–41.

20 Gross and Dziewanovski, 1986, p. 361; Karjahärm, 2003, p. 58.

21 Voionmaa, 1971, pp. 191–192.

22 Post World War II foreign policy planning. 1520-H-19. Soviet Union: Baltic States; Foreign relations: Soviet-Baltic relations, 15.6.1943.

23 Gross and Dziewanovski, 1986, pp. 357–358, Valenta, 1995, p. 349; Mazover, 1999, p. 204.

like, for example, Protocol 10 of the Estonian Foreign Delegation issued in January 1943, persistently relied on the Atlantic Charter and was confident on the prospects for a restoration of Estonian independence.[24]

Peace as the Purpose of European Cooperation

Warma rightly saw his plan as a radical reform rendered possible by the context of the war: "the immediate past has scarcel[y] (*sic*) ever offered better possibilities for such efforts than the future of mutilated, starved and woebegone Europe". With his plan, Warma explicitly linked a reorganization of Europe into both federations of small states and the preservation of peace. This is obvious in the title and in the way he describes peace as a general natural law and war as a disturbance: "general European peace preservation requirements" should be a basis for the way in which regional unions would be formed. In this way, Warma's plan finds its place among a host of wartime plans proposing to ensure European peace through the unification of Europe by one form or another.

The unions would lead to coordination of production and trade and Warma took prospected economic advantages for granted. He touched them very shortly but what he missed in length came back in conviction: "Undoubtedly, it would also make for easier and more elastic coordination in labour and to some extent also in trade with its positive economic consequences."

Economic results, however, were not the most significant priority in Warma's justifications: "incorporating the small states as regi[o]nal (*sic*) confederations should promote and develop social thinking and have it replace a so-called own-corner patriotism. That is very important for European social evolution." For Warma, the regional unions would also be efficient in preventing war through the development of a European mentality. Warma here followed in the footsteps of Tõnisson and Pusta regarding their arguments in the League of Nations in 1931.

Although Warma's primary idea was to coordinate the actions of small states by creating regional unions, he also wished to prevent the isolation of these entities by developing coordination and contacts. A reward for avoiding isolation was for example an improved security through defense unions. "Neighboring federations should be so formed that if on[e] (*sic*) of the member States should be threatened by an outside power, it would affect strategically the neighbouring regional federations of States." For example, an attack against Estonia would mobilize Scandinavian, Central European and Russian unions, depending on which state

---

[24] BA. Warma 3. Eesti Vabariigi välisdelgatsiooni protokoll No. 10, 16.1.1943.

had initially attacked. This compulsory, mutual defence union would bind unions together based on "direct, real political reasons" rather than just moral grounds.

Furthermore, the actual realist agreement would make them feel a sense of unity. In other words, realist and idealistic were in constant interaction and, according to Warma, practical cooperation could alter mental assumptions. The new political structures would change fundamental thinking and reciprocally this structure would "act more effectively due to the increased mentality of general interests, which would emerge and forcibly gain impact within it".[25] This was in line with the idea of making regional unions and federations as similar as possible, since the federations already had a sense of national identity.

Nevertheless, Warma did not totally believe in his idea of European networks, and he proposed a partially centralized European organization. In his third main point, he suggests a "higher international controlling organ", endowed with the right to impose sanctions. The organization should be formed based on its member states' equal rights and equal status. In line with his partial defiance towards centralization, Warma devoted much less space to it than to his first two points. He particularly stressed the fact that such an organization should respect the independence of member states. In comparison to de Gruben's proposition, who wrote that "the collective agency of (this) European federation will have the double duty of administering common interests and intervening in the affairs of the different groups", Warma's European organization clearly had a more limited authority, at least without the right to intervene in the states' affairs.

Warma remained unclear as to how such an organization would function, and how its resolutions and its constitution would be implemented: a network could emerge based on mutual interests, but a formal organization would seem to require outside authority. This is alluded to in the fourth point, which demands the fair and ineluctable adaptation of the Atlantic Charter for all nations and states. The Charter required among other things the "establishment of a wider and permanent system of general security".[26] Warma's last point completed his system with small states, regional federations, a European organization, and the possibility of intervention from outside powers such as the Western allies or the United States as external guarantors.

---

[25] Also Baron de Gruben stressed this immaterial result: "finally their rivalries are absorbed into an awareness of shared interest." (Ajax (Baron Hervé de Gruben), 1942.)

[26] Atlantic Charter, 14.8.1941.

In addition to this reference to the Atlantic Charter, Warma had a clear picture of how his plan would have an impact on the world and humanity beyond Europe. Warma saw the war as "the greatest known catastrophe in the history of mankind, [both] spiritually and materially". His world view was Eurocentric since, by implication, Europeans would have "duties and tasks we owe to the future of mankind". Moreover, although the war had started in Europe, it concerned the entire world.

Warma's Influence in Finland and in the United States

In Finland, where he lived, Warma had contacts mostly with private Estophile individuals, who were not particularly interested in foreign affairs. Warma's official position in Helsinki was unclear, as the Finns refused to reopen the Estonian legation. In addition, since Estonia was occupied by Germany, Finland's co-belligerent, the Finns were not eager to officially associate themselves with Warma. Despite this, he managed to bring his plan to the attention of various Finnish personalities within the emerging Finnish peace opposition, for example, Väinö Voionmaa.

Initially, Warma approached Voionmaa, because he had taken part in the peace talks with Stalin in Moscow in 1940. Additionally, Voionmaa was a distinguished member of the Finnish Social Democratic Party and as a former Foreign Minister their leading expert on international politics. At the time of Warma's approach, he was chairman of the Finnish Parliament's Committee for Foreign Affairs. He was not, however, a member of the core of Finnish decision-making but rather one of a sort of reserve group with, for example Juho Kusti Paasikivi, who became Finnish President after the war.[27]

Voionmaa had mixed feelings on both Estonia and Warma. He was a partisan of Nordic cooperation and emphasized Nordic features in Finnish culture during, as well as before, the war. Partly because the Germans were placing Finland as the leading Nordic nation and thus neglected the idea of equal Nordic cooperation, Voionmaa disliked the idea of New Europe. Furthermore, he thought about Sweden more than Estonia as a partner for future collaboration. Alternatively, Voionmaa also acknowledged the importance of Estonian independence for Finnish security, and seemed to pity Estonia's fate: "Poor Estonia is so close to my kindred-sensitive heart."[28]

27 Halila, 1969.

28 Halila, 1969, pp. 212–215, 232–234, 304; Voionmaa, 1971, pp. 200, 225.

Warma met Voionmaa regularly after May 1940. In the letters he sent to his son, Voionmaa mentioned a total of five meetings, though obviously more went unrecorded. Voionmaa referred to Warma for the first time in his letters on November 23, 1942, and already then Voionmaa called Warma "our friend". They discussed, for example, Estonian exiles and Finnish relations with Washington, but he also made reference to Warma's plan, with which Voionmaa seemed to sympathize greatly: "What an enormous vision and still how practical and feasible", he stated.[29] Warma's plan had excellent timing, because in the winter of 1942–1943, the Finnish peace opposition increased its activities. This eventually led to the foundation of a special committee at the Finnish foreign ministry, which studied various alternatives for Finnish foreign policy from late 1943 to the summer of 1944.[30] Yet the influence of Warma's ideas does not seem to extend to the end of the war, when the European connection disappeared even in Voionmaa's letters, and he stressed the Nordic countries, especially Sweden, as Finland's closest allies and most important partners.

Although Warma's plan failed to influence Voionmaa in the later stages of the war, it probably influenced an old friend of Estonia, Urho Kaleva Kekkonen. Kekkonen would later be President and at that time was the chairman of the Finnish-Estonian Society, and met regularly with Warma.[31] Kekkonen had already been Minister of Interior but lacked an official position during the war. Although he had become known as a fierce opponent of the Finnish far right, he indirectly supported Nazi New Europe. Kekkonen was active in Finnish sports organizations and, as a consequence, he became involved in the formation of the European Sports Union. He tried to find support for this idea from President Ryti as late as 23 September, 1942, when Ryti was already trying to take distance from Germany.[32] In his writings in March 1943, Voionmaa identified two kinds of New-Europeans, the genuine fascists and faking opportunists, but unfortunately he did not name them.[33] Nonetheless, Voionmaa might well have seen Kekkonen as one of the latter.

After Stalingrad, Kekkonen started to approach the peace opposition, drawing on similar themes to those exposed by Warma in a column entitled "Small Nations and Europe" he wrote in February 1944 under his pen-name, Pekka Peitsi, for the magazine *Suomen Kuvalehti*. This article

29 Voionmaa, 1971, pp. 172, 177, 183, 191–192, 266.

30 Halila, 1969, pp. 325–330; Voionmaa, 1971, pp. 192, 252, 262, 269–270, 286–287.

31 Warma, 1971, for example p. 190. For Kekkonen's relations with Estonia, especially during World War II, see Lilja and Raig, 2006, pp. 67–89.

32 Ryti, 2006, p. 211.

33 Voionmaa, 1971, p. 225.

had much in common with Warma's plan: it required equality between states, made larger states responsible for the war, and stressed the importance of small states. Finland, as the only remaining small state that had emerged from World War I, had, according to Kekkonen, a special obligation to speak on their behalf. Yet contrary to Warma, Kekkonen was willing to sacrifice the sovereignty of nations in order to maintain peace.[34]

Johannes Klesment refers to articles published in Finnish magazines under pseudonyms by Estonian writers but does not mention Warma as one of them.[35] Thus, it remains plausible that the article was actually written by Warma, not Kekkonen, whose ideas on foreign policy were always based on good relations with a greater power, Germany or Russia, and not on international organizations. On the other hand, Kekkonen was at the time retreating from German influence and the article would fit well with his changing stream of thought, which nevertheless continued with Kekkonen becoming a strong advocate of trustful relations with the Soviet Union.

It is most likely that the European situation was discussed between Warma and Kekkonen in Helsinki, and they also heard about the plans from Western representatives. Indeed, one of the important consequences of Warma's plan was his influence on American conceptions related to the post-war reconstruction of Europe. Warma seems to have had a good relationship with Schoenfeld, the American Ambassador in Helsinki. Voionmaa also referred to Bruce Hopper, who seemed to be President Roosevelt's personal envoy in Stockholm, as a contact of Warma. Since Warma visited him, Voionmaa believed the Estonian's plan would be further developed in Hopper's "academy". However, the Finn was disappointed to learn that Hopper lacked official status, and was merely "a master of propaganda".[36] In actual fact, Bruce Hopper was more than that, as he worked for the OSS in Stockholm.[37] The Chargé d'Affaires in Helsinki, Vice Consul Robert McClintock, seems also to have been very close to Warma, and they also maintained a friendship after the war.[38]

Warma's plan was eventually considered by the U.S. State Department's Advisory Committee on Post-War Foreign Policy, which was initiated in January 1940. The Subcommittee on Political Problems was the senior subcommittee and met regularly with President Roosevelt. Among

---

34 Peitsi, 1944.

35 Klesment, 1959, p. 25.

36 Warma 1971, for example pp. 181–182; Voionmaa, 1971, pp. 177–178, 192, 224.

37 Smith, 1983, p. 125.

38 BA. Warma 22. Correspondence with R. McClintock 1945–1951.

its three special subcommittees, one concentrated on the "Problems of European Organization". The subcommittees were disbanded in 1943 and replaced by the Division of Political Studies and its Inter-Divisional Country and Area Committees, amongst which the committee on Russia-Poland dealt with the Baltic states.[39] Warma's plan landed on a fruitful soil, as the same themes of European and regional unions were being discussed in Washington as well.

The minutes, dated on February 19, 1943, considered the question of federations based on a memorandum, which stated that "regionalism is undesirable and dangerous". This statement was however rejected by the rest of the Inter-Divisional Committee on Russia-Poland, which preferred "regionalism in order to frame a policy. Regional organizations should be subordinate to world organization and might perform important supplementary functions". Germany could be included in such a bloc on the basis of equality and European cooperation would also prevent an Anglo-American policy of "divide and conquer".[40]

It is probable that this position does not derive directly from Warma's plan, most likely the Estonian's ideas simply found the U.S. administration engaged in the same kind of reflections. While Warma's plan certainly echoed aspirations for closer cooperation in Europe that also existed among the U.S. leadership at the time, the idealistic tinge of his plan, his talks of general natural law and collective sentiments, and his numerous misspellings in the English language could only warrant that this draft by an unknown Estonian quickly fell into oblivion amongst American planners.

Additionally, Warma's country of origin was a problem from an American perspective. Estonia was a small, occupied country in Eastern Europe, which was not considered alone but was connected with its neighbours, and about which the U.S. Advisory Committee had only little information. Various examples of this American uncertainty on the Baltic states can be found during these years. The reactions to the Polish-Czechoslovak Agreement of January 23, 1942 and to a similar agreement between the Yugoslavs and the Greeks on January 15, 1942 are two such examples.[41] In late 1942, the U.S. Advisory Committee focused hopes on these agreements because they were to form a basis for regional units, which would later join together. "The territory in the Union would be

39 Mark, 1987.

40 Post World War II foreign policy planning. 850-R-52. Minutes, 19.2.1943.

41 Gross and Dziewanovski, 1986, pp. 354–355; Valenta, 1995, pp. 334–336; Zgorniak, 1995, pp. 346–48; Łaptos and Misztal, 2002, pp. 29–52.

all of Europe west of Russia, except Finland, Norway, Sweden, possibly Denmark, Spain and Portugal."[42] One cannot find anything here on the Baltic states: would they be included in this union, or merged with Russia? That question surfaced a month later under a new form: "Are the Baltic states tied by trade more to Russia or the Continent?" That the latter would be true was assured soon afterwards.[43] Later on, in April 1943, the Baltic states featured prominently on a map of problematic territories in Europe drafted by American planners. It showed a total of 33 areas between France and Russia, most of them involved in border disputes, such as, for example, Memel/Klaipėda. The Baltic states were represented as a single large problem and they were by far the single biggest contested territory. Next in line were the problematic areas of Karelia and Petsamo, on the Finno-Soviet border.[44]

The possibilities of federations discussed in Warma's plan were also discussed in Washington. The U.S. Advisory Committee offered federation as a solution in the case of Finland, although maintaining independence was seen as the most desirable solution when Finland was discussed in June 1943. A federation with Sweden or all of Scandinavia was clearly preferred to other alternatives of neutralization or incorporation within the Soviet Union.[45] While the Swedes showed little interest for such adventures,[46] the leaders of Finland, such as President Ryti, were aware of these U.S. plans but showed interest only for cooperation with Sweden.[47]

One of the biggest difficulties for federation drafts during the war was the Soviet and communist opposition.[48] This was especially true for Warma's plan, since from Moscow's point of view, his country officially joined the Soviet Union during the war. Even in December 1941, Stalin would not consent to retreat from the borders established the previous summer and previously agreed with Hitler. Victory in Stalingrad quite surprisingly moderated Stalin's demands, and in the spring of 1943 he seemed to have accepted regional alliances in Central and Eastern Europe.

---

42 Post World War II foreign policy planning. 850-R-52. Minutes, 20.10.1942 and 4.12.1942.

43 Post World War II foreign policy planning. 850-R-52. Minutes, 8.1.1943.

44 Post World War II foreign policy planning. 850-R-13. Problem areas. (map), 15.4.1943.

45 Post World War II foreign policy planning. 1520-H-18. Foreign relations: international status of Finland, 15.6.1943.

46 Gross and Dziewanovski, 1986, p. 361, Łaptos and Misztal, 2002, pp. 60–61.

47 Ryti, 2006, for example p. 267.

48 Gross and Dziewanovski, 1986, p. 361; Mazover, 1999, p. 204; Łaptos and Misztal, 2002, pp. 59–65.

Nevertheless, he shortly returned to demands for a universal organization and opposition to regional solutions, which he saw as modified *cordons sanitaires* against the Soviet Union.[49]

This reality of Stalin's aspirations became increasingly problematic for the U.S. Already in June 1943 it was stated that "It might be awkward for the United States to challenge the good faith of the Soviet contention that the incorporation had taken place in legal form and at the request of the peoples concerned." Later on in the war, these conceptions evolved, and U.S. foreign policy planning came to involve the possibility of "independent Baltic states with provision for Soviet military facilities on their territory" without plebiscites and incorporation.[50] The slippery slope reached its bottom when the Inter-Divisional Committee on Russia and Poland recommended in January 1944 "that the United States not make a vital issue of the re-incorporation of the Baltic states into the Soviet Union, but that it not give approval to such re-incorporation."[51] This line of not recognizing the Baltic states' annexation by the Soviet Union remained official U.S. policy throughout the Cold War.

One unknown peculiarity in European unification history is the rhetoric of Europe in Soviet propaganda during World War II. One example of this was *Народы Европы против Гитлера* (European Nations against Hitler), which was translated into Estonian in 1943 and published by the Estonian Soviet State Publishing in Moscow; most likely it was translated in other European languages as well. The book underlined that the common battle against German aggression does not actually promote unification but separately presents resistance activities in various European countries.[52]

Wartime relations also brought difficulties to the above-mentioned Coudenhove-Kalergi's Paneuropean Union, which had moved in August 1940 to New York. In February 1942 he was given an organizational base, as a Research Seminar for a Post-War European Federation was initiated at New York University. He summoned from emigrated liberals a steering committee to organize the Fifth Paneuropean Congress in March 1943. Former Finnish Foreign Minister Rudolf Holsti was on the committee.[53]

49 Mazover, 1999, pp. 217, 228–231.

50 Post World War II foreign policy planning. 1520-H-19. Soviet Union: Baltic States; Foreign relations: Soviet-Baltic relations, 15.1.1944; 1579–14 Baltic States. Political Problems.

51 Post World War II foreign policy planning. 712-TS-79. Soviet Union: Baltic States. International Status of Estonia, Latvia and Lithuania.

52 Ponomarev, 1943.

53 Lipgens, 1986, p. 788.

He wanted to include Pusta and another (unknown) Estonian diplomat, most likely Consul General Johannes Kaiv, but Coudenhove-Kalergi didn't want "to embarrass the U.S. in their position toward their Russian ally." Nevertheless he promised to call them to the Congress but neither of them ultimately attended it.[54]

After the war, Europe was not united according to Warma's plan. On the contrary, Europe was divided, and the Eastern part, including Estonia, fell into the Soviet realm. Unification was initiated in the West, but in quite a different fashion compared to what Warma had pictured. He could claim to have been right only in the case of the re-implementation of a German federation. Yet, Warma did not draft a prophecy, but rather a plan for action. His stance on European unification did not end with the formation of the Eastern Bloc. Already in May 1946, he drafted an article with almost the same title "On Structures of Cooperation for European States to Consolidate Peace", which was more abstract and theoretical, and was probably never published. His "Theses", dated July 1948, again presented centralized Germany and Russia as threats to Europe. The purpose of these manuscripts remains unknown.[55] A few years later, Warma would return to European unification with the European Movement, which organized a conference in Hamburg to discuss the German question in 1951. While there, Warma drafted a statement which underlined the themes of decentralization and democracy. The same as had been the case nine years earlier.[56]

54 KA. Holsti 80. Coudenhove-Kalergi to Holsti, 9.1.1943.

55 BA. Warma 25. Euroopa riikide koostöövormist rahu konsolideerimiseks, May 1946; Teesid, 3.7.1948.

56 NLE. ERN 400. Rei to Retinger, 13.9.1951.

Chapter 3

Estonia in the New Europe

During World War II, Estonian came to learn the hard way that German promises of a secure future for conquered nations within the framework of New Europe was just another propaganda scheme. It was not about integration and cooperation but occupation and submission. The experience of New Europe brought out a reaction first in the homeland and as the information reached diplomats abroad, they also reacted.

In Estonia, German occupation was perhaps not liked but it was preferred after the Soviet annexation. Thus, very little resistance emerged against the Nazi New Europe; however criticism can be detected from various publications. The most prominent articles related to European international politics were written by Jaan Tõnisson in 1940 and Edgar Kant in 1942. Although it might be coincidental that these were their last published articles, the fact underlines the hope placed on a united Europe against both the totalitarian, Soviet or Nazi, systems.

In exile, Alexander Warma's plan for consolidating European peace was not an exception. There were many plans for Europe drafted during World War II, all included unification procedures in one form or another. These plans aimed at presenting alternatives first to the failed interwar system, and secondly to the radical European unification presented by the racist New Europe of the Nazis, and to the ideas of Soviet Russia. Warma's idea of networking Europe ran contrary to the European concentration envisaged by these hierarchical ideologies.

Warma's draft found its way from Helsinki through the local consul to the U.S. State Department, where plans of European unification for the post-war period were also considered. Warma's plan found its way to a fertile soil, and regional unions were emphasized in Washington mostly after the plan was sent to American representatives. Warma's plan accompanied this change towards more support for European regional unification schemes but with many misspellings while details on natural law gave no considerable reason for this change. On the contrary, the general themes of Warma's plan were common in most of the plans of post-war Europe.

Warma attempted to give his plan a universal tone, leaving Estonia unmentioned and writing about small states in general. Nonetheless, his plan reflected, in many ways, his national Estonian background. First of all, it recalled previous Estonian projects of international cooperation. It also drew several distinctive features from Estonian experiences of the 1930s and 1940s, like the lack of state intervention in the economy. In addition, Warma named the Soviet Union and Germany, the two occupants of Estonia in 1940 and 1941, as the enemies of European peace. Yet, not all Great powers were necessarily evil: the signatories of the Atlantic Charter, the United States and Great Britain were needed to implement the plan. Warma's moderation towards these countries was only partly intended to flatter potential benefactors; the Estonian also genuinely wanted to promote values of democracy and the unaltered national borders that Washington and London defended.

Despite these national peculiarities, Warma's plan had many similarities with other blueprints formulated by exiled politicians coming from elsewhere in Europe. Compared to Western counterparts, the federalists from the East were both more visionary and idealistic partly due to technical reasons. In the same fashion Warma stayed clear of calculations and economic considerations, but emphasized the national feelings behind his plan and its possible immaterial outcomes. However, his plan shares the most with the ideas proposed by the Belgian Hervé de Gruben, more than with plans drawn in Eastern Europe. The key point in Warma's plan is a united Europe that functions as a network of small nations, although he considered a higher-level organization ultimately necessary to control international life and prevent the next war.

Although Warma's plan failed to materialize, its ideas reflected previous Estonian politics during the interwar period. The plan lived on through the 1950s with Warma's involvement in the European Movement. More importantly, the plan and its unique aspects serve as an example about ideas of peaceful international relations as imagined during World War II.

Part III

Estonian Emigrants in the European Movement

Chapter 1

The Estonian National Committee of the European Movement

On October 23, 1957, Aleksander Warma gave a lecture in Stockholm with the title "Movement for European Unification and Emigrants Within it". After specifying his topic to the Estonian point of view, he began unabashedly: "It is complex to answer this".[1] Despite these words of warning, the end of the book has a task very similar to Warma's lecture: to investigate the Estonian activities and attitudes in the European unification process during the Cold War years. The first aim is to demonstrate that the main focus of the Estonian exiles' foreign affairs efforts concerned European unification. Secondly, I aim to show that they were disappointed with unification efforts as they were seen at the time of the lecture. This was, of course, the year when European integration is usually considered to have begun with the Treaty of Rome.

The two themes of the latter half of the 20th century Europe are discussed in this section, both European integration and the Cold War. Research on these major phenomena has developed into sub-fields of their own, but only few enquires combine these approaches. Both sub-fields are gradually moving away from the statist character,[2] thus also shedding light on previously marginalized groups, such as emigrants from the Eastern bloc. So far research has been dominated by the work of the emigrants themselves, but critical studies are now being increasingly found in the field. The Estonians were undeniably a small group, but their activities provide an interesting perspective for both themes.

According to Alan Milward, ECSC integration began in Western Europe in order to secure and rescue the nation state by surrendering some of each state's sovereignty to the joint organization. European and national goals did not rule each other out.[3] Although Milward concentrated on economic reasons while the Estonians were addressing the question ideologically, however the point of departure was fundamentally the

1 Warma, 1958, p. 15.

2 Kaiser and Varsori, 2010.

3 Milward, 1984; Milward, 1994.

same. European unification was valuable for Estonians only as a means of achieving their primary goal. That remained, as the Estonian "guidelines for a foreign political battle" in the spring of 1951 declared, "the liberation of the occupied homeland". Exceptions or vacillations were not approved, but the methods and sources for foreign assistance could be changed according to general tendencies.[4] Although liberation meant, firstly, the breakup of the Soviet Union, it also included establishing a new international system, which would guarantee national security. The difference is that combining national goals with European unification worked in the West but not in the East, and Estonians were forced to search for other channels.

On the other hand, underlining the national tone reveals the danger of the martyr-like image of a common front. However, in recent years, critical views on the importance and influence of the exiled governments have emerged.[5] Just as in how previous studies on the history of European integration stressed the impact of the resistance movements, nowadays such views of the exile governments are also dismissed as teleological and idealist. The research on Baltic emigration has hitherto concentrated on social issues and is only now turning to political activities.[6] Due to the initial nature of the research on exile politics, comparisons between different emigrant groups (or National Committees of the European Movement) will have to wait for further research.

Here the activities of the Estonians in the European Movement are presented in a chronological manner: it starts from the troublesome first steps and then goes on to detail Estonian ambitions in the European Movement in general and especially in the Central and East European Commission. Gradually they were degraded as observers in the process and thus they changed their focus to other organizations without, nevertheless, leaving the idea of unification completely. Appeals to European institutions were sent all the way until 1980s.

---

4 "Meie välispoliitilise võitluse sihtjooni," in *Eesti Teataja*, 28.4.1951, p. 2; also *Eesti Rahvusfondi Teated* 12 (October 1951), p. 11 and for the following year, "Mis teha, kuidas teha," in *Eesti Teataja*, 18.10.1952, p. 3.

5 Convay, 2001; Goddeeris, 2005; Made, 2008.

6 Furthermore, the research on Baltic exile politicians has mostly considered the pressure on the American and Canadian authorities, for example, Danytė, 2005 and Janauskas, 2008.

Chapter 2

Creating Contacts and Joining

An Estonian at The Hague Congress

After the Soviet Union invaded Estonia in September 1944, roughly 70,000 Estonians fled to the West. Approximately 20,000 of them remained in Sweden, while others travelled via DP camps in Germany mainly to the U.S., Canada and Australia. Politically, questions surrounding the legitimacy, continuity, and importance persisted in this community throughout the Cold War period. Nevertheless, the Estonian National Council (ENC) became the main exile centre in Sweden. It was a sort of exiled parliament, where the parties of democratic Estonia of pre-1934 were represented. The leaders of the Council remained the same throughout the entire period. The leader, August Rei, had been Head of State and Foreign Minister in the independent Estonia. Former envoy in Helsinki, Aleksander Warma, became the most important foreign affairs commentator and actor of the ENC.[1]

Additionally, Rei continued to maintain the legal status of the Estonian republic. Therefore, he assumed the position of the "Prime Minister in capacity of the President of the Republic in exile" and established a government-in-exile in Oslo on January 12, 1953. Warma became Foreign Minister, and other ministers included Johannes Sikkar, Tõnis Kint and Arvo Horm. Rei justified his authority, because he was the oldest minister of the last, short-lived, government in Estonia of September 1944. Rei's stance was supported by the majority of Estonians in Sweden but at the same time, Alfred Maurer established a parallel government-in-exile two months later in Augustdorf, Germany, which died with him a few years later. Overall, there was not even a consensus among Estonian diplomats for establishing the government-in-exile, and thus it never took an active role but remained as the bearer of national symbols and credentials.[2]

1 Lane, 2003; Orav and Nõu, 2004; Mälksoo, 2006; Made, 2008; Tammaru, Kumer-Haukanõmm, Anniste, 2010; Ant, 2012, pp. 265–269.

2 Made, 2008; Ant, 2012, pp. 254–257, 274–283, 285–287.

The Estonians that immigrated to Sweden had a domestic policy of educating refugees and maintaining contact with the local authorities, but the main focus of the ENC was abroad. There, the method remained the same: to inform the West about the suffering of the Estonian people. This information would somehow indirectly create international pressure against the Soviet Union, which would then be compelled to adopt a more lenient policy towards Estonia. Emphasis on the information policy is evident in the name of the Estonian National Fund (ERF), which worked in close cooperation with the ENC. Under this Estonian name, it collected funds. However, the English name – the Estonian Information Centre – reveals the purpose of the organization. It published journals for the Western world, *Newsletter from Behind the Iron Curtain* being the most widely circulated.[3]

The forums where this information was to be delivered changed over the years. The most important forums were the remaining foreign legations, in that they enabled the exiles to show continuation of the state. The international connections between political parties were almost equally significant. Right after these, before the United Nations and others, was the European Movement (EM).[4]

The EM was the manifestation of the increased ideology of unification in Western Europe after World War II. It was a joint initiative by (originally five but soon eight) private organizations from various countries and political backgrounds (Union européenne des fédéralistes, United Europe Movement, Conseil Français pour l'Europe Unie, European League of Economic Cooperation, Nouvelles Equipes Internationales, Socialist Movement for United States of Europe, the Liberal International, and the International Peasant Union). First EM worked as The Joint International Committee for European Unity until it was formally established in October 1948. Briton Duncan Sandys became President and his father-in-law, Winston Churchill, was elected as Honorary President along with Léon Blum, Alcide De Gasperi and Paul-Henri Spaak, all former or then current Prime Ministers of their respective states.

Its major achievement in the propagation of unification was the Congress of Europe in The Hague in May 1948. August Torma,[5] the remaining Estonian Ambassador in London, learned about the forthcoming

3 *Eesti Rahvusfond*, 1952, pp. 5–8; *Estonian information centre ten years*, 1956, p. 3; *Eesti Rahvusfondi Teated* 12 (October 1951), p. 11; Ant, 2012, pp. 258–274.

4 "Meie välispoliitilise võitluse sihtjooni," in *Eesti* Teataja, 28.4.1951, p. 2; "Mis teha, kuidas teha," in *Eesti Teataja* 18.10.1952, p. 3.

5 Torma had changed his name from Schmidt in 1940.

conference and additionally he had the impression "that the participation of our people is not certainly totally impossible" at least as observers. Torma seemed to support the Estonian representation in The Hague and urged the ENC to contact the organizers by letter if a personal delegation was out of question.[6]

The ENC had both economic and other difficulties and thus they drafted a telegram to The Hague, just in case, in order to make their voice heard in this European event. The telegram politely wished success to the Congress and stressed that Estonia's fate was shared by 100 million Europeans. "Freedom and cooperation in Europe are impossible, if the freedom of the Baltic Sea is not guaranteed." Furthermore, the freedom and future of Europe were possible only after the decentralization of the whole Eurasian continent, which was a candid way to require the dissolution of the Soviet Union.[7] The telegram was most likely drafted by Warma, who attended the meeting of the Liberal Union instead during the same month, but he stressed the importance of European unification there as well.[8]

The official invitation received by the Estonians to attend the Congress came via the International Federation of Workmen's Associations. Once they also joined in financing the journey, it became considerably easier for Estonians to reply positively. The Baltic Humanist Association also paid for part of the effort.[9] In addition to financial difficulties, time had also become a factor, as the Congress was approaching fast.[10] Consequently, the Estonian attendant was left off the list of participants. The telegram was eventually not sent but personally conveyed to the Congress by the Estonian delegate, Arvo Horm. This was translated – as the first, Horm boasted – to the rest of the delegates.[11]

Arvo Horm had studied economics and law in Tartu and Stockholm, graduating in 1938. In 1943, he migrated to Sweden, where he later helped newcomers. He was administrative director of the ENC from 1948 until

6 BA. Rei 9. Torma to Rei, 18.3.1948. Also Torma to Rei, 4.5.1948.

7 "Vaba Baltikumita pole Euroopa koostööd," in *Eesti Post*, 21.5.1948, p. 3; "Rahvusnõukogu märgukiri Churchilille ja kongressi delegatsioonidele," in *Eesti Teataja*, 15.5.1948. p. 2; also "Euroopa enesekaitsel ja meie," in *Eesti Teataja*, 8.5.1948, p. 1.

8 Warma, Aleksander, "Välispoliitilisi marginaale," in *Eesti Teataja*, 30.6.1948, p. 2.

9 "Mis tulemused olid Euroopakongressil?" in *Välis-Eesti*, 23.5.1948, pp. 2, 8; "Euroopa-uniooni kongress Haagis," in *Stockholm-Tidning eestlastele*, 8.5.1948, p. 1; Horm, Arvo, "Antikommunistlikud organisatsioonid tihedamale koostööle," in *Teataja*, 8.12.1962, p. 8.

10 Mnd, "Euroopa enesekaitsel ja meie," in *Eesti Teataja*, 8.5.1948, p. 1; also Horm, Arvo, "Märkmeid Euroopa konverentsilt Haagis," in *Eesti Teataja* 15.5.1948, p. 2.

11 Horm, Arvo, "Parantamatu viga, et ei olnud rohkem Balti esindajaid Haagis," in *Stockholms-Tidning eestlastele*, 16.5.1948, p. 2.

his death in 1996. Politically, he belonged to liberal circles, but he leaves the impression of an office clerk more than an inspiring politician.[12]

In his report in an exile newspaper, Horm connected the Estonian fate with the European dimension. He stressed that Europe was a whole, and that half a continent was not allowed to join the Congress. He reinforced this point with reference to the opening speeches by Churchill, Romanian Grigore Gafencu, and particularly the Dutch Senator Pieter Kerstens: "Our continent must be free and united from Balticum to Iberia, from Scandinavia to Greece."[13]

The same evening, Horm was among guests from other occupied nations at the reception hosted by Princess Juliana. After a suggestion made by Gafencu, Horm entered the reception by the name of all three Baltic nations. Princess Juliana seemed delightedly surprised to meet the Estonian, Churchill seemed ambiguous or indifferent, but Paul Ramadier, former French Prime Minister and the head in charge of organizing the Congress, promised boldly: "Baltic nations – voilà – soon you will be in our company." During the same reception, Horm joined with Polish and Czech delegates to thank Churchill personally, but they could not find him.[14] On Sunday evening, Horm participated in the press conference organized for the Eastern Europeans.[15]

Although the discussion between delegates was unproblematic, in an interview Horm criticized the attitude of the Congress towards the Eastern European delegates as "vague and confused" from the beginning. They were first categorized as observers with low standards; they were transformed into delegates only after Duncan Sandys' intervention, which was preceded by Polish claims of Spanish representation.[16]

Colonel, former Chief of General Staff, Juozas Lanskoronskis of the Lithuanian Liberation Council arrived from Paris to The Hague only on Sunday,[17] so he was not included on the list of participants. The two representatives from the Baltic managed to pull together a joint declaration by the Movement of Baltic Federation. Written with obvious haste, they

12 "Arvo Horm 50-a.," in *Teataja*, 5.10.1963, p. ii.

13 Horm, Arvo, "Märkmeid Euroopa konverentsilt Haagis," in *Eesti Teataja*, 15.5.1948, p. 2.

14 *Ibid.*

15 Horm, Arvo, "Parantamatu viga, et ei olnud rohkem Balti esindajaid Haagis," in *Stockholms-Tidning eestlastele*, 16.5.1948, p. 2.

16 "Mis tulemused olid Euroopakongressil?" in *Välis-Eesti*, 23.5.1948, pp. 2, 8; Lane, 2005, pp. 193–194.

17 "Mis tulemused olid Euroopakongressil?" in *Välis-Eesti*, 23.5.1948, pp. 2, 8; Horm, Arvo, "Parantamatu viga, et ei olnud rohkem Balti esindajaid Haagis," in *Stockholms-Tidning eestlastele*, 16.5.1948, p. 2.

expressed thanks on behalf of all three Baltic states for being accepted to the Congress, which was starting a new phase in the long history of European unification. Furthermore, they expressed the willingness of the Baltic states to uphold both the sovereignty and national autonomy within the true European values of democracy, freedom for the individual, and solidarity among nations. Consequently, they demanded an end to occupation of their countries and cooperation within Europe as a whole.[18] The declaration as such is the only proof of Horm's and Lanskoronskis's presence in The Hague.

Surprisingly, Horm did not mention anything later about what was a most visible occurrence of Baltic cooperation at the Congress. Instead, he regretted the lack of cooperation among politicians from the occupied countries. Their underlining attitudes were nevertheless the same. Horm, however, was satisfied with the change of ideas during the conference, and he anticipated deeper collaboration in the future, this included cooperation among Baltic activists.[19]

On the other hand, in his report Horm praised the cooperation received from Swedish delegates. Horm shared an airplane to Holland with a Swedish delegate, James Dickson, from whom he later received the conference papers.[20] Due to this assistance, the Dutch perhaps treated Horm as a member of the Swedish delegation.

Horm's report also stressed that the Congress was "completely informal". Nevertheless he was disappointed that ENC had missed this occasion of propaganda on a larger scale.[21] Rei on the other hand was pleased with the Estonian representation. He explained to Torma that Horm had had an opportunity to "discuss with numerous prominent individuals from multiple countries, provide them with our propaganda material, and even create very useful contacts."[22]

The immediate results from The Hague Congress of Europe for Estonians in Stockholm were rather small. It was meaningful for them in a sense that they became aware of other aspirations towards European unification. The newspapers of émigré Estonians started to refer to European unification on a reasonably regular basis. In September 1948, one of few examples

---

18 HAEU. ME 1179. Horm is misspelled as "Anro Halm".

19 "Mis tulemused olid Euroopakongressil?" in *Välis-Eesti*, 23.5.1948, pp. 2, 8.

20 Horm, Arvo, "Märkmeid Euroopa konverentsilt Haagis," in *Eesti Teataja*, 15.5.1948, p. 2.

21 Horm, Arvo, "Märkmeid Euroopa konverentsilt Haagis," in *Eesti Teataja*, 15.5.1948, p. 2; also, Horm, Arvo, "Parantamatu viga, et ei olnud rohkem Balti esindajaid Haagis," in *Stockholms-Tidning eestlastele*, 16.5.1948, p. 2.

22 BA. Rei 9. Rei to Torma, 4.6.1948.

concentrated on the implementation of the Marshall Plan and the Interlaken conference of Coudenhove-Kalergi's European Parliamentary Union.[23] The process started in the Congress of Europe was not mentioned and not even the end result of the establishment of the Council of Europe in May 1949 evoked large publicity. This was notified only briefly as the first step on the long way to the actual goal of a United States of Europe, and clearly as a minor organ compared to NATO or the OEEC.[24]

A Baltic Detour to Europe

Even before the Congress of Europe and without the EM the Estonians were prepared to move towards unification. As early as April 1947, Harald Perlitz, an emigrated physicist, approached, apparently on his own initiative and privately, the United Europe Committee in Britain and wanted to attend their next meeting but he was denied.[25] Allegedly, the working problem of ENC in 1947 had a similar goal: "In foreign political cooperation we must pursue a European confederation."[26] The ENC statute that was adopted was presented as objective 2.3: "to pursue informative activities with the object of promoting European collaboration and unity." It is not clear whether this aim or formulation was present in the original statute on January 26, 1948 or amended later on February 5, 1950.[27] Moreover, the ERF listed as one of its most important fields of activity "propagation among Estonian refugees the idea of a United Europe."[28]

Despite their enthusiasm, the Estonians were ignored by the central European powers. For example, in March 1948, the EM sent Raoul Dautry to make contacts with politicians in Scandinavia but apparently he did not meet with exiled Estonians. Neither did Swedish authorities want to encourage Estonians to work for European unification in Sweden.[29] In August, Torma came across the difficulties of Estonian membership in EM organizations. "It received strong objections from many parties." Only after

23 "Miks koostöö ei edene," in *Eesti Teataja*, 5.9.1948, p. 1.

24 AL, "Esimesed sammud ühendatud Euroopa poole," in *Eesti Teataja*, 5.3.1949, p. 4; AL, "Ühendatud Euroopa," in *Eesti Teataja*, 13.8.1949, p. 4.

25 HAEU. ME 348. Perlitz to United Europe Committee, 13.4.1947 and United Europe Committee to Perlitz, 18.4.1947.

26 Warma, Aleksander, "Euroopa valiku ees," in *Eesti Teataja*, 17.5.1952, p. 3; also, BA. Warma 27. Presentation on the E.K. meeting, 21.5.1950.

27 *Estonian National Council 1947–1957*, 1957, p. 11. The statute was also amended on 29.6.1954 and 11.3.1956.

28 *Estonian information centre ten years*, 1956, p. 3; *Eesti Rahvusfond 1946–51*, 1952, pp. 8–9.

29 HAEU. ME 897. Note by Raoul Dautry on his trip to Scandinavia, 12.3.1948; Heikkilä, 2012.

the appeals by Polish and Rumanian representatives, a "decision in principle" was achieved so that the Baltic states could become members, but only with one representative.[30]

British diplomat Hughe Montgomery Knatchbull visited Scandinavia in October 1948 on a similar journey as Dautry half a year earlier. He had been an envoy in Tallinn before World War II and his old contacts encouraged businessman Heldur Tõnisson, son of Jaan Tõnisson, to contact him. Nevertheless Knatchbull did not support the Baltic politicians in taking action. Only the Dane Karl Bøgholm became involved and began co-operating with them.[31] Bøgholm contacted the former Finnish Foreign Minister, Hjalmar Procopé, who had been involved in the unification effort since the 1920s and was living at the time in Stockholm. Procopé provided Bøgholm with some names from the Baltic states.[32]

In November 1948, the ENC contacted the United Europe Movement, which replied that they are working only in Britain but forwarded the letter to the EM. Their Secretary General, Joseph H. Retinger, was already coming to Stockholm to meet Procopé and he informed the Estonians that he would be anxious to meet them as well.[33] The Estonian emigrants met with Retinger who visited Stockholm in January 1949. In the discussion with Rei, Warma, and another former Foreign Minister, Hans Rebane, Retinger was also reluctant to admit the Estonians directly to the EM. Retinger told that "the Balts cannot be taken into the European Movement with the way things are now." He proposed that they concentrate on a European club for exiles, which was going to be established. According to Procopé, Warma was "extremely dissatisfied" to hear what sounded like a plan to divide Europeans into two groups.[34] According to Retinger's report, he "welcomed this idea, but explained that no official recognition could be given, since such a club would be outside the general plan of the European Movement."[35]

Retinger, who himself was of Polish descent, had personal reasons to involve emigrant politicians into the EM even by bending the rules and ignoring the official opinion of the organization. In March, Retinger once again assured Estonians that he was looking for any method for inviting

30 BA. Rei 9. Torma to Rei, 31.8.1948.

31 HAEU. ME 650. Hughe Knatchbull Hugessen to Duncan Sandys, 16.10.1948.

32 KA. Procopé KAY 6636. Procopé to Bøgholm, 20.11.1948.

33 NLE. ERN 401. Hare-Scott to Rei, 29.11.1948; HAEU. ME 348. Retinger to Rei, 31.12.1948.

34 KA. Procopé 24. Diary, 12.1.1949.

35 HAEU, ME 270. Report on a visit by Dr. J.H. Retinger to Stockholm, January 1949; also Retinger to Rei, 17.1.1949.

the representatives from Eastern Europe to the EM. Retinger cast the blame on technical reasons, as to why only six of them were members at the moment. The Estonians had proposed some kind of alternative method, and although Retinger noticed that this violated the principles of the EM, he was warmly welcoming of this back door approach if it brought Estonians inside.[36]

Despite disagreements during their first meetings, Retinger continued cooperation via correspondence. In the following month, the ENC wrote directly to the executive committee of the EM and asked for membership or to assist the EM in fulfilling its aim of unifying the whole of Europe.[37] In addition, the Estonians visited London twice before Retinger returned to Stockholm in November.[38]

Retinger may have referred to the mentioned club for exiles but the Estonians may also have introduced an idea of creating a Baltic council as a sort of middle organization. Either way, the road for Estonians to membership in the EM flattened in May 1949, when Procopé conveyed greetings to the Baltic emigrants from Duncan Sandys, chairman of the International Executive Committee of the EM. He proposed to form a joint Baltic European group that could join the EM.[39] Sandys visited Stockholm soon afterwards with the same message, and both the Baltic Council and the separate national committees were founded within the next few months.[40] The EM had, from the beginning, a preference of treating the small Baltic states together. Already the organizers of the Congress of Europe had desired a joint Baltic delegation, but their Latvian connections were reluctant to associate themselves with the Congress. The Lithuanians had disagreements on the content of the delegation and thus the idea had been dropped.[41]

The official application was signed on June 1, 1949 and sent on the following day. The Baltic Council of the European Movement asked for representation from the three Baltic states, Estonia (signed by Rei and Warma), Latvia (Mintauts Čakste and Mikelis Bukss), and Lithuania (Stasys Žymantas and Vladas Žilinskas). Since politicians in their occupied countries were unable to participate, the exiled democratic politicians

36 HAEU. ME 807. Retinger to Rei, 17.3.1949.

37 BA. Warma 32. ENC to European Movement Executive Committee, 13.2.1949.

38 "Tunnustus Eesti iseseisvuse taastamise voitlusele," in *Eesti Teataja*, 4.2.1950, pp. 1–2; HAEU. ME 807. Retinger to Warma, 2.5.1949.

39 KA. Procopé 24. Diary, 30.5.1949.

40 "Euroopa kui terviku vabastamiseks ja ühendamiseks," in *Eesti Teataja*, 4.2.1950, p. 6.

41 HAEU. ME 1179. Letter to K. Valdmanis, 16.4.1948. Also, BA. Rei 9. Torma to Rei, 4.5.1948.

asked to represent them in the EM. The signatories solemnly consented to the aims and methods of the EM, and referred in the end to the EM's own declaration of Europe as a whole, without borders and barriers, which nevertheless existed. They "hope that these barriers would be no obstacles whatever for the admission of the Baltic Council of the European Movement to the European Movement."[42]

The application caused some confusion within the EM. Sandys considered that "they obviously cannot be recognized as a National Council but could be as a National Committee." Instead of a council Sandys wanted "the Baltic Committee for recognition as a National Committee of the European Movement, in respect of Latvia, Lithuania and Estonia."[43] Moreover, Retinger wanted to be sure to avoid surprises in the forthcoming meeting to guarantee a positive decision. Therefore, he sent the list of the members of the council to the British Foreign Office to clarify "whether – as far as you know – their political record during the war is satisfactory." Retinger also asked for the eligibility of these persons and organizations within their emigrant communities.[44]

Retinger told also Rei that certain Estonians in London did not accept his leadership. The problem was common for all emigrant groups and this increased their mutual troubles. Retinger referred apparently to diplomat and economist Villibald Raud, who had already crossed swords with many Estonians. After the Estonians had become members, Rei accused in *Eesti Teataja*, how "a renowned Estonian figure in London" had, by unjustified allegations of unreliability of the ENC, caused perplexity within the EM, which had then postponed the Estonian membership for six months. Furthermore, these insinuations could be traced to "a clique" in Stockholm.[45]

The leadership of the EM was not sure that the location of the Baltic committees might be ideal for their actions. Rei dispelled these suspicions that the work of the committees was based on the cooperation between experts, who in any case, are dispersed around Europe and met each other only once a year. Apparently, a greater critique dealt with Stockholm (against London or Paris) and Rei defended it as having the highest density of emigrants and good opportunities for preparatory research.[46]

42 NLE. ERN 400. Minutes of the Meeting for the purpose of setting up the Baltic Council, 1.6.1949; HAEU. ME 807. Conseil Balte. Lettre adressée au Mouvement Européen 2.6.1949. Also, KA. Procopé KAY 6639. Procopé to Duncan Sandys, 2.6.1949.

43 HAEU. ME 807. Sandys to Curtis, 9.6.1949.

44 HAEU. ME 807. Retinger to Pomien, 5.1.1950 and Retinger to Foreign Office, 13.1.1950.

45 HAEU. ME 807. Retinger to Rei, 17.3.1949; "Tunnustus Eesti iseseisvuse taastamise voitlusele," in *Eesti Teataja*, 4.2.1950, pp. 1–2.

46 BA. Rei 6. Rei to the President, 18.4.1950; NLE. ERN 400. Warma to Pomian, 20.6.1950.

The EM soon replied to Stockholm that the Executive Committee would make the decision at the next meeting, even twice, because Retinger wanted to personally express his interest in the Baltic organization as well as satisfaction for the accomplished work. When the final decision was postponed during the following six months, the anxious Balts asked many times, when this next meeting was going to be held. Retinger explained the delay as related to the obligation related to the ignition of the Council of Europe and asked for the list of members of the Estonians involved with the EM, which was soon delivered.[47] Additionally, Procopé wrote his letter of recommendation to Sandys on Baltic emigrants: "Among them there is a very sincere interest in everything that concerns European unity and that they are anxious to contribute to the movement."[48]

Meanwhile, during the same autumn, the Baltic Council had already managed to act as a member organization of the EM, even before official approval. It sent the Lithuanian, Vaclovas Sidzikauskas, and the Latvian, Olgerds Grosvalds, for a meeting of International Council of the EM in Strasbourg in August 1949 (coinciding with the first assembly of the Council of Europe).[49]

However, at the same time, in September 1949, the Baltic representatives were not wholly satisfied with a joint council as they were seen to "ask to have a separate representation in the European Movement" for each country, Estonia, Latvia and Lithuania. The letter, written most likely by Sidzikauskas, presented Abbot Jean Krivickas and Sidzikauskas as the provisional Lithuanian committee, Brūno Kalniņš, Čakste and Bukss for the Latvians and Rei, Warma, Sikkar and Johannes Mihkelson for the Estonians.[50] Krivickas soon wrote to Georges Rebattet, Secretary-General of the EM in London, whether the application for the Lithuanian Committee was approved. However, Rebattet sought calm, telling him to wait for the next meeting of the International Council.[51]

In October 1949, another letter from Stockholm was sent to Retinger stating that Estonian and Latvian "councils are now formed as independent bodies and they cooperate only under the name of the Baltic Council."

---

47 HAEU. ME 807. Curtis to Baltic Council, 27.6.1949, Retinger to Rei, 11.7.1949, Retinger to Horm, 27.10.1949, Retinger to Rei, 23.12.1949; HAEU. ME 914. Retinger to Horm, 27.10.1949; BA. Warma 8. Baltic Council of the European Council to Retinger, 4.10.1949; NLE. ERN 400. Retinger to Rei, 26.9.1949; Members of the ENCEM (5.1.1951).

48 KA. Procopé KAY 6639. Procopé to Sandys, 13.7.1949.

49 HAEU. ME 807. Liepins to Retinger, undated.

50 HAEU. ME 807. Note. Représentation des Baltes, 3.9.1949.

51 HAEU. ME 807. Krivickas to Rebattet, 23.9.1949 and Rebattet to Krivickas, 14.10.1949.

According to their information, Sidzikauskas had sent a similar note a few months earlier on behalf of the Lithuanians.[52] The exact date for establishing the Estonian National Committee of the European Movement (ENCEM) cannot thus be defined as anything closer than the autumn of 1949. Additionally, the Lithuanians worked alone without their Baltic partners during the Conference of European Culture in Lausanne in December 1949. The "Lithuanian Directory in exile" sent an appeal, which pointed out the danger approaching from the east: the "horrors of the Soviet concentration camp" had already captured the Lithuanian nation. On the other hand, the three Baltic nations joined with the Ukrainians in another appeal to raise the status of these occupied nations. Former Foreign Minister, Karl Selter, signed the document for Estonians.[53]

Thus, when the International Executive Committee finally approved the membership of the Baltic committees on January 19, 1950, it did so simultaneously for the three committees and not for the joint council, which had officially applied for membership. The meeting decided additionally that "the Baltic states should be jointly entitled to representation in the European Movement on the same footing as the countries of Eastern Europe and Spain."[54]

Mintauts Čakste thanked Retinger for his personal efforts in approving the membership on behalf of the "Latvian National Council of the European Movement".[55] Sidzikauskas, on behalf of the Lithuanian committee, had written a similar response a few days earlier.[56] Rei compared the acceptance of Estonians to the de jure recognitions of Estonian independence by the Western powers, which had coincidentally occurred by date 29 years earlier.[57]

Three months later, the three Baltic committees were also added as members within the Central and East European Commission of the EM. During the first meeting held in June, there was confusion about the

52 BA. Warma 8. Baltic Council of the European Movement to Retinger, 4.10.1949.

53 HAEU. ME 807. Appel de l'Élite Lithuanienne à la Conférence Européenne de la Culture, 8–12.12.1949; "Balti pagulasesindajate memorandum Euroopa kultuurkonverentsile Shveitsis," in *Välis-Eesti*, 25.12.1949, p. 12.

54 HAEU. ME 278. Meetings of the international executive bureau and international executive committee, London 19–21.1.1950; NLE. ERN 400 Retinger to Rei, 24.1.1950.

55 HAEU. ME 807. Čakste to Retinger, 13.2.1950.

56 HAEU. ME 807. Retinger to Sidzikauskas, 29.3.1950. Also, Retinger to MacMillan, 30.3.1950.

57 "Tunnustus Eesti iseseisvuse taastamise voitlusele," in *Eesti Teataja*, 4.2.1950, pp. 1–2; also, Warma, Aleksander, "Euroopa uuendatud tunnustus Eestile," in *Eesti Teataja*, 4.2.1950, p. 2.

publications, which still lacked any mention of the newest members. As a solution, a slip correcting the issue was attached to subsequent postings. A year later, the publication still lacked any remarks on the Baltic committees.[58] When updating the leaflet, Rebattet asked for the list of members of the Baltic Council from Stockholm in June 1950. He was in fact also abandoning the council and preferred the names of each of the national committees, by doing so keeping contacts would be easier.[59]

The EM organizational structure consisted of the International Council and the International Executive Committee. The former originally included 160 members, and the national committees had different numbers of seats: for example, Sweden had four and Estonia had one. The latter had 50 members, and the Baltic states were given only one seat. After changes were made in July 1950, the council had 65 members and the committee had 18 members.[60] The Baltic representative was elected "in alphabetical order"; thus, the seat was first given to Estonians, who selected Rei to take the position.[61]

After direct Estonian membership had been achieved, all references to the Baltic Council were erased. The statute of the ENCEM was changed without delay in April 1950.[62] This did not, however, mean the end of the Baltic Council, which would later recur from the European centre as an embarrassment for the Estonians. Neither did Baltic cooperation cease, but Latvian and Lithuanian exile centres and politicians remained the most important partners in foreign enterprises.[63] The ENCEM was always ready to admit Baltic and Finnish assistance in gaining membership.[64] The Lithuanian, Stasys Bačkis, worked intensively for unification in Paris. Little correspondence between him and the Estonians has survived, but these letters indicate very strong cooperation. Occasionally he represented

---

58 HAEU. ME 642. Réunion de la Commission de l'Europe centrale et orientale, 30.3.1950 and 27.6.1950; NLE. ERN 400. Rei to Retinger, 5.4.1951.

59 HAEU, ME 807. Rebattet to Secrétaire général du Conseil national Pays Baltes de Mouvement Européen, 16.6.1950.

60 Warma, Aleksander, "Euroopa uuendatud tunnustus Eestile," in *Eesti Teataja*, 4.2.1950, p. 2; "Euroopa kui terviku vabastamiseks ja ühendamiseks," in *Eesti Teataja*, 4.2.1950, p. 6; "Euroopa peab oma jõud ühendama," in *Eesti Teataja*, 19.8.1950, p. 1; "Sõda Euroopas ebatõenäolik," in *Välis-Eesti*, 20.8.1950, p. 10; "Okupeeritud maade vabad esindajad tihedamas kontaktis Euroopa liikumisega," in *Eesti Teataja*, 17.4.1951, p. 3.

61 "Abi nõutamine Eesti ülesehitamiseks," in *Eesti Teataja*, 12.1.1952, p. 1.

62 BA. Warma 20. Statute of the ENCEM.

63 "Mis teha, kuidas teha," in *Eesti Teataja*, 18.10.1952, p. 3.

64 "Balti küsimused Euroopa liikumise foorumile," in *Eesti Teataja*, 15.4.1950, p. 3; Warma, 1954, p. 3; BA. Warma 19. Warma to Torma, 23.3.1954.

the Baltic committees in the meetings of the EM, when Rei was unable to travel to Central Europe.[65]

Rei would continue to stress good relations between the Baltic nations to the EM leadership. In April 1950, he wrote on behalf of, what he now called the collaborative committee, to chairman Sandys and wanted to avoid "any misunderstanding that may be detrimental both to the intimate and sincere cooperation of our three committees, if necessary to the good of our peoples and for the preservation and strengthening of Western civilization."[66]

In addition, other kinds of regional imagination remained among the Estonians. Journalist Evald Uustalu envisioned a "future European political organization" that would start by regional agreements. The three Baltic states were too small, so he decided to build a bridge across the Baltic Sea and proposed a defence union of the Nordic states. Furthermore, unions like this "would play in coordination with other regional alliances among Central European states their own part in the organization of united Europe based on the balance of power."[67] Proposals like this were also typical among other exile groups of the early 1950s, like the Central European Federal Clubs and consequently the Central European Federal Movement – Estonian Evald Jakobson was for a while president of the Federal Club in London.[68]

Others, such as Kaarel Robert Pusta, were now critical towards the regional approach and desired cooperation within Europe as a whole.[69] Additionally, Professor Nikolai Kaasik, in one of his last articles written in May 1949, criticized the idea of a separate Intermarium federation of Central Eastern Europe. "There is no reason not to welcome it, as collaboration between Intermarium and the Western Union appears assured in the future and both would inevitably be transitional stages on the road to

65 BA. Warma 19. Torma to Rei, 24.2.1951; Warma to Torma, 28.2.1951; Torma to Warma, 10.3.1951; Warma to Torma 12.3.1951; Torma to Warma, 16.3.1951; BA. Rei 2. Rei to Bačkis, 13.9.1951; Bačkis to Rei, 28.9.1953; NLE. ERN 400. Horm to Bačkis, 11.10.1949; Rei to Retinger, 5.4.1951. More on Bačkis, see Streikus, 2007.

66 BA. Rei 6. Rei to the President, 18.4.1950.

67 Uustalu, Evald, "Balti riigid ja tulevane Euroopa," in *Eesti Teataja* 17.11.1951, pp. 3, 6; also BA. Warma 10. P.M. Conference on Eastern and Central Europe, 12.1.1952; "Need, kes ei saa kuuluda Euroopa Uniooni," in *Eesti Teataja*, 31.10.1948, p. 1.

68 NLE. ERN 400. Rei to Morton 8.12.1951; Horm, Arvo, "Vahemehe ülesanded," in *Eesti Teataja*, 2.4.1949, p. 1; "Kesk-Euroopa föderatsiooni taotlemas," in *Eesti Teataja*, 26.4.1952, 3; Lane, 2005, pp. 195–196; Lane, 2008, pp. 309–310; Łaptos, 2008, pp. 318–322; Lukasiewicz, 2010, pp. 384–388.

69 BA. Warma 17. Pusta to Warma, 19.8.1953; BA. Rei 25. East-Central European Committee for European Union (third meeting), 11.8.1953.

European union." He considered the recent agreements in Western Europe only as obligatory replies to urgent needs but not necessarily as "an example for the future". The general European problem remained unanswered and actually "such a duality would lengthen and weaken the process of unification and withhold the support so necessary for the growth of these tendencies in Eastern Europe, the place where, politically and psychologically, they are required most." Eastern Europe consisted of small nations, which had a long tradition of international cooperation and now strived for "a form of union enabling them to constitute a political entity in the future, strong enough to guarantee their integrity."[70]

70 Kaasik, Nikolai, "Europe indivisible," in *Baltic Review* 1949:3, pp. 3–8.

Chapter 3

Inside the European Movement

The Central and Eastern European Commission

It had taken roughly two years from the time of initial contact for the Estonians to achieve membership in the EM. It was not getting any easier to work as a member organization within the EM. The Estonians remained as committed as ever to the European idea. According to the statute, the object of the ENCEM was "to endeavour to establish an intimate political and economic union between the free peoples of Europe and the peoples of Europe who are struggling for their freedom". As an organization, it was subjugated to the ENC, or in alternative formulation, the ENC "collaborates closely with the Estonian National Committee of the European Movement, where all political parties are equally represented."[1]

The ENCEM arranged the first meeting on April 5, 1950 for which Rei was elected chairman and Warma as a foreign representative. In the beginning, the organization summoned 113 members.[2] During the process of application, the Estonians provided the EM with a list of all members; this list included 131 names in total.[3] By December 1952, ENCEM membership had reached 185.[4] The ENCEM held an annual meeting, where it approved leadership and a lecture was given. As an example, in December 1951, Warma talked about the EM and Central Europe to an audience of 38 people. In May 1953 the current situation of the EM was discussed after speeches by August Rei and Arvo Horm.[5]

The Estonian commitment to the EM becomes evident by their international participation. According to historical reviews, during the first decade of activity, ENC members took part in approximately 70 international

---

1 NLE. ERN 398. Statutes of the ENCEM; *Estonian National Council 1947–1957*, 1957, p. 4.

2 BA. Warma 20. ENCEM (invitation), 31.3.1950; "Euroopa kui terviku vabastamiseks ja ühendamiseks," in *Eesti Teataja*, 4.2.1950, p. 6; "Balti küsimused Euroopa liikumise foorumile," in *Eesti* Teataja, 15.4.1950, p. 3.

3 NLE. ERN 400. Members of the ENCEM, 5.1.1950.

4 HAEU. EM 807. Warma to Morton, 9.1.1952.

5 BA. Warma 10. ENCEM, 5.12.1951; NLE. ERN 399. ENCEM annual meeting 27.5.1953. Invitation.

European events; nearly half (32) of them were organized by the EM.[6] During the same time, the EM organized 16 conferences and Estonians attended six of them: the Congress of Europe in The Hague in May 1948 (Arvo Horm), "Germany and Europe" in Hamburg in September 1951 (Rei), the Central and Eastern Conference in London in January 1952 (16 Estonians),[7] the second Congress of The Hague in October 1953 (Rei), the second Economic Conference in London in January 1954 (Eduard Poom and August Torma), and the second Congress of Europe in Rome in June 1957 (Warma).[8]

The London Conference on Central and Eastern Europe, which took place January 21–24, 1952, was particularly important for the Estonians. Their eagerness and strong emphasis was evident from the beginning. August Torma received the first draft for the conference programme in January 1951 and asked for a reply from Stockholm. Warma rapidly produced five pages of considerations and proposals. Torma was surprised and went beyond his authorities by formulating a "pretty and general", yet positive, reply himself. Warma's longer draft was utilized a year later in the actual conference.[9] Eventually the Estonian delegation consisted of 16 individuals and was among the largest at the conference. The ENC had prepared a total of 64 pages of material in English to present on both exile activity in Sweden and the situation in occupied Estonia.[10]

The actual work of the EM was undertaken by the Economic and Cultural Commissions, which were followed in the autumn of 1949 by the Central and East European Commission (CEEC).[11] The CEEC was

6 *Eesti Rahvusfond 1946–51*, 1952, pp. 22–24; *Eesti vabaduse eest II*, 1956, pp. 36–39.

7 Arvo Horm, Tõnis Kint, Johannes Mihkelson, Ilmar Mikiver, Harald Perlitz, Villibald Raud, August Rei, and Aleksander Warma in the official delegation; Gert Helbemäe, Evald J. Jakobson, Adelaida Lemberg, Helene Purre, August Torma, Evald Uustalu, Theodor Vellend, and Arved Viirlaid as observers.

8 HAEU. ME 80. Liste des participants aux congrès, conférences et réunions internationales du Mouvement Européen. NB! The list contains obvious mistakes.

9 BA. Warma 19. Torma to Rei, 24.2.1951; Warma to Torma, 28.2.1951; Torma to Warma, 10.3.1951; Warma to Torma, 12.3.1951; Torma to Warma, 16.3.1951.

10 BA. Warma 10. ENCEM Summary on the London Conference, 20.2.1952; HAEU. ME 641. The Eastern and Central European Conference, 16.8.1951; "Abi nõutamine Eesti ülesehitamiseks," in *Eesti Teataja*, 12.1.1952, p. 1; "Arvukas Eesti delegatsioon Londonis," in *Eesti Teataja*, 19.1.1952, p. 1; Beta, "Londoni konverentsi tähtsusest," in *Eesti Teataja*, 9.2.1952, p. 2; Horm, Arvo, "Haagist Londonini," in *Eesti Teataja*, 9.2.1952, p. 3; "100 Pagulasjuhti Londonisse," in *Välis-Eesti*, 20.1.1952, p. 3; "Uut lootust ikestatud rahvastele," in *Välis-Eesti*, 3.2.1952, pp. 1, 5; Łaptos, 2008, pp. 337–339.

11 Warma, Aleksander, "Euroopa uuendatud tunnustus Eestile," in *Eesti Teataja*, 4.2.1950, p. 2; "Euroopa kui terviku vabastamiseks ja ühendamiseks," in *Eesti Teataja*, 4.2.1950, p. 6; "Okupeeritud maade vabad esindajad tihedamas kontaktis Euroopa liikumisega,"

initially discussed as early as August 1948, when Torma had heard about them in London.[12] A year later, Retinger asked Baltic representatives "to join the Eastern European Study Group which we are forming now" and attached some confidential plans to his letter before they were even in the EM.[13]

Prominent British Conservative, Harold MacMillan became the chairman of the CEEC, and his memorandum in 1950 created the guidelines for the commission. It aimed at "constantly reaffirming, as a matter of principle that these countries will not be given up forever." Accordingly, progress for unification in the West should always take these countries into consideration as well. By continuously invoking the idea of Europe as a whole, the actions of the EM would strengthen the individual efforts of the emigrants. When the division of Europe would eventually come to an end, this work would pay off, as the plans for "political, moral, cultural, and psychological" reconstruction would be ready.[14]

In the CEEC Council, each national committee included two representatives. The Estonian envoy in London, August Torma, before being officially nominated, acted as the Estonian representative, and would also afterwards represent Estonia if the meetings took place in London. Aleksander Aspel was teaching literature at French universities[15] and he attended meetings in Paris. Occasionally, Rei or Warma would travel from Stockholm to the location.[16] On the other hand, it could appear that Baltic committees had only one representative, since the Baltic council also received a representative, and Torma started to plan the rotation cycle with Bačkis and others. Each country was to have a seat for two years and another seat would rotate annually. Torma preferred to have three Baltic representatives and promised to work towards that goal. Apparently, he succeeded in this with help of Chairman MacMillan.[17]

in *Eesti Teataja*, 17.4.1951, p. 3; "Sõda Euroopas ebatõenäolik," in *Välis-Eesti*, 20.8.1950, p. 10; Łaptos, 2008, pp. 332–339; Hick, 1990, p. 323; Lane, 2005, p. 194.

12 BA. Rei 9. Torma to Rei, 31.8.1948.

13 HAEU. ME 807. Retinger to Rei, 11.7.1949.

14 HAEU. ME 643. Eastern and Central European Section, 25.1.1951; Macher, 2009.

15 Tamm, 1998.

16 HAEU. ME 642. Réunion de la Commission de l'Europe centrale et orientale, 8.5.1950, 27.6.1950, 16.10.1950, 25.9.1951, 25.11.1951, 7.1.1952; KA. Procopé 24. Diary, 16.10.1950. For example, "Balti esindus Euroopa liikumise koosolekul," in *Eesti Teataja*, 20.5.1950, p. 3; "Hea tahe Saksamaa suhtes," in *Eesti Teataja*, 6.10.1951, p. 1.

17 BA. Rei 9. Torma to Rei, 30.6.1951; Torma to Rei, 24.9.1952; HAEU. ME 642. Réunion de la Commission de l'Europe centrale et orientale, 16.10.1950; NLE. ERN 398. Torma to Warma, 3.7.1967.

The Estonians had some cooperation with the Swedish committee[18] that invited Macmillan to Stockholm. Macmillan also paid a visit to the ENC on March 6, 1951, when the Latvian and Lithuanian representatives were also present. This gave Rei an opportunity to underline the CEEC as the protector of "the interests of currently oppressed countries in the European Movement, and it keeps their issues on the agenda."[19] Furthermore, the ENC acknowledged the CEEC as the most important partner for the Estonians, especially by publicizing the situation in the occupied countries.[20]

The London Conference was the climax of the CEEC and for exiles in the EM, but Rei and Warma were forced to explain the meagreness of the results even earlier. As early as August 1950, Rei defended the EM, stating that "large innovations of revolutionary importance are not carried out quickly or easily."[21] Six months later; Rei excused the lack of action by referring to issues relating to organizational changes.[22]

Warma first appeared frustrated at the Hamburg Conference held in September 1951, complaining that the conference had offered the same ambitious resolutions of supra-national sovereignty, but once again, "without a strict form and precisely identified programme". It also, he argued, avoided the real underlying problems, those based on agreements made in Yalta and Potsdam.[23] At the moment, Warma could nevertheless see clearly the benefits of belonging to the EM and being active there, as it kept Estonians among other Europeans: "Although we are there in the role of a so-called poor relative, because we do not have the strength and power behind us, which other countries possess, we are not badly treated, poor relatives but totally the opposite."[24] In the EM, they became part of that strength and power.

The London Conference was hailed as a success in the immediate Estonian reports both publicly and inside the ENC. For example, even the

---

18 For example, BA. Rei 3. Horm to Rei 24.10.1953; "Balti küsimused Euroopa liikumise foorumile," in *Eesti Teataja*, 15.4.1950, p. 3; "Kontakt Euroopa Liikumise Rootsi Rahvuskomiteega," in *Eesti Teataja*, 1.3.1952, p. 6; "Euroopa Nõukogu toetab Eesti vabadustaotlusi," in *Teataja*, 26.6.1954, pp. 1, 8.

19 "Harold Macmillan Eesti rahvusnõukogus," in *Eesti Teataja*, 10.3.1951, p. 1; also "Okupeeritud maade vabad esindajad tihedamas kontaktis Euroopa liikumisega," in *Eesti Teataja*, 17.4.1951, p. 3.

20 "Euroopa kui terviku vabastamiseks ja ühendamiseks," in *Eesti Teataja*, 4.2.1950, p. 6.

21 "Euroopa peab oma jõud ühendama," in *Eesti Teataja*, 19.8.1950, p. 1.

22 "Meie välispoliitilise võitluse sihtjooni," in *Eesti Teataja*, 28.4.1951, p. 2.

23 Warma, Aleksander, "Hamburgi konverentsi tulemusi," *Eesti Teataja*, 13.10.1951, p. 2.

24 "Euroopa peab oma jõud ühendama," in *Eesti Teataja*, 19.8.1950, p. 1.

usually critical *Välis-Eesti* recognized increased conviction in the idea of a united Europe on both sides of the Iron Curtain.[25] However, by the time the London Conference was held, the unification process was already moving away from the EM and the Council of Europe after the Schuman Declaration and the emerging Coal and Steel Community.[26] This was noticed by Warma, who recognized how the commitment to the Council of Europe had caused the EM to fall into stagnation.[27] *Välis-Eesti* also commented that due to this connection, "the EM, as the godfather of the Strasbourg Parliament, lost a certain importance among the Western powers."[28] The author writing under the pen name, Observer, was convinced that although the EM was "currently going through certain signs of a crisis", this could not affect the activity of the CEEC. His article confidently predicted that "the London Conference will become both the first and last great summit of East European politicians during the exile days."[29] He turned out to be right, although he was certainly anticipating the end of the exile days and not of the summits of East European politicians.

A year later, Warma had to explain, why "we have heard little about that commission". The London conference had been a great effort and success in introducing idea and function of the commission but now there were changes in the organization, which hindered the work.[30] The Western concentration on the Defence Community was another good excuse for delays in the CEEC.[31] Warma also privately expressed his faith in a forthcoming new start to Kaarel Robert Pusta, grand old man of Estonian diplomacy: "they are beginning to [...] overcome the stagnation that has characterized the commission during the last half year."[32]

Warma did not lie about there being organizational changes. One part of the reorganization was to increase the autonomy of the CEEC from the EM. The new statute was formulated and approved in November 1952, which separated the statutes of the CEEC from other commissions.

---

25 BA. Warma 10. ENCEM Summary on the London Conference, 20.2.1952; "Uut lootust ikestatud rahvastele," in *Välis-Eesti*, 3.2.1952, pp. 1, 5.

26 Messenger, 2006.

27 BA. Warma 27. European Movement and the Europe In-between. Presentation on the ENCEM general meeting, 11.12.1951.

28 "100 Pagulasjuhti Londonisse," in *Välis-Eesti*, 20.1.1952, p. 3.

29 Observer, "Ida-Euroopa konverents," in *Eesti Teataja*, 19.1.1952, p. 2; *Eesti Rahvusfondi Teated* 13 (January 1952), pp. 7–8 included the same formulation.

30 "Uuendatud start", in *Eesti Teataja*, 21.3.1953, p. 3.

31 BA. Warma 31. ENC. Foreign activities 1953/1954; also, "Kas 1954.a. on 'suhtelise rahu' aasta?" in *Teataja*, 21.2.1954, p. 6.

32 BA. Warma 17. Warma to Pusta, 11.3.1953.

There were both geographical and political justifications for this, as the CEEC was described as an anti-communist exile organ. The Estonian comments believed that the new arrangement would increase the efficiency of the commission.[33] However, their greatest fear of two parallel unions had actually materialized.

The isolation of Eastern Europeans from a European organization was not an isolated incident. Emigrated social democrats founded between themselves the Socialist Union of Central-Eastern Europe, which later became an associated organization in the Socialist International. Christian democratic politicians had started to exclude parties from Central Eastern Europe even during World War II and preferred Western European cooperation, which they continued quite successfully during the Cold War.[34]

With its new autonomy, the CEEC made efforts towards new initiatives the following spring, and the vice-chairman, the Hungarian Pál (Paul) Auer, drafted a new organizational chart including new committees. In general, the ENC welcomed the proposal in its comments. It was concerned about exiles on other continents outside of Europe and proposed an opportunity for them to join cooperation initiatives.[35] The representatives for economic, agricultural, moral, and church committees were elected in June.[36]

The ENCEM also wrote their considerations on the matter directly to the CEEC. They wanted to firstly improve the role of the national committees and secondly connections to Western governments. They also proposed a common stand by the emigrants at the forthcoming conferences of the great powers on the questions of Central and Eastern Europe. Finally, they wished to have another conference among the emigrants but with a more concrete programme than in London a year earlier. The CEEC replied politely "several of the points you mention are already being put into effect by the Commission and you may be sure that the others will be very carefully considered."[37]

When this did not seem to materialize, the Estonians also took their own initiative and, in August 1953, Warma drafted a demand of new

33 "Euroopa liikumise Kesk-ja Ida-Euroopa komisjon tuleb ümberkujundamisele," in *Eesti Teataja*, 13.12.1952, p. 3.

34 Lane, 2005, pp. 196–198; Kaiser, 2007, p. 161.

35 BA. Warma 32. ENCEM Proposal for reorganizing the structure on the meeting in London, 21.2.1953.

36 BA. Rei 3. Horm to Rei, 7.11.1953.

37 NLE. ERN 399. ENCEM to CEEC, 27.3.1953 and Law to Rei, 21.4.1953.

proposals and joint action by the exiles to solve the European problems. The CEEC would otherwise lose its authority and become outdated. He desired a perspicuous and concrete programme that would be sent on behalf of all exiles to the governments of the great Western powers. His draft included the now familiar prerequisites for the liberation of Central and Eastern Europe to fulfill human rights and national self-determination. In the draft, Warma accused the CEEC of being preoccupied with technical details and forgetting its actual mission but this was dropped from the final proposal. Instead, it appealed to the Western powers, stating that it would lower their prestige and "weaken the morale of Western self-defence" if they were to approve the violations of human rights and national self-determination in Eastern Europe, which remained the most significant hindrances to the United Europe.[38]

The demands asking for a joint declaration were calls of desperation, since Warma already knew about the disagreements in London.[39] Gradually disagreements started to influence the actions of the CEEC. By February 1952, Torma had already attended a meeting of the council of the CEEC, which he described as "exquisitely embarrassing". The Poles, who dominated the CEEC, had threatened to leave the entire organization altogether. As such, the meeting was not able to come to a consensus on the themes or time for an additional conference, despite a broad agreement concerning its necessity.[40]

Harold MacMillan left the CEEC in September 1952, and was succeeded by his fellow Conservative Richard Law.[41] Quite soon afterwards, he voluntarily resigned after internal disputes. The Belgian Étienne de la Vallée-Poussin became the new chairman in March 1954. The rapid changes revealed difficulties in the CEEC and decreasing funding had already disrupted its work. Torma was afraid the CEEC would move away from London and work only from Paris – which eventually happened. He despondently regarded the "commission as currently in the state of 'suspended animation.'"[42] After this, the CEEC did not appear in Estonian correspondence until 1967, when Torma described it with the same definition. The only issue worth reporting was the attempt to remove two Baltic representatives from the council two years earlier but Torma had

38 BA. Warma 20. Draft to the CEEC, August 1953; NLE. ERN 399. Warma to CEEC, 23.9.1953.

39 BA. Warma 27. European Movement and Europe In-between. Presentation, 10.3.1952.

40 BA. Warma 19. Torma to Rei, 10.2.1955.

41 BA. Rei 9. Torma to Rei, 10.9.1952; "Selgeid sõnu raudeesriidetagustele rahvastele," in *Eesti Teataja*, 11.10.1952, p. 3.

42 BA. Warma 19. Torma to Warma, 27.3.1954. Also, Torma to Warma, 14.4.1954.

been able to prevent this.[43] The long delay convincingly shows the disappointment by the ENCEM towards the special commission dedicated to their cause. As the CEEC had been isolated from the EM, the emigrants were to also abandon it by the mid-1950s. The most surprising detail is that the CEEC was still to exist in 1967.

The Special Committee in the Council of Europe

While the EM had segregated the Eastern emigrants within the CEEC, a similar development took place in its subsequent organization, the Council of Europe. Overall, the Estonian attitude towards the Council of Europe remained belittlement. It was rarely mentioned in the press, and was usually linked to other institutions, such as when the new chairman de la Vallée-Poussin attempted to guide the CEEC back into the lap of the EM and the Council of Europe.[44]

In an attempt to establish a meeting place that would be acceptable to the whole of Europe, not merely the liberal West, the Council resolved in August 1949 that empty seats in their meetings would represent the absent Eastern Europeans. The Council then established a separate section for the Eastern Europeans in August 1950, called the Special Committee to watch over the interests of European nations not represented in the Council of Europe. Initially, it followed the EM on the task of supporting the emigrants in promoting the idea of European unity and preserving their national cultures.[45] It was chaired for a long time by a Swede, Karl Wistrand, which made it easier for Estonians to keep contact with the Committee.

Despite their attitude, Estonians naturally would not turn down any opportunity to discuss their national cause within a European institution. Social Democrat, Johannes Mihkelson, was heard as an expert by the Committee in April 1952 for improving the publicity of the Council of Europe in the non-member states. In September same year, the Council released a resolution on the matter. Considering the current broadcasts by the national stations inadequate, the Council recommended its own programmes.[46]

After lobbying by exile politicians, in May 1954, the Council gave a declaration on the "Future of the subject European Nations" which underlined "genuine national independence and freedom" on both sides

---

43 NLE. ERN 398. Torma to Warma, 3.7.1967.

44 "Euroopa Nõukogu toetab Eesti vabadustaotlusi," in *Teataja*, 26.6.1954, pp. 1, 8.

45 Lane, 2005, pp. 194–195.

46 CACE. AS/SNR (3) PV 5 (box 341); Resolution 39 (1952) [http://assembly.coe.int/Mainf.asp?link=/Documents/AdoptedText/ta52/EREC39.htm#1].

of the Iron Curtain as a prerequisite for lasting European peace. The council assured moral support for the Eastern Europeans and anticipated "the day when they may become an integral part of the free European community". Rei acknowledged the "relatively large fundamental importance" of the declaration.[47]

During the following year, the Special Committee made the resolution to invite exile politicians as members. Warma had apparently exaggerated the magnitude of the resolution and straightforwardly proposed Rei as the Estonian representative. In its reply to Warma, the committee was less eager to follow its decision. Subsequently, additional members were rejected on the basis of earlier experiences in the process aiming to select the suitable persons to represent the emigrants. The committee nevertheless was willing to use Rei, or other persons from the Baltic states as experts.[48] Next spring it was not Rei, but Stasys Lozoraitis, Head of the Lithuanian Diplomatic Service, who presented the situation occurring in a Baltic country to the Committee.[49]

In 1957 the committee adopted a new, slightly shorter name, Committee on European Non-Member Countries, which coincided with its soul-searching. For example, a memorandum drafted by the new Chairman, Brit Peter Kirk, asked the essence of the committee, how to accomplish its task more efficiently and what that task actually was. The ultimate goal of liberation seemed, after the Hungarian revolt, out of reach. The Committee produced a considerable amount of documents discussing the situation behind the Iron Curtain, which nonetheless remained inside the room. Kirk wanted to expand the scope of the committee from Eastern Europe by practically prolonging the Cold War to the more promising prospects of Spain and Portugal, but as explicit note on Baltic states, "we have a duty to keep an eye on conditions there".[50] In the following years, the Committee concentrated on connections to churches in the Soviet bloc as well as cooperation with Comecon.

The Estonians, meanwhile, were to eventually lose their last interest in the Council. On its tenth anniversary, Warma described the Council as

---

47 CACE. Resolution 47 (1954) [http://assembly.coe.int/ASP/Doc/XrefViewPDF.asp?FileID=15448&Language=EN]; "Euroopa Nõukogu Resolutsioon orjastatud Euroopa rahvaste vabadusest ja tulevikust," in *Teataja*, 26.6.1954, p. 7; "Euroopa Nõukogu toetab Eesti vabadustaotlusi," in *Teataja*, 26.6.1954, pp. 1, 8.

48 CACE. AS/SNR (7) 8, Warma to Wistrand, 25.8.1955; Special Committee Minutes, 13.9.1955 (box 338); BA. Warma 9. Warma to Wistrand, 25.8.1955.

49 CACE. Special Committee Minutes, 24.3.1956, box 338; AS/SNR (7) 35.

50 CACE. AS/NR (9) 19, Box 338. Memorandum on the future work of the Committee, 13.11.1957.

a minimal power. Europe had all the mental and material preconditions to become an actor in world politics but the Council was not a necessary uniting spine.[51]

On the other hand, Estonian newspapers *Teataja* and *Välis-Eesti* were pleased to see – and tell – when the Council of Europe took the Baltic issue into consideration. In September 1960 the committee gave a resolution "on the situation in the Baltic states on the twentieth anniversary of their forcible incorporation into the Soviet Union", which among other sentiments expressed "sympathy with the sufferings of the Baltic peoples and assures them that they are not forgotten by their fellow Europeans".[52] In September 1963, the Committee again reminded the Council of the fate of the Baltic states, which in turn instructed the committee to carry on its studies on Eastern European countries. Two years later the Council's exile commission visited Stockholm and the Estonians used the opportunity to promote the question of double citizenship.[53] Since the mid-1950s, the Council of Europe reached Estonian publicity only when the American Assembly of Captive European Nations had meetings in Strasbourg.[54]

The CEEC's other connection to the Council of Europe was the "Committee of Cultural Actions" created at the London Conference. It was intended to cooperate with the Cultural Commission of the EM and consult with EM members on Eastern culture. The funding would come from the Council of Europe.[55] Warma enquired about the progress in Paris

---

51 Warma, Aleksander, "Kümne aastat Euroopa Nõukogu," in *Teataja*, 2.5.1959, p. 2; Warma, Aleksander, "Kas 'kelirikko' Euroopa välispoliitikas?" in *Teataja*, 24.10.1959, p. 1; Warma, Aleksander, "Saagu Euroopa…" in *Teataja*, 8.10.1960, p. 2; Warma, Aleksander, "Välispoliitilisi mõtisklusi peale Strassburgi," in *Teataja*, 1.6.1963, p. 2; Warma, Aleksander, "Käidud tee," in *Teataja*, 17.10.1964, p. 2; "Prantsusmaa hoiak Baltikumi suhtes püsib," in *Teataja*, 28.5.1966, p. 1; Warma, Aleksander, "Prantsusmaa ei tunnusta Soveti vägivalda Baltikumis," in *Teataja*, 19.11.1966, p. 1.

52 CACE. Resolution 189 (1960) [http://assembly.coe.int/Mainf.asp?link=/Documents/AdoptedText/ta60/ERES189.htm]; "Baltikumi küsimusi Euroopa Nõukogus," in *Teataja*, 30.7.1960, p. 1; "Euroopa Nõukogus meenutati Balti riikide okupeerimist," in *Teataja*, 1.10.1960, p. 1.

53 "Euroopa Nõukogu mõistab hukka Kremli kolonialismi," in *Teataja*, 6.10.1962, p. 1; Warma, Aleksander, "Mida oodavad eesti, läti ja leedu rahvad Euroopa Nõukogult?" in *Teataja*, 29.6.1963, p. 2; "Euroopanõukogu erikomisjon uuris Balti küsimusi," in *Teataja*, 13.7.1963, p. 3; "Euroopa Nõukogu põgenikekomisjon külastab Rootsit," in *Välis-Eesti*, 23.6.1966, p. 4; "Baltlaste topeltkoda kondsuse probleem esitati Euroopa põgenikekomisjoni esimehele," in *Välis-Eesti*, 25.8.1966, p. 3; Warma, Aleksander, "Euroopa probleeme," in *Teataja*, 13.6.1970, p. 2.

54 Pusta, Kaarel Robert, "Euroopa ikestatud rahvaste delegatsioon," in *Välis-Eesti*, 10.5.1959, p. 4; "Euroopa Nõukogu oli koos," in *Teataja*, 29.5.1965, p. 3.

55 BA. Warma 10. ENCEM Summary on the London Conference, 20.2.1952; Horm, Arvo, "Haagist Londonini," in *Eesti Teataja*, 9.2.1952, p. 3.

in October 1952 and in January 1953, receiving no response to either enquiry.[56] Apparently Vallée-Poussin's initiatives influenced the matter, as the cultural foundation re-emerged in May 1954, and the EM issued a recommendation supporting a common European culture.[57] After six months, the ENCEM got tired of waiting; it had heard rumours to the contrary concerning the attitude of cultural activities which were damaging for the political struggle. The Estonians saw them as complementing each other, and as proof, they sent the Council of Europe their review of "10 years of Estonian Cultural Activities in Sweden", which included budgets, plans and results of various cultural organizations.[58] The Council of Europe drafted a memorandum concerning the Cultural Fund of the Exiles briefly after this, but soon the ENCEM felt it necessary to remind the Council in April to save the initiative from oblivion.[59] The Committee of Cultural Actions never materialized.

Later in 1959 the founding of the European Court of Human Rights was covered in *Teataja*. Although the short news flash was merely reviewing the history and functions of the Court, in the end the paper commented boldly: "It is hardly necessary to underline that the birth of the Court of Human Rights will develop into an essential link in the process of European unification."[60]

Indirectly inherent to the Cultural Commission of the European Movement was the European Cultural Foundation, founded by Denis de Rougemont in 1954. It gave rise to Estonian publicity in 1960 when it had a conference in Copenhagen, although there were no Estonian representatives attending. *Teataja* presented the Foundation as the cultural organization for the developing unification.[61]

European Culture and Anti-Communism

Although the emigrants were isolated from the diplomatic unification of the EM, the Estonians did not withdraw from the movement. This can be explained by the notion of common European culture, which Estonians shared despite being degraded in the EM and the Soviet occupation of their homeland. The question of European culture also evoked discussion

56 BA. Rei 1 and Warma 20. Memorandum – European Movement Central and Eastern European Commission, 19.1.1953; "Selgeid sõnu raudeesriidetagustele rahvastele," in *Eesti Teataja*, 11.10.1952, p. 3.

57 "Euroopa Nõukogu toetab Eesti vabadustaotlusi," in *Teataja*, 26.6.1954, pp. 1, 8.

58 BA. Warma 10. ENCEM Memorandum to the Council of Europe, 5.12.1954.

59 BA. Warma 10. ENCEM. P.M, 19.4.1955.

60 "Inimõiguste Kohtukoda Euroopas," in *Teataja*, 7.2.1959, p. 2.

61 "Euroopa kultuuri rahaallikas," in *Teataja*, 5.11.1960, p. 4.

within the Estonian diaspora. The emphasis on culture was not because of being isolated from diplomatic or economic unification, thus leaving culture as the only thing available. On the contrary, common culture was perceived, like during the interwar period, as the fundamental prerequisite for unification at other levels.

After World War I, the Estonians had already combined their striving for national independence with the new, firmer European system. While in the EM, the Estonians remembered their national goal. Warma stated clearly that "it is evident, may I repeat this that the United Europe is not the goal as such, but a tool, which among other tools should contribute to the security of those nations, who belong to the United Europe."[62] He later emphasized that Estonians had "the right but also the duty, to participate in the discussion on the European question due to our national rights" because "the fate of our nation depends on the general fate of European nations."[63] This, in large measure, reflected the old slogan of "Let's be Estonians, but let's also become Europeans" by Gustav Suits, who engaged briefly with the European Movement before his death.[64] Arvo Horm considered unification "simultaneously a national and also a European mission".[65]

Warma pondered the content and form of the forthcoming European Union. He preferred to start with the federalist approach: "We believe that there are greater chances to affect a political union of Europe in the first place and as a quasi-confederation it might then develop into an economic and political whole."[66] The positive development would constitute Europe "in confederative form, in which participating states would retain the rights of a proud independent state." Even a customs union with a common currency "would respect the natural facilities and characteristics for economic production." The confederation would consist of independent and equal states that, on the other hand, would enjoy greater security, thanks to the common defence system and a higher standard of living by virtue of a coordinated economic policy.[67] Independence should be restricted as little as possible concerning "European general interests". As an Estonian, he underlined "only in a European confederation will a

62 Warma, Aleksander, "Välispoliitilisi marginaale," in *Eesti Teataja*, 30.6.1948, p. 2.

63 Warma, Aleksander, "Euroopa uuendatud tunnustus Eestile," in *Eesti Teataja*, 4.2.1950, p. 2.

64 "Selgeid sõnu raudeesriidetagustele rahvastele," in *Eesti Teataja*, 11.10.1952, p. 3.

65 Horm, Arvo, "Meie osa vastupanurindes," in *Eesti Teataja*, 26.9.1948, p. 2.

66 BA. Warma 20. Considerations of the Estonian Committee, 11.10.1950.

67 BA. Warma 28. Speech on European Unity, undated. Also BA. Rei 19. Warma, "European problems from the Viewpoint of a European," 31.10.1952; BA. Warma 10. Positions on the materials of the London conference, undated.

small state be able to achieve normal self-realization which will enrich both its own nation and the whole of humanity."[68]

For Estonians, unification was not only material reconstruction but "the major task of re-building of Eastern countries and their inclusion in Western civilization, mentally, politically and financially."[69] The delegation to London underlined the "respect for the characteristically European, Christian-humanitarian ethical principles that constitutes the spiritual and moral strength of United Europe and is its most vital condition of existence."[70]

As the single attempt to gain public support for the unification, the ENCEM sold pins, or buttons, with the EM symbol in early 1952. The price was five Swedish Krona. At least 500 items were sold. According to *Välis-Eesti*, this could be seen "as a nice coincidence, the large letter E symbolizes both free Europe and free Estonia."[71]

Even a review of emigrant literature mentioned European politics. According to the editor, Bernard Kangro, the publication activities were "at the same time a struggle for complete free Europe and human basic rights for all nations."[72] The next edition in Swedish in 1971, when European unification was not any longer an Estonian priority, lacks such a reference.[73]

Warma saw the reality of the modern day world in the "political and economic units in continental dimensions". It was "about illusions" to rely on national self-sufficiency. The idea of unification had indeed won support but "official politics still spasmodically trudge by habit on the road of today's policy of appeasement". A united Europe was the only way to guarantee freedom and a better future for European nations and "to give them back their heritage and share in the larger community of the peoples of the world."[74] Warma talked about "the ideology of sovereignty based on egocentrism",

---

68 Warma, Aleksander, "Euroopa valiku ees," in *Eesti Teataja*, 17.5.1952, p. 3; also, BA. Warma 27. European problems in Strasbourg. Presentation, 24.10.1952; "Uuendatud start," in *Eesti Teataja*, 21.3.1953, p. 3.

69 "Mis teha, kuidas teha," in *Eesti Teataja*, 18.10.1952, p. 3.

70 BA. Warma 10. P.M. Conference on Eastern and Central Europe, 12.1.1952; "Eesti delegatsiooni seisukohad," in *Eesti Teataja*, 19.1.1952, p. 1.

71 "Euroopa Liikumise märkidemüük," in *Välis-Eesti*, 20.1.1952, p. 1; BA. Warma 20. Proposal for the ENCEM working program; *Eesti Rahvusfondi Teated* 12 (October 1951), p. 11.

72 *Eestiläinen kirja vapaassa maailmassa*, 1957, p. 4. The German edition *Das Estnische Buch in der freien Welt* had a similar formulation but the English version *Estonian books published in exile* referred to more generally "universal struggle to defend spiritual freedom and human rights against the totalitarian onslaught."

73 *Den Estniska boken i den fria världen*, 1971.

74 Warma, Aleksander, "Euroopa valiku ees," in *Eesti Teataja*, 17.5.1952, p. 3; also, BA. Warma 27. Presentation on the E.K. meeting, 21.5.1950.

which the Estonians had tried to oppose at the League of Nations in 1931. However, the effort had failed then and, by this time, the "idea of an authoritarian state with autarkic tendencies and drift for expansion" prevailed.[75]

Warma was not alone among Estonians considering the meaning of Europeanness and nations in Europe. Part of the younger generation, spearheaded by Vahur Linnuste, looked for the solution to the international questions in the federalist ideas of Pierre-Joseph Proudhon, which were subsequently developed and exercised by Henri Brugmans, the rector of College of Europe in Bruges. For them, European unification was only half a task as state organizations ought to be divided into local and European levels. Small practical steps with television networks, roads, tourism etc. would develop into new forms of politics and economics across prospectively outdated national borders. The liberation of Eastern Europe was essential for preserving European culture.[76]

Federalists were against nationalism and the idea of nation states as the fundamentals of international politics. In an exceptionally stern opinion of Andrus Saareste "current sovereign nation states are becoming the gravediggers of Europe".[77] Vahur Linnuste was more amicable and emphasized the dual nature of nations and Europe, as both could not survive without the other. "The question is to find balance, to unite the maximum of sovereignty with the maximum of solidarity." Federalism was not picking sides but accepting the complex totality of the situation.[78]

Warma got into discussion with these federalists on this topic. Eino Tubin confronted Warma's idea of superiority of nationality with the supranational idea: "The most positive progress during the latest years [...] has been the progress towards European federation." Current units have expanded from smaller ones whether they were economic, military or cultural in nature and would continue to do so, due to following benefits. Tubin pointed out the recent development in Western Europe, "where great national priority does not exist any longer, or it is disappearing." To enhance nationalities runs against the idea of European unity, and Tubin

---

75 BA. Warma 27. Presentation on the E.K. meeting, 21.5.1950; Warma, Aleksander, "Euroopa valiku ees," in *Eesti Teataja*, 17.5.1952, p. 3.

76 "Ühendatud Euroopa poole," in *Vaba Eesti*, 1952:5, p. 1; Linnuste, Vahur, "Noor Euroopa," in *Vaba Eesti*, 1953:6, p. 1; Linnuste, Vahur, "Euroopa Ühendriigid – Me suur võimalus," in *Vaba Eesti*, 1954:1, pp. 1–2; Saareste, A., "Uue ajastu lävel," in *Vaba Eesti*, 1955:2, p. 12; Lasberg, Max, "Idülline federalism," in *Vaba Eesti*, 1958:2, pp. 2–3; Taagepera, Rein, "Euroopa Ühendriikide lävel," in *Vaba Eesti*, 1962:4/5, pp. 54–55; Tubin, Eino, "Euroopa uus kurss," in *Vaba Eesti*, 1962:3, pp. 34–36; Tõnus, 2000.

77 Saareste, Andrus, "Uue ajastu lävel," in *Vaba Eesti*, 1955:2, p. 12.

78 Linnuste, Vahur, "Noor Euroopa," in *Vaba Eesti*, 1953:6, p. 1.

preferred policy the framework of ideology rather nationality; improving Estonian nationality interested very few in Sweden but the goal of protecting human rights was shared by many others.[79]

In his reply, Warma referred to Spanish diplomat and philosopher Salvador de Madariaga, "that united Europe does not mean, figuratively speaking, a palette where all the colours have mashed into a grey mass, but a palette where individual colours increase the common glow." Tubin asked in return: "When individual colours mean political nationalism and extended passion on one's nation, would not the glow be more than disharmonious"? In his final reply, Warma underlined the difference between the concepts of natural and political nationalism, how certain politicians exploited national feelings, which were instinctively for mutual cooperation.[80]

In addition to these youngsters, there was very little public discussion on European unification. The limited elitism is further highlighted by the fact that even prominent politicians, who kept contact with the ENC, were quite unaware of its European aspirations. Karl Ast had been in the Estonian Social Democratic Party while a member of the Estonian Parliament and also in the Estonian Paneuropean Society. He was also a renowned fictional writer, under the pseudonym Karl Rumor. Additionally, he wrote numerous travel books and after World War II settled in Rio de Janeiro, where he became the Estonian Consul. He wrote several times on European rebirth in federalist form and the Estonian necessity to take part in it. Unlimited sovereignty had been the cause of the failure of peace and it had to be stalled.[81]

In 1953, Ast wrote to his old party colleague August Rei and pointed him in the direction of these guidelines. "Neither will the Baltic states return as international units as they once were, but they will have to enter the European general orchestra. Their general concert will also define our political structure and economical position." Rei assured that the EM was already a high priority for his foreign policy. "Politically free, non-totalitarian Europe is feasible to emerge and remain only as European general orchestra, where also Estonian and other Baltic states must have their fixed place."

79 Tubin, Eino, "Rahvuslus ja ideoloogia," in *Teataja*, 14.1.1961, p. 5. Warma's original editorial was: "Milleni jõutud…?" in *Teataja*, 7.1.1961, p. 2.

80 Warma, Aleksander, "Rahvuslus ja ideoloogia," in *Teataja*, 28.1.1961, p. 5; Tubin, Eino, ""Rahvuslus ja ideoloogia,"" in *Teataja*, 4.2.1961, p. 4; Warma, Aleksander, ""Rahvuslus ja ideoloogia,"" in *Teataja*, 11.2.1961, p. 2.

81 For example, Ast, Karl, "Tänapäevasus ja tuleviku mõeldavusi," in *Vaba Eesti*, 1962:2, pp. 27–29.

On the other hand, he emphasized the troubles and work ahead before finding the correct place for the instruments and players.[82]

Kaarel Robert Pusta, who had been in the U.S. since 1940, returned to Europe at the end of 1953 and took the post of Estonian Ambassador in Madrid. He had been involved with the Free Europe Committee in New York, when it initiated the European Integration Project in the early 1950s. Pusta was nevertheless disappointed as it was soon closed down. At the same time, he became interested in the EM and gave advice to Warma: "I'd presume that it is the last hour to educate our people to think common of European problems; the fate of our country and nation depends totally on their solution."[83] Warma had written virtually identical sentences only a few years earlier and, at this time, he was already ready to withdraw from the EM.

Warma was not happy with the EM's tautological definitions of Europe, which were founded on two premises: a specific mentality characteristic to Europeans and a space where this mentality is typical. Warma preferred combining Europeanness with human rights and the commitment to fasten them. This bordered the Soviet Union as outside Europe.[84]

Like all emigrant groups, Estonians wanted to foster their democratic undertone by joining Western organizations.[85] The ENC justified their application to the EM: "Primarily this fact would help to preserve internal self-esteem and inspire other necessary psychological preconditions for the idea of European unification in European nations suffering under totalitarian pressure, in this case among Estonians, both in their home country and among their numerous political refugees."[86] Warma tirelessly underlined the democratic traditions and procedures in Estonian politics, defining them as European. In general, it was difficult for emigrants to directly condemn the authoritarian Päts regime of the late 1930s, because many of them had stayed in office and, despite its flaws, because it had nevertheless been a constitutional, independent state. Warma could mildly criticize the preceding government as fundamentally giving the state to the Soviet Union in 1940. This was proof that only democracy could protect Estonia's sovereign independence.[87]

---

82 BA. Rei 2. Ast to Rei, 10.4.1953; Rei to Ast, 7.5.1953.

83 BA. Warma 17. Pusta to Warma, 23.2.1953; Pusta to Warma, 20.7.1955. "Uudiseid Lääne-Euroopast," in *Teataja*, 25.3.1956, p. 7; Pusta, Kaarel Robert, "Meie rahva tuleviku väljavaated," in *Välis-Eesti*, 3.5.1953, pp. 2, 7.

84 Warma, Aleksander, "Suur-Euroopa," in *Teataja*, 21.8.1965, p. 2.

85 Lane, 2008, pp. 302–303.

86 BA. Warma 32. ENC to European Movement Executive Committee, 13.2.1949.

87 BA. Warma 28. Speech on European Unity, undated; Warma, Aleksander, "Jäägem eurooplasteks," in *Eesti Teataja*, 5.11.1949, p. 2; Warma, Aleksander, "Euroopa uuendatud tunnustus Eestile," in *Eesti Teataja*, 4.2.1950, p. 2.

There was, however, a contradiction between the fundamental democratic undertone of unification and certain elitist methods used to strive towards it, which also continues in the present European Union.[88] Only a small elite of the Estonian exile community participated in the European discussion and all of them stressed the importance of unification, since the best political minds, including Winston Churchill and Paul-Henri Spaak, were involved with it.[89] In addition, Rei once defended his frequent travels to conferences abroad: "Europe's fate is not decided by the public at football matches or with gymnastics, but by European and American statesmen."[90]

According to Arvo Horm, democracy and unification were complimentary elements, which supported each other. The international relations of political parties were an important factor for creating a new European leadership and therefore Estonians had to also take part in these cooperation actions. "Along with this, the prospective European federal structure empowers European nations against authoritarian and totalitarian ideologies of both the left and the right like nothing else."[91]

Aksel Mark criticized Horm's zeal for democracy and underlined that it did not appear to be an essentially European element. European capitals, like Rome, Berlin, and Moscow, had tried to export an opposite kind of ideology only recently. Additionally, Central European countries, like Belgium, had also lost their democracy and subsequently received it back only from their Western liberators; that was the difference with Estonia. On the contrary, Finland shined as an example of the democratic European periphery. Mark also questioned the process of the parties becoming similar in every European country. According to him, national communities were still far more important than ideological visions. The fact that Horm was writing in the exile Estonian, and not a Swedish liberal, newspaper was proof of this. In his response, Horm saw Mark's comments as evidence of Europe still being "over-saturated with nationalism", which were preventing evident unification. Horm did not see Europeanism contradicting nationalism and ended by citing Gustav Suits.[92]

---

88 Delanty and Rumford, 2005, p. 67; Raik, 2003, p. 230.

89 For example Warma, Aleksander, "Jäägem eurooplasteks," in *Eesti Teataja*, 5.11.1949, p. 2; "Sõda Euroopas ebatõenäolik," in *Välis-Eesti*, 20.8.1950, p. 10; Observer, "Ida-Euroopa konverents," in *Eesti Teataja*, 19.1.1952, p. 2.

90 "Euroopa peab oma jõud ühendama," in *Eesti Teataja*, 19.8.1950, p. 1.

91 "Euroopa poliitiline struktuur," in *Eesti Teataja*, 22.11.1952, p. 3.

92 Mark, Aksel, "Noored on olnud koos," in *Eesti Teataja*, 24.1.1953, p. 6; Horm, Arvo, "Noored ja Euroopa…" in *Eesti Teataja*, 31.1.1953, p. 8.

Other Estonian organizations did not have connections to the EM. The exception verifying the rule took place during the London Conference, when Villibald Raud for the World Organization of Free Estonians (WOFE) associating himself with the Estonian delegation despite the opposition of the ENCEM. According to Raud, his organization was "representing the majority of Estonians in exile", while the ENC "does not represent the average political opinion of the Estonians in exile". Consequently, he demanded the EM to nominate two delegates to the WOFE. Raud's demands were backed by a letter from Osvald Viirsoo of the Estonian Farmers' Union in Lund, who refused to cooperate with the "militant left-wing socialists" of the ENC.[93]

The incident revealed the tensions within the emigrant community. Warma was forced to explain to the organizers the structure of Estonians in exile and portrayed the WOFE as a non-political refugee organization, with the Farmers' Union portrayed as untrustworthy separatists.[94] Rei had even earlier described WOFE to Retinger more bluntly as fascists, who had denounced the democratic manners of the ENC.[95] Raud could not see any benefit in approaching the ENC personally and asked for the invitation directly from the EM, who wanted delegations to be as versatile as possible. The ENC criticized the way internal disputes were taken into an international forum but tried to make the situation best for itself: the opponents that came to the conference showed the importance of unification and was thus also an appreciation of the Estonian unifiers as well.[96] Eventually Raud gave a presentation on European economic unity. However, ENC reports from London disparagingly described Raud's contribution as rather paltry; only *Välis-Eesti* offered Raud an opportunity to reply and he criticized all the Baltic delegations for both their restraint and passive participation.[97]

Building opposition against the communist Soviet Union was the common aim of emigrants.[98] The ultimate goal was nothing less than the partial dissolution of the Soviet Union, and the Estonians looked for like-minded company with the same or a similar goal. "It goes without

93 NLE. ERN 399. Raud to Morton, 13.12.1951 and Viirsoo to Morton, 17.12.1951.

94 HAEU. EM 807. Warma to Morton, 9.1.1952.

95 BA. Rei 6. Rei to Retinger, 6.8.1949.

96 BA. Warma 10. ENCEM Summary on the London Conference, 20.2.1952; Observer, "Kaks kaebajat," *Eesti Teataja*, 12.2.1952, p. 2; Observer, "Ida-Euroopa konverents," in *Eesti Teataja*, 19.1.1952, p. 2; Beta, "Londoni konverentsi tähtsusest," in *Eesti Teataja*, 9.2.1952, p. 2.

97 "Uut lootust ikestatud rahvastele," in *Välis-Eesti*, 3.2.1952, pp. 1, 5; BA. Warma 10. ENCEM Summary on the London Conference, 20.2.1952.

98 Lane, 2008, pp. 307–312.

saying that the centre has to present Estonian problems on a larger scale, not separately, but in connection with Baltic and Eastern European problems and while preserving a non-communist way of life." This was also in line with the underlying democratic values being pursued.[99] Partially and purposely misrepresenting a quote by Proudhon, Warma stated: "XX or "20th" century is the century of European federation. Otherwise she will go through the purgatory of a thousand years." He could not help referring to the argument that the Eastern part was already living in this purgatory.[100]

Apparently, there was initially both sincere uncertainty and hope among some that the Soviet Union would return to building "socialism in one country" and retreat from Central Europe, Estonia included. However, the events of February 1948 in Prague revealed its continuing policy of expansion and violence.[101] Thus, the Soviet threat became a major factor justifying European unification among Estonians. In May 1952, Warma underlined that "as long as nearly 1/3 of European people are forced to endure Soviet despotism, the consolidation, in any form it is aspired to, remains only as a pretty intention."[102] Half a year later, his formulation had changed to a more alarming "almost half".[103]

Another example of this juxtaposition between the EM and the Soviet Union was the way their criticism was used as evidence of the effective actions of the EM.[104] For example, according to Warma, radio broadcasts from the London Conference had reached their targets in Central and Eastern Europe because the "Kremlin had ordered its satellite governments to send protests to London."[105] Warma could not have had any evidence of this kind of line of command. He later used the same line of reasoning with Johannes Mihkelson, when they reported on the Treaty of Rome in 1957 and of Soviet criticism, the latter making the statement: "This demonstrates that Europe is on the right track."[106]

---

99 *Estonian information centre ten years*, 1956, p. 3; *Eesti Rahvusfond 1946–51*, 1952, pp. 8–9.

100 Warma, Aleksander, "Liigub siiski," in *Teataja*, 27.5.1961, p. 2.

101 J.K., "Quo vadis, Europa?" in *Eesti Teataja*, 10.1.1948, p. 2; "Vene pealetung äratab Euroopa liitumise mõtteid," in *Eesti Teataja*, 31.3.1948, p. 2.

102 Warma, Aleksander, "Euroopa valiku ees," in *Eesti Teataja*, 17.5.1952, p. 3.

103 "Mis teha, kuidas teha," in *Eesti Teataja*, 18.10.1952, p. 3.

104 For example, "Euroopa liikumise Kesk-ja Ida-Euroopa komisjon tuleb ümberkujundamisele," in *Eesti Teataja*, 13.12.1952, p. 3.

105 BA. Warma 10. ENCEM Summary on the London Conference, 20.2.1952.

106 Mihkelson, Johannes, "Väike-Euroopa sünd," in *Teataja*, 6.4.1957, p. 2; also Warma, Aleksander, "Mis edasi…?" in *Teataja*, 16.2.1957, pp. 2–3; Beta, "Euroopa majandusunioon äratab poliitilisi lootusi," in *Teataja*, 29.9.1962, p. 3.

Such strong words could rarely be attributed to domestic factors, since Sweden had recognized the Soviet annexation of the Baltic states in 1940. Rei, therefore, referred to the "danger threatening the whole free world" or the "totalitarian thief state."[107] The most extreme words were used by "AL" to pit unification "against that power which aspires not only to destroy states and nations, but also culture and civilization, the way of thinking of Europe and the whole Christian world."[108]

Periphrases were not used during private occasions such as the meeting of the ENCEM where the goal "of liberation from the burden of violent forces of the Soviet Union" could be expressed freely.[109] The ENC also did not mince its words in a memorandum to the London Conference where it stated that "among the most essential prerequisites for the creation of the feeling of security and stability in East and Central Europe is [...] the dissolution of the Soviet Union. In our opinion, the conference should summon up the courage to state this fact plainly and unambiguously."[110] The actual declaration did not go that far. On the other hand, it demanded restoring personal freedom and national independence but at the same time wished a lasting settlement with the Soviet Union. Estonians learned here to moderate their claims and in a memorandum written to the EM in 1953, Warma asked to straighten out the fact "that the people of Central and Eastern Europe, suppressed by the Soviet Union's terror and violence, must have back their kidnapped freedom. To this end, the Soviet military and civilian authorities must retreat from those countries in order for the people to implement their will."[111]

The intensification of action towards the Soviet Bloc appeared to be contradictory to the broader aim of unifying a divided continent. Rei felt it necessary to remind the EM that "it would be most undesirable to establish two parallel unions, one for the West and another for Eastern and Central Europe". The division was dangerous to the West alone, since its security remained vague. "Europe, integral and free, is not imaginable as long as broad belt of nations is cut off from it arbitrarily."[112] Warma searched for justification from another level, as "the European economic

107 "Euroopa peab oma jõud ühendama," in *Eesti Teataja*, 19.8.1950, p. 1.

108 AL, "Ühendatud Euroopa," in *Eesti Teataja*, 13.8.1949, p. 4.

109 BA. Warma 27. European Movement and the Europe In-between. Presentation on the ENCEM general meeting, 11.12.1951.

110 BA. Warma 20. Considerations of Estonian Commitee, 11.10.1950.

111 BA. Warma 20. Draft to the CEEC, August 1953.

112 BA. Warma 10. Conference on Eastern and Central Europe, Afternoon Session. Speech by Rei, 21.1.1952.

sphere" was an entity and not divided into two halves. A separate customs union at either side of Europe would disrupt this natural condition and was therefore bound to fail.[113] On the other hand, they were not contradictory, because "the struggle to unite Europe is simultaneously the struggle to liberate Central and Eastern European nations."[114] Europe could simply not be united without these countries and liberation was a prerequisite for unification.

In addition to political/ideological reasons, the Estonians also had practical, geographical/national reasons to promote unification on a European scale. An Estonian declaration at the London Conference stressed that "under no circumstances does Estonia want to belong to any 'Russian nations' federation."[115] The regional unions of the Baltic Sea Region were promoted during the early 1950s for the same reason.

The federalism of the youngsters proposed in the journal, *Vaba Eesti*, was also by default anti-communist. According to them, the unification would result in such economic growth that the appeal for Communism in Western society would disappear. In the longer run, this would lead towards both economic and ideological pressure against the socialist regimes in Eastern Europe and eventually the Soviet Union itself. On the other hand, the Soviet threat had forced Western Europe to take action. Eino Tubin prophesied: "One day it will be reported that the only achievement of communist terror was to unite Europe."[116] This prophecy has certain ground based on historical facts but not entirely positive, as the fall of Communism resulted in the Eastern enlargement of the European Union but it also deleted a fundamental reason for the unification. With the lack of a convincing image of an enemy it is considerably more difficult to justify the transfer of national rights and tasks to a European level. This has led to attempts to define a common identity within Europe but has also, on the other hand, intensified the search for external enemies, mostly from the Islamic world.

It is hard to determine whether all anti-Soviet claims were also Russophobic. At least Aldo Lattik, Deputy Chairman of the Estonian National

---

113 BA. Warma 20. Considerations of the Estonian Commitee, 11.10.1950.

114 "Eesti delegatsiooni seisukohad," in *Eesti Teataja*, 19.1.1952, p. 1; also, BA. Warma 27. European Movement and Europe In-between. Presentation, 10.3.1952; BA. Warma 10. P.M. Conference on Eastern and Central Europe, 12.1.1952.

115 BA. Warma 10. Positions on the materials of the London conference, undated.

116 Linnuste, Vahur, "Euroopa Ühendriigid – Me suur võimalus," in *Vaba Eesti*, 1954:1, pp. 1–2; Tubin, Eino, "Euroopa uus kurss," in *Vaba Eesti*, 1962:3, pp. 34–36; Grabbi, Hellar, "Eesti rahva väljavaadetest maailmapoliitilise olukorra taustal," in *Vaba Eesti*, 1962:4/5, pp. 50–53.

Council in Canada, who visited Stockholm in August 1955, explicitly demanded deeper cooperation with Germany, since it was the rising power against the Soviet Union. At the same time, he also underlined the importance of good relations with the Russians, as they would still be neighbours for the Estonians after the fall of Communism.[117]

The Long Last Years in the European Movement

After Stalin's death in March 1953, the new Soviet leadership tried to restrain the Cold War. The Estonians, among other emigrants, tried on their behalf to warn Western politicians against a "smiling policy".[118] Related to this activity, the Estonians demanded new action from the CEEC "in order to avoid an eventual standstill or differing attitudes in the activities of the National Committees."[119] Shortly afterwards, in June 1953, the EM organized a meeting in Strasbourg to agree on a common response to the intensified Soviet diplomacy. Rei was invited, since the question obviously interested him.[120] The meeting was going to accept a German proposal for the resolution on the partial and phased liberation of Central and Eastern Europe. By working together, Rei, Auer, and Gafencu managed to prevent this. For them, that would not have led to a halfway point, but to a dead-end.[121] Furthermore, the Second Economic Conference that was held in London in January 1954 drafted a resolution without mentioning the countries behind the Iron Curtain. "Nevertheless, Torma's energetic and fast action soon gave results on this issue", as the second attendee, Eduard Poom, in *Teataja* coloured the event.[122]

During the preparations for the Second Congress of The Hague in 1953, Rei and Stasys Bačkis had heard rumours that every Baltic committee would not be invited. Rei desired to see the end of the special case of the Baltic nations. "At the beginning, when we were admitted to the European Movement, we were forced to content ourselves with a state of inferiority compared to other countries, but this time our inequality becomes unbearable." Rei could see the situation damaging the whole

117 "Saksamaa relvastumine on realiteet," in *Välis-Eesti*, 7.8.1955, p. 8.

118 For example, "Vene 'rahupoliitika' ja Eesti problem," in *Teataja*, 10.5.1953, p. 1.

119 BA. Warma 10. Rei to Central and Eastern European Commission, 21.1.1955.

120 BA. Rei 6. Rebattet to Rei, 30.5.1953; Rei to Rebattet, 3.6.1953; Rebattet to Rei, 12.6.1953; Rebattet to Rei, 22.6.1953; Rebattet to Rei, 7.7.1953; Rei to Rebattet, 9.6.1953; HAEU. ME 2155. Rei to Rebattet, 9.7.1953.

121 "Ida-Lääne läbirääkimised ja okupeeritud rahvad," in *Teataja*, 12.7.1953, p. 1; HAEU. ME 475. Réunion du Bureau exécutif international à Strassbourg.

122 "Uus Euroopa ilma tollipiirideta," in *Teataja*, 7.3.1954, p. 1.

organization of the EM but his main concern was national: "It is also dangerous in terms of the national interests of our country, since it implies the idea that the claims of freedom and independence of our peoples are less firmly established and less absolute than those of other peoples."[123]

Bačkis promised to work for an invitation for all three Baltic committees, and eventually they were called[124] and attended the Congress. Despite these difficulties in preparations, the Congress left Rei a positive impression, as soon as the resolutions and declarations will be authorized and popularized within the wider audience.[125] However, his enthusiasm did not last long.

As early as 1950, the ENCEM proposed to circulate a questionnaire among the national committees in order to discover the abilities and preferences for systematic operations for all member organizations as well as proposals for how to implement these better.[126] The questionnaire finally materialized in August 1954. The ENCEM's response did not attempt to hide its criticism, but underlined the contradiction between the aims and actions of the EM. Unsurprisingly, the primary criticism focused on forgetting the Eastern part of Europe and on the work that, during the previous three years, had only concentrated on "Little Europe" and which had not borne any fruit. Instead of increasing enthusiasm for Europe, the EM was bound to follow the Council of Europe. Consequently, the idea of unity was "more confused and vague," and on the contrary, the original zeal was "decreasing and turning into the weariness of disillusion." The ENCEM proposed more drastic methods such as attempting to directly influence teachers and other educators when the "wide masses adopt this idea," which, on the other hand, was a prerequisite for final unification.[127]

For Warma, the failure of the European Defence Community in August 1954 had been another sign of the growing difficulties concerning "the cooperation of the European framework". Post-World War II development in this area had a long record of "political bustle back and forth". More importantly, it showed a lack of spirit towards an "internal conviction of the necessity of cooperation". Without it, cooperation became nothing more than mechanical.[128] Warma's pessimism was justified, as the re-armament of

123 BA. Rei 6. Rei to (Bačkis), 9.9.1953.

124 BA. Rei 6. Drapier to Rei, 2.10.1953; Rei to Drapier, 6.10.1953.

125 BA. Rei 3. Rei to Horm, 16.10.1953.

126 BA. Warma 20. Considerations of the Estonian Commitee, 11.10.1950.

127 HAEU. ME 2271. ENCEM to Rebattet, September 1954. Similar criticism was voiced by Poles (Lane, 2005, p. 198).

128 Warma, Aleksander, "Euroopa Ahhillesekand," in *Teataja*, 18.9.1954, p. 2.

Western Germany consequently created two German states, thus fostering the general European division which also left Estonia more permanently behind the Iron Curtain.[129] Pusta, on the other hand, wanted to remain optimistic. In ten years, Western Germany had become an essential element in Western defence against Communism and in the future its influence would spread across its borders.[130]

The failure of the European Defence and Political Communities was also a great disappointment to the young federalists. Vahur Linnuste considered this frankly the end of the strategy, "where the common army and the need to control it were points of departure to guarantee human rights, coordinate economic life and have a common foreign policy by establishing the European Political Community [...] the perspectives for European unification are darkened."[131]

Linnuste took over from Aleksander Aspel and started to teach Estonian in Paris while ceasing with the political writings. He would return briefly to the cultural dimension of European unification in the late 1970s, when the Council of Europe adopted "An die Freude" by Ludwig van Beethoven as the official anthem. The French wanted to translate the text by Friedrich Schiller to other European languages and asked Linnuste to take task for his language.[132] His work was somewhat in vain, as the current hymn of the European Union is an instrumental version.

Reports from the EM meetings got smaller. The International Council of the EM was summoned to Versailles in June 1955, Aspel and Pusta both attended. They did not contribute anything to the meeting documents, although the situation in Eastern Europe was discussed widely there. Even *Teataja* published only the final resolution of the conference.[133] Estonian appreciation towards the EM was probably not evoked either, when Rei was mentioned as a Latvian during the meeting of the Executive Commission in Paris in June 1956.[134]

In early 1957, Warma confessed to Torma that he had also lost faith in the possible resurrection of the CEEC. The member committees were

129 Messenger, 2006.

130 Pusta, Kaarel Robert, "Saksamaa ja meie," in *Välis-Eesti*, 6.2.1955, p. 3.

131 Linnuste, Vahur, "Euroopaföderalism muutunud olukorra ees," in *Vaba Eesti*, 1955:1, p. 3; also, Saareste, Andrus, "Uue ajastu lävel," in *Vaba Eesti* 1955:2, p. 12.

132 Viivik 2008.

133 HAEU. ME 1088. Conseil International Versailles, 11–12.6.1955, pp. 2–5; HAEU. ME 2520; "Euroopa küsimused tulevad korraldada nende tervikus," in *Teataja*, 19.6.1954, p. 9.

134 BA. Warma 10. Compte-Rendu de la Réunion du comité exécutif de la Commission de l'Europe Centrale et orientale, 4.6.1956.

ridden with internal conflicts, a common vision for Eastern Europe was missing. The CEEC was also short on money.[135] Although the CEEC still continued to operate, its significance quickly faded.[136] As mentioned earlier, it existed at least in 1967.

Publicly, the ENCEM and the politicians within it avoided criticizing the EM for a long period of time – they simply did not say anything about it. As early as May 1953 European unification faded into silence, when *Teataja* organized a questionnaire on the new international situation. Among the respondents (for example Rei, Pusta, Torma, Ast) only Warma mentioned the EM. Additionally, his reference was due to a then current youth conference and he mostly emphasized distributing information "on all international forums" in the West and cooperation between emigrants.[137] Three years later, Estonian students organized an event on the topic of foreign orientation, where Warma and Laretei, among others, attended as invited speakers. The published information did not make any references to European unification or organizations aiming at it.[138]

The issue of unification disappeared from annual foreign policy reviews[139] and it was also erased from preceding reviews. In 1957, the ENC produced an updated leaflet on its activities, structure, organization and historical background, which did not mention Europe or unification at all but focused attention solely on general anti-communist activities. The updated ENC statute aimed at merely "European collaboration".[140]

In January 1955, Tõnis Kint, the expert on agriculture, who had not been involved with the EM but had attended numerous conferences of the European Confederation of Agriculture, announced the poor state of European affairs in *Teataja*. International development was pushing Central European and Estonian questions to the marginal and Kint demanded new methods to promote their national cause.[141] Two years later,

135 BA. Warma 19. Warma to Torma, 28.2.1957.

136 Łaptos, 2008, p. 334.

137 "Vene 'rahupoliitika' ja Eesti probleem," in *Teataja*, 10.5.1953, pp. 1, 3; "Võitlus peab jatkuma," in *Teataja*, 25.5.1953, pp. 1, 5.

138 "Välispoliitiline orjenteerumine," in *Teataja*, 27.5.1956, p. 7.

139 "Aktiivne välispoliitilise tegevuse aasta," in *Teataja*, 11.7.1954, p. 1; "Suurenenud välispoliitiline aktiivsus," in *Teataja*, 19.6.1955, p. 5.

140 "ERN hoogne tegevusaasta," in *Teataja*, 19.6.1955, p. 5; *Estonian National Council 1947–1957*, 1957, p. 1.

141 Kint, Tõnis, "Koostöö ja sisepoliitiline ühtlus," in *Teataja*, 24.4.1955, p. 2; For example, "Euroopa Põllumajandusliidu kongress Amsterdamis," in *Teataja*, 4.9.1965, p. 4; "CEA Kongrssil Helsingis," in *Teataja*, 9.8.1969, p. 1; "Mere alt võidetud maal," in *Teataja*, 13.10.1979, p. 4.

Johannes Mihkelson, a Social Democrat and trade unionist, invoked the international connections of his party as an effective way of reminding everyone of the fate of the Estonians. In addition, Mihkelson referred to the dualism of pretty words and few results, mostly notably in his descriptive statement of how "the European Movement, which started with a great fuss, [...]is withering away like the Amu-Darya River to desert sand before reaching the Caspian Sea."[142] Mihkelson's metaphor is sadly weakened by the error that Amu-Darya empties into Lake Aral.

Although they had been involved in the ENCEM, Agrarian Kint and Social Democrat Mihkelson had other preferences. Warma, who had been in charge of foreign policy, finally announced his disappointment in a public lecture mentioned earlier in October 1957. He briefly reviewed the history of the CEEC, focusing on the London Conference and concluded: "Its management has subsequently gone from hand to hand, but its initiatives have been more than restrained."[143]

Concurrently, the Estonian membership in the EM stagnated and lost its previous vitality. The EM organized the Second Congress of Europe in Rome in June 1957. Rei was invited, but after his refusal and persuasion by the EM,[144] Warma attended the conference but did not take a very active role there. The only comment he made on the papers of the congress concerned a tribute to the "heroic Hungarian fighters" of the previous year in Budapest.[145]

In the following years, Estonians took distance from the EM. One of first signs of their return was the plan by the ERF to start cooperation with the European Youth Campaign in 1960. They were probably unaware that it had ceased from activity two years earlier.[146] There are only a few implications of Estonians in the Youth Campaign prior this. Estonians had participated in various Youth seminars for example in Caen, France, in June 1953 and a special national committee for the Estonian youth within the EM was considered in 1957.[147]

142 Mihkelson, Johannes, "Väike-Euroopa sünd," in *Teataja*, 6.4.1957, p. 2.

143 "Välisvõitluse seminar algab," in *Teataja*, 12.10.1957, p. 1; Warma, 1958, p. 25; also, Warma, Aleksander, "Vaheriideta Euroopa Strassburgis," in *Teataja*, 18.5.1957, p. 3.

144 BA. Warma 9. Schendel to Rei, 10.5.1957; Warma to Schendel, 13.5.1957; HAEU. ME 2153. Schendel to Warma, 15.5.1957.

145 BA. Warma 10. Movimento Europeo, Congresso d'Europa. Warma's collection contains protocols also from five consequent EM conferences, but they are without any comments. Also HAEU. ME 830. Congrès de l'Europe; Warma, Aleksander, "Euroopa end sirgu ajamas…?" in *Teataja*, 6.7.1957, p. 2; Warma, Aleksander, "Euroopa Kongress Roomas," in *Teataja*, 6.7.1957, p. 3.

146 *Eesti Rahvusfondi Teated* 35 (February 1960), p. 10; Palayret, 1995.

147 NLE. ERN 398. EL Eesti noorte Rahvuskomitee (1957); NLE. ERN 403. European Youth Conference 1953. Programme; Vaher, Ilmar, "Euroopa Liikumine ja eesti noored," in

Arvo Horm wrote the history of the ENC in 1982, in which he referred to the "newly activated" ENCEM in 1962–1968.[148] Indeed, the EM made a comeback during the early 1960s. However, it was firstly not a continuous activity and secondly its return was not all positive news for the Baltic emigrants. The EM drafted recommendations for reforms in its organizational chart. The representatives of national committees were invited to the Congress in Brussels in June to discuss these recommendations. Rei was asked to nominate one representative from the Baltic committees but he frankly rejected to do this. Rei considered the invitation as discrimination towards the Baltic nations, especially since the Estonians had previously been active in the EM. "This means that some national committees are less favoured than others, which would be a mistake. To do such would be both political and psychological misconduct". While there were practical difficulties in arranging a joint representation but his main reason was ideological: "The notion of the Baltic countries is only a geographical concept, like for example Scandinavia, not a political or international abstraction."[149]

Apparently there was no Baltic representation in the Congress. In his proceeding article in *Teataja*, Warma did not hide his disappointment towards the organization, which had started so greatly in The Hague and had afterwards become a mere spectator on events. Any changes in the organization chart were not going to be enough but emphasizing the national committees and creating contact with the wider society was required. Currently the EM was a "military headquarters without an army". Warma still desired a concrete programme to distinguish the EM from other organizations working for unification.[150] A review of the foreign activities of ENC a few years later mentions only how they provided "a longer justification, which stressed the need for a more active explanation of the problems in European cooperation in Scandinavia".[151]

The next EM Conference was organized in Munich in May 1962. Warma mentioned the meeting only briefly in his long editorial, although

---

Teataja, 7.6.1953, p. 2; "ERN. Euroopa noorte konverents," in *Teataja*, 10.5.1953, p. 6; "Olev Mikiver föderalistide esimeheks," in *Välis-Eesti*, 9.5.1954, p. 7.

148 *ERN 1947–1982*, 1982.

149 BA. Warma 9. Rei to Schendel, 28.3.1961; Schendel to Warma, 3.5.1961; Rei to Schendel, 16.5.1961; BA.. Warma 8. Pusta to Warma, 26.6.1961; "Eesti Rahvusnõukogu välistegevusest aastal 1962," in *Teataja*, 15.6.1963, p. 5.

150 Warma, Aleksander, "Liigub siiski," in *Teataja*, 27.5.1961, p. 2; "Euroopa Liikumise reorganiseerimise konverents Brüsselis," in *Teataja*, 17.6.1961, p. 1; "Brüsselis toimub," in *Välis-Eesti*, 17.6.1961, p. 1.

151 *Eesti Rahvusnõukogu välispoliitilise tegevuse kroonika*, 1965, p. 26.

he eventually attended it. *Teataja* reported on the meeting only afterwards and Warma wrote his report, where he listed some of the declarations on the necessity of joint organizations and a European constitution.[152] The contradiction between words and reality was evident.

Apparently, the increased interest in the EM resulted partly in a new person entering foreign exile politics. William Muld was not a young man any longer and had established a career in Sweden as physicist and teacher but became involved in politics and European affairs in mature age. His comments during the ENC annual meeting in 1963 remind of the same optimism in the European unification as that shown by Warma and others 15 years earlier: "Estonia's freedom depends to a large extent on the realization of the idea of European unification. This is the direction we need to pay our attention to. While we want to liberate our home country, we have to be advocates of a United Europe."[153]

Muld repeated his theses five years later in a public event organized by the ERF. He envisioned a "free and independent Estonia within the family of United European states." With the enthusiasm of a newcomer he wanted to get involved in the activities of the EM: "Estonians ought to fight for the concept and idea of a United Europe, not only in words but also in deeds." Everyone agreed except diplomat, Valter Kotsar, who expressed doubts as to whether it was worthwhile to cooperate with the EM and whether it would assist the Estonian cause. He got responses not only from Muld but also from ethnologist, Gustav Ränk, who preferred the EM as a group of small nations compared to directly influencing the great powers. He was accompanied by Arvo Horm, who underlined the West German interest in the EM and hoped for intensified cooperation with the Germans in any case, especially if the U.S. continued to withdraw from European issues.[154]

The Estonians as well as emigrants in general were forced to continue defending their place in the EM. In December 1963, the CEEC was planning to discuss the status of the Baltic states. The Estonians heard about this from other diplomats. None of them were invited to the meeting. Furthermore, the EM was preparing to start corresponding with the socialist

152 BA. Warma 8. Warma to Philippovich, 23.5.1962; Warma 9. Horm to Schendel, 30.5.1962; Warma, Aleksander, "Euroopa mõte ja selle realiseerimine," in *Teataja*, 2.6.1962, p. 2; "Min. Warma Euroopa Liikumise kongressile," in *Teataja*, 16.6.1962, p. 2; "Euroopa maad peavad liituma poliitiliseks uniooniks," in *Teataja*, 30.6.1962, p. 1.

153 "Elavad vaidlused ERN üldkogus," in *Teataja*, 15.6.1963, p. 3.

154 "Aeg töötab balti rahvaste vabaduse kasuks," in *Teataja*, 13.4.1968, p. 3; "Euroopa liikumine ja Eesti," in *Teataja*, 22.5.1968, p. 4; "Ka Eesti peab kuuluma ühendatud Euroopasse," in *Teataja*, 22.5.1968, p. 3.

states of the Central and Eastern Europe. This sounded too much like "the betrayal of Yalta" and it resulted in various protests by the Baltic emigrants. Warma himself personally contacted the Secretary-General of the EM, Robert van Schendel, and the Estonians joined a memorandum with emigrant organizations against these tendencies and attempts. Although the Baltic committees were eventually invited, they rejected the opportunity to participate in the CEEC Congress in Brussels in January 1964. Additionally, Kaarel Robert Pusta received an invitation to that event but he also declined.[155] Soon after, Warma described the EM as "in the shadow of death".[156]

The disagreements were settled before the next EM Conference in Cannes in October 1965. The Baltic committees were happy to cooperate again and Warma attended the conference. The declaration also paid attention to Central and Eastern Europe in a roundabout way and assured that they will eventually unite with the rest of Europe. Warma was seemingly pleased with the resolution and the new activity but also compared it to a drowning dog, which would only start swimming after its ears got wet.[157]

Unification did not disappear from exile discussion. For example, in February 1966 publicist Esmo Ridala referred to occasional claims that "the direction of Estonian foreign policy should be participation in cooperation within the framework of united Europe". Ridala himself agreed on the general level with the goal and how it could solve Estonian security problems but doubted the practical methods for achieving it. Nevertheless, unification presented a threat; first as specific national interests could be sacrificed for bigger European benefits and secondly, echoing the doubts of Professor Tammekann thirty years earlier, Estonia was in danger of "melting away and disappearing into organizations of other states with the loss of its own identity." Under these premises Ridala assured: "We should not hope too much from European unification, as a battle for life between nations and other groups goes forever on."[158]

---

155 BA. Warma 7. Jurgis Baltrusaitis to Warma, 27.5.1964; Warma to Baltrusaitis, 29.5.1964; Warma to Kappel, 7.12.1964; Warma 8. Warma to Kütt, 18.12.1963; Pusta to Warma, 13.12.1963; Pusta to Torma, 23.1.1964; BA Warma 9. Warma to Schendel, 16.12.1963; Schendel to Warma, 13.2.1964; Warma to Schendel, 28.3.1964; "Protestid Euroopa Liikumise hoiaku vastu," in *Teataja*, 25.1.1964, p. 1; Lane, 2005, p. 199.

156 Warma, Aleksander, "Suur-Euroopa," in *Teataja*, 21.8.1965, p. 2.

157 BA. Warma 9. Warma to Schendel, 12.10.1965; "Eesti delegaadid väliskongressidel," in *Teataja*, 16.10.1965, p. 1; Warma, Aleksander, "Parem hilja kui ei kunagi," in *Teataja*, 16.10.1965, p. 2; "Eesti Rahvusnõukogu välistegevus 1964–1965," in *Teataja*, 13.11.1965, p. 3.

158 Ridala, Esmo, "Mõtteid Stokholmi ja Tallinna vahelt," in *Teataja*, 12.2.1966, p. 5; also ER, "Euroopa majanduslik koostöö sügavas kriisis," in *Teataja* 21.12.1983, p. 2.

Muld lectured on European cooperation to the Estonian youngsters in 1966 and twice in spring 1968. He was dissatisfied with the few practical results of the many noble ideas which derived from the interwar period; he particularly mentioned the Pusta and other Estonian involvements in the Paneuropean Union. Afterwards technological development, the benefits of larger economic units and the threat of the Soviet Union had improved the preconditions for unification but rather than being unified, Europe had joined in three camps: Comecon in the east, EFTA in the north-west and the EEC in the centre; while NATO and the Warsaw pact divided the continent at the military level. "Stubbornness, jealousy and greed of individual states" remained the obstacle for unification. More recently, unification has repeatedly attempted to find new ground and has prepared on many occasions to take the next steps despite frequent negative French opinion.[159]

During the mid-1960s the organizational structure of the ENC was reformed and a new foreign committee introduced. The close relation between the ENC and the ENCEM was intensified by the uniting of their leadership. The "questions connected with the forming of a United Europe" constituted nevertheless the most important field in their activity. Warma was naturally displeased with the degrading of emigrant committees as observers, and he came close naming them as bastard sons of the EM and the Western committees as legitimate heirs. Despite their limited resources, the emigrant committees were, nevertheless, crucial in popularizing the idea of unification on both sides of the Iron Curtain. Nonetheless, Warma was happy to see the EM gaining more momentum in 1967 with the revised constitution. It was his logic that as the U.S. was forced to concentrate on the war in Vietnam, Europeans ought to take charge of their own politics.[160] Furthermore, in the same paper, veteran Heinrich Laretei underlined cooperation within Europe in fighting for Estonian independence with this also meaning moving "to declare that we desire to belong to the composition of United Europe."[161]

The new constitution was adapted and administrative changes made in the EM. The exiles now became mere associate members but at least the role of the Baltic committees was clarified. Once again, they were to hold a joint representative at the Executive Committee but Horm, nonetheless,

---

159 "Kommunism on muutunud suureks maailmaprobleemiks," in *Teataja*, 29.1.1966, p. 1; "Euroopaliikumine ja Eesti," in *Teataja*, 22.5.1968, p. 4.

160 NLE. ERN 398. Warma to Schendel, March 1967; Torma to Warma, 3.7.1967; Warma to Schendel, 19.8.1967; Warma, Aleksander, "Sõna on nüüd eurooplastel," in *Teataja*, 18.3.1967, p. 2.

161 Laretei, Heinrich, "Meie välispoliitiline aktiviteet," in *Teataja*, 18.3.1967, p. 6.

valued this position as an improvement.[162] To draft the plan of action to propagate the idea of unification, the new international council met in January 1968 in Rome. William Muld, now the secretary of the ENCEM, was in attendance. The meeting wanted to expand the EM firstly with the EEC, when that time would come, but Muld emphasized the need for increased interest in the countries behind the Iron Curtain. Accordingly, West-East contacts would strengthen the opposition working within these states and nations; this would in turn distance them from the Soviet Union. Additionally, the framework of the united Europe in the West functioned as a pull factor to the East.[163]

Muld also visited a similar meeting in West Berlin in April 1971. Despite the new initiative, contradictions between national committees and the central organization prevailed. A clear and new programme for action as well as funding to achieve the main goal were together unanimously required. This was going to be the topic for the next meeting.[164] The next annual meeting in Bonn in May 1972 pleased Muld much more. He perceived the EM as having returned to the core of the unification debate. The most relevant emphasis was placed on the establishing of the European Parliament instead of various councils consisting of parliamentarians in other European organizations. The meeting also considered the European Currency Union with full-scale economic union not being seen as far from there.[165]

Warma had resigned as the chairman of the ENCEM in April 1970. He handpicked August Koern, the Estonian consul in Copenhagen, as his successor. Muld resigned as secretary due to his professional obligations, and he could not concentrate on this task as much as he wanted. The EM was nevertheless the most crucial sector in the foreign activities of Estonian emigrants and "temporary lows [...] must not distract us to pessimism in our pursuit towards united and free Europe." Muld remained as deputy chairman, and Aleksander Terras inherited his post as general secretary. Arvo Horm was named as organization secretary. Koern expressed hopes "that our good cooperation will fix the tangled European issues."[166]

---

162 NLE. ERN 398. Horm to Sivers, 17.5.1974; Lane, 2005, p. 199.

163 NLE. ERN 398. Conseil Federal; "William Muld Euroopaliikumise konverentsil," in *Teataja*, 27.1.1968, p. 1; Muld, William, "Euroopa Liikumise konverentsilt," in *Teataja*, 24.2.1968, p. 7; "Euroopaliikumine ja Eesti," in *Teataja*, 22.5.1968, p. 4.

164 "W. Muld konverentsile L-Berliini," in *Teataja*, 10.4.1971, p. 1; "Berliinis nõuti Euroopa Liikumise reorganiseerimist," in *Teataja*, 8.5.1971, p. 1.

165 NLE. ERN 398. Terras to ERF, 21.4.1972; "V. Muld sõidab Bonni," in *Teataja*, 6.5.1972, p. 1; "Euroopakongress Bonnis," in *Teataja*, 3.6.1972, p. 1.

166 BA. Koern 17. Warma to Koern, 5.12.1969; Koern to Warma, 9.12.1969; Warma to Koern, 27.1.1970; HAEU. ME 2153. Horm to Schendel, April 1970 (also BA Warma 9); NLE. ERN 398. Koern to Muld, 5.2.1970; Muld to ENCEM, 10.2.1970; "Euroopaliikumise

It did not help the activities that the leadership was divided between two countries. Koern asked for documents from Stockholm but Horm replied that the position is purely nominal and "actually such a committee does not exist." Koern renewed his demand two years later, when he learned on the activities from newspapers instead of official correspondence! Frictions were clear and nothing more is known from the ENCEM. In 1981 the ENCEM was still registered as one of the Estonian organizations but it did not report any activities of the previous year or plans for the subsequent year either.[167]

New kinds of activities were also to emerge outside the EM. One example was the European congress in Saarbrücken in November 1969, which Arvo Horm visited. The general feeling was certain dissatisfaction with the then current status of unification. The official institutions were not invited but the conference was organized by (mainly German) organizations wanting to return the unification process to a mass movement; they were later joined as the European Action Committee. Public support had faded as unification became characterized by institutions. Horm had paid attention to the younger generation, which had earlier been in favour of unification but now the young protested against colonization and did not take to the streets for Europe. On the contrary, united Europe could deal more effectively with the problems of the Third World as well.[168] Aleksander Terras continued Horm's reasoning and anticipated the forthcoming advantages in unification, when the euro-enthusiastic young had grown in 20 years into political leaders.[169] Another Estonian comment envisaged membership of the former colonies in the EEC from a national point of view. Thus, Europe would become an overwhelming power in international politics. "Wide perspectives open... that question could start to play an essential part also in the development of Estonian destiny."[170]

During the early 1970s, there were many excursions from Sweden to European organizations or invitations to European actors to visit Sweden to inform the political youth organizations about unification efforts. The biggest was organized in Rome in May 1972, where 25 Estonian youth

Eesti Rahvuskomitee," in *Teataja*, 4.7.1970, p. 1; "Eesti Rahvusnõukogu tegevusest 1970.a." in *Teataja*, 28.11.1970, p. 3.

167 BA. Koern 17. Koern to Horm, 18.5.1970; Horm to Koern, 8.7.1970; Koern to Horm, 8.4.1972; NLE. ERN 398. Information on Estonian organizations 1981.

168 "Euroopakongress Saarbrückenis," in *Teataja*, 1.11.1969, p. 7; "Euroopakongress nõudis uut hoogu Euroopa ühinemistaotlusisse," in *Teataja*, 29.11.1969, p. 2; "Eesti Rahvusnõukogu tegevusest 1970.a." in *Teataja*, 28.11.1970, p. 3.

169 "Euroopa ühinemine – kuivõrd Eesti päästmine?" in *Teataja*, 27.2.1971, p. 5.

170 Uu, "Ühendatud Euroopa," in *Teataja*, 7.11.1970, p. 2.

leaders were invited and with Estonian presenters the amount of participants grew to 44 persons. The most significant event in Sweden was the symposium in Linköping in February of the same year with presentations by Walter Hallstein and others.[171]

The EM, along to the Paneuropean Union, tried to increase to popularity of the forthcoming elections for the European Parliament in 1979. As Horm and Terras were unable to travel, Fanny (de) Sivers, who worked in *Centre National de la Recherche Scientifique* in Paris, became the Estonian contact person within the EM and participated in at least three meetings. She was doubtful as to whether the old men of the EM could find contact with the European public, when there was not even a press conference for the meeting. At this moment, the exile representative had only a consultative role in the EM but Sivers nevertheless pointed out the importance of belonging to such organizations, when the future could bring pleasant surprises. Sivers was not merely paying lip service for the public, as she showed the same optimism in a private letter to Horm: "Despite the difficult crisis it seems the wind is turning favourably."[172]

Eventually the European Parliament also became a target of Estonian appeals. Tõnis Kint used his connections with Agrarian politicians and Johannes Mihkelson promoted the idea in the Socialist Union of Central-Eastern Europe. In 1981, the Estonian government-in-exile contacted at least two German representatives, Paul Schnitker and Otto von Habsburg. According to the letter, the Estonians had high hopes for the Parliament and wished that their situation be taken into its agenda. "May the united Europe us not forget and consider the fact that we as well belong to the free Europe." Although Estonians were apparently working alone, they reminded that the question concerning them also dealt with the whole Baltic.[173]

---

171 NLE. ERN 398. Europa-symposium 3–5.2.1972; "Euroopaseminaar eesti noortele Roomas," in *Teataja*, 5.2.1972, p. 1; "Euroopasümposium Linköpingis," in *Teataja*, 5.2.1972, p. 3; "Linköpingi Euroopasümpoosium oli edukas," in *Teataja*, 26.2.1972, p. 1; "Euroopaseminaar Roomas," in *Teataja*, 6.5.1972, p. 8; "Ulatusliku programmiga eesti noorte europaseminar Roomas," in *Teataja*, 3.6.1972, p. 1; "Koolide Peavalitsuse Euroopa-konverentsil," in *Teataja*, 13.5.1974, p. 1.

172 NLE. ERN 398. Sivers to Horm 19.6.1975. "Euroopa Liikumise nõukogu kokkutulek," in *Teataja*, 3.8.1974, p. 1; Sivers, Fanny, "Kui noori oleks," in *Teataja*, 19.7.1975, p. 2; "Euroopa Liikumise Nõukogu Pariisis," in *Teataja*, 9.7.1977, p. 10.

173 BA Kint 47A. Kint to Antonius John, 7.11.1980; NLE. ERN 428. Kint to Schnitker, 20.3.1981; Mark to von Habsburg, 30.4.1981. Reprinted in Orav and Nõu, 2004, pp. 385–391; "Baltikum peab saama vabaks!" in *Teataja*, 16.5.1981, p. 5; Kint, Tõnis, "Euroopa Põllumajandusliidu kongress," in *Teataja*, 19.12.1981, p. 4; "Euroopaparlament nõuab omariiklust Eestile, Lätile ja Leedule," in *Teataja*, 22.1.1983, p. 1; "Balti riikide vabadusvõitlus täiesti loomulik ülesanne," in *Teataja*, 5.3.1983, p. 5; "Euroopaparlamendi Balti resolutsioon saadeti Rootsi Riigipäeva liikmetele," in *Teataja*, 2.4.1983, pp. 1, 15.

The aspirations of emigrants collided conveniently with the dissident movement emerging in the Baltic states. 45 Lithuanian, Estonian, and Latvian dissidents had joined on August 23, 1979 to condemn the Molotov-Ribbentrop Pact 40 years earlier and demanded the restoration of national governments. When the European Parliament adopted the resolution on January 13, 1983, it directly referred to this "Baltic appeal". The resolution condemned the occupation and wished an "attempt to form a common favourable approach" to the Baltic situation. Unfortunately, four months later, German Foreign Minister Hans Dietrich Genscher declined any common effort from European foreign ministers due to the poor prospect of positive results. On the contrary, any attempt seemed to harm the cause. This action nevertheless brought the Baltic question back to European forums, when new resolutions on Baltic issues were later introduced in the European Parliament and also, after two decades, in the Council of Europe.[174]

[174] Hough, 1985, pp. 438–440; Karlsson, 2003, pp. 176, 180–181; Elsuwege, 2008, p. 36.

Chapter 4

The Outsider's View

Relations with American Organizations

Since the late 1940s, the ENC's foreign activity was constantly criticized by the authors of *Välis-Eesti* and especially by its foreign commentator, Heinrich Laretei, former Estonian envoy in Stockholm. He could follow the ENC that "the problem of Estonian security is not actually a specifically Estonian problem, which could be solved separately from the overall European security problem." On the other hand, he rejected associating purely with European organizations and considered the U.S. as the sole guarantor of the liberal West against the Soviet Union. Therefore, he wanted to join Transatlantic cooperation through any way possible.[1]

There were many private organizations in the U.S. promoting American involvement in Central Eastern Europe. One of them was the American Committee on United Europe, which operated in Europe through Radio Free Europe and the *Collège de l'Europe Libre* in Strasbourg and even secretly funded the EM.[2] National groups worked as the National Committees for Free Europe.[3] The names reveal that the efforts were not directed at unification but rather at the liberation of Central and Eastern Europe, which was nevertheless considered the prerequisite for unification by the emigrants. The Free European University provided grants for exile students and Estonian newspapers loyally published these calls. These grants were cancelled in 1958. The current students were allowed to

---

1 Laretei, 1954, p. 206. Newspaper articles for example, P.J., "Kui kaugel on Euroopa Ühendriigid?" in *Välis-Eesti*, 17.10.1948, p. 10; Laretei, Heinrich, "Idealism ja egoism välispoliitikas," in *Välis-Eesti*, 16.3.1952, p. 2.

2 "Sõda Euroopas ebatõenäolik," in *Välis-Eesti*, 20.8.1950, p. 10; "Vaba Euroopa Ülikooli suvekursus Stassburgis," in *Teataja*, 26.10.1957, p. 4; Wilford, 2003, pp. 225–237.

3 BA. Warma 17. Pusta to Warma, 20.7.1955; Warma to Pusta, 19.10.1956; Horm, Arvo, "Tee lääne demokraatiate juurde," in *Eesti Teataja*, 10.2.1951, pp. 3, 7; "Okupeeritud maade vabad esindajad tihedamas kontaktis Euroopa liikumisega," in *Eesti Teataja*, 17.4.1951, p. 3; "Meie välispoliitilise võitluse sihtjooni," in *Eesti Teataja*, 28.4.1951, p. 2; "L. Vahter Nõuandva Kogu esimeheks," in *Eesti Teataja*, 12.1.1952, p. 1.

finish their studies normally.[4] Many Estonian youngsters, such as Vahur Linnuste, attended courses in Strasbourg.[5]

The Estonians were to find a new organization in the Assembly of Captive European Nations (ACEN), which was the American umbrella organization for emigrants from Central and Eastern Europe founded in September 1954. The United States wanted to use it primarily as a propaganda tool to influence Eastern Europe, secondly, as a source of information and, thirdly, to gain support in Western Europe for its policy toward Eastern Europe. Its actual aims were thus quite humble compared to the full liberation preached and hoped for among the emigrants. The control over the ACEN was exercised jointly by the CIA and the Department of State. Because they funded the organization, they could easily connect it with the official U.S. foreign policy of maintaining the status quo. For the emigrants, changing the status quo was the ultimate goal of their activities. This gap between the two ideals was evident from the beginning, and it gradually increased. Governmental funding was drastically cut first in 1960 and later in 1965 and since then the ACEN lived a still life before being shut down in 1972.[6]

However, in a partial sense, the EM and ACEN had similar goals. The first ACEN session in 1954 declared that Captive Nations "fully realize that their national survival hinges on their integration into an all-European community. Their freedom can only be secured within a continental federated unit."[7] The topic was also discussed later on. For example, their European sessions in 1958, where Estonia was represented by Pusta, Warma, Laretei and others, dealt with "European integration and politics of Council of Europe".[8]

ACEN scheduled their European sessions in Strasbourg to coincide with the meetings of the Council of Europe. In 1955, Estonians tried to convince the EM to cooperate with this tactic underlining how this joint action would "form a more powerful and certainly also more significant manifestation for the benefit of the peoples behind the Iron Curtain".

4 "VE ülikool ei anna tänavu stipendiume," in *Teataja*, 13.9.1958, p. 8; "Eestlased 'Vaba Euroopa' suvekursusel," in *Teataja*, 9.9.1961, p. 1; "Eesti Rahvusnõukogu välistegevus 1964–1965," in *Teataja*, 13.11.1965, p. 3.

5 Linnuste, Vahur, "Kas on võimalik kohandada majanduselu humanistlikele sihtidele?" in *Vaba Eesti*, 1955:3, pp. 1–2; Sepp, Reino, "Ülikool põgenikele," in *Vaba Eesti*, 1957:1/2, p. 3.

6 Gadomski, 1995; Mazurkiewicz, 2009, pp. 167–185.

7 *Assembly of the Captive European Nations. First Session*, 1955, pp. 125–128.

8 "Ikestatud Rahvaste Täiskogu konverents Strassburgis," in *Teataja*, 19.4.1958, p. 1; Warma, Aleksander, "Ikestatud Rahvaste esindajad Strassburgis," in *Teataja*, 17.5.1958, p. 1.

Claiming administrative difficulties, the EM declined to participate.[9] After this, Estonians appealed to ACEN to postpone their conference until the autumn; however, this was also in vain.[10] Estonians placed the blame entirely on the EM. This was another example of their inability to effectively demonstrate against the oppression of Eastern Europe. Only with American assistance had a joint meeting been possible and this further highlighted "the weakness of European exiles".[11]

At first, Warma had been dubious of American organizations and insisted that "European policy can still be made only in Europe."[12] On the other hand, he acknowledged U.S. support and assistance to the European unification many times.[13] It did not take a long time for ACEN to contact the ENC at the turn of the year in 1954/1955, at which point cooperation increased.[14] Warma was one of six Estonian delegates at the ACEN conference in Strasbourg in May 1957 with, among others, Heinrich Laretei, who considered its main focus of the liberation on Eastern Europe essential to "integration, i.e. to create some kind of United Europe," which was not possible "before solving the question of captured nations."[15]

By that time, the former ENCEM activists had also jumped on the bandwagon and followed their opponents to ACEN. During his lecture in October 1957, Arvo Horm disparaged European liberation efforts, which were nothing close to those conducted in the U.S. Instead, ACEN "is currently without a doubt the largest and most fundamental international political centre for emigrants."[16] Rei and Horm visited the U.S. in the spring of 1957 to strengthen connections there.[17] Although Warma had also shifted his focus from European to Transatlantic organizations, he kept his old initiatives alive. In 1957, he once again requested funding for

---

9 BA. Warma 10. ENCEM to CEEC, 21.1.1955; CEEC to ENCEM, 5.2.1955; NLE. ERN 401. Horm to Pomian, 26.2.1955; Pomian to Horm, 1.3.1955.

10 BA. Warma 8. Rei to Masens, 15.3.1955; Warma 10. ENCEM to ACEN, 19.4.1955.

11 BA. Warma 10. Warma to Torma, 21.5.1955.

12 "Selgeid sõnu raudeesriidetagustele rahvastele," in *Eesti Teataja*, 11.10.1952, p. 3; also, "Mis teha, kuidas teha," in *Eesti Teataja*, 18.10.1952, p. 3; Horm, Arvo, "Ameerika ja Euroopa," in *Teataja*, 16.8.1953, p. 2.

13 For example, Warma, Aleksander, "Mida kõnelevad tõsiasjad," in *Eesti Teataja*, 1.11.1952, p. 2.

14 "Suurenenud välispoliitiline aktiivsus," in *Teataja*, 19.6.1955, p. 5.

15 Laretei, Heinrich, "EIRE konverentsi kokkuvõte," in *Välis-Eesti*, 12.5.1957, p. 2; "EIRE kolmas erakorraline kokkutulek Strassburgis," in Teataja, 18.5.1957, p. 1; Warma, Aleksander, "Vaheriideta Euroopa Strassburgis," in *Teataja*, 18.5.1957, p. 3.

16 Horm, 1958, pp. 8, 12.

17 "A. Rei ja A. Hormi edukas tegevus USA-s," in *Teataja*, 4.5.1957, p. 1; Ant, 2012, pp. 292–304.

Eastern European reconstruction from Paul-Henri Spaak, who was then Secretary-General of NATO.[18]

NATO had meanwhile become the most important guardian of the national right to sovereignty. It constantly reminded that Central and Eastern Europe will not remain under the Soviet rule forever. At the same time, Warma wished for both mental and psychological weapons for affecting minds in both the East and the West in working towards this goal. He constantly spoke of the "barrier of the occupation in Central and Eastern Europe", which referred to strengthening resistance in these countries.[19]

During the 1960s, Heinrich Laretei continued to emphasize the crucial meaning of American influence on European unification; the change of American focus to Asia and Vietnam seemed to curiously correspond with the halt in the process of unification. NATO was the only organization consisting of all Western European democratic states, whilst economically the EEC and EFTA were still keeping them apart. Here he blamed Charles de Gaulle's policy of preventing British membership in the EEC and neither could he follow his reasons to flirt with the Soviet Union but, in the long run, a single man was powerless against the rapid development in the technical sphere and could not ignore the steps which were already taken towards unification: "European integration has become inevitable, and in spite of difficulties Europe is going forward steadily, albeit slowly toward this goal." European nations had already given up such significant portions of their sovereignty, which was previously considered indivisible, that the only possibility was to continue on the same road. Once united, Europe would be an overwhelming counterforce against communist powers.[20]

At the same time, while the ENC's foreign policy moved from Europe to America, it also encouraged increased regional cooperation with refugees from other Baltic states. This had practical reasons, as demonstrations during "the meeting of the big four" in Geneva and simultaneously in Stockholm in June 1955 required special arrangements. This gave impetus

---

18 BA. Warma 23. Correspondence with H. Spaak 1957; "Aktiivse välistegevuse aasta," in *Teataja*, 31.5.1958, p. 1.

19 Warma, Aleksander, "Aasta vahetusel," in *Teataja*, 11.1.1958, p. 2; "Atlandi Liidu liikmed ei lepi Ida-Euroopa orjastamisega," in *Teataja*, 11.1.1958, p. 7; Pusta, Kaarel Robert, "Ikestatud rahvaste küsimus NATO konverentsil," in *Teataja*, 11.1.1958, p. 1; "Atlanti kongress soovitab suuremad efektiivsust ideoloogises sõjas," in *Teataja*, 27.6.1959, p. 1; Warma, Aleksander, "Euroopa julgeoleku probleeme," in *Teataja*, 27.3.1963, p. 2.

20 Laretei, Heinrich, "Euroopa ühinemise teel," in *Välis-Eesti*, 20.1.1962, p. 2; Laretei, Heinrich, "Euroopa integratsiooni suunas," in *Välis-Eesti*, 27.1.1962, p. 2; Laretei, Heinrich, "Tõke Euroopa ühinemisteel," in *Välis-Eesti*, 9.2.1963, p. 2; Laretei, Heinrich, "Sündmusterikas aasta," in *Välis-Eesti*, 11.1.1964, p. 2; Laretei, Heinrich, "Uus olukord Euroopas," in *Välis-Eesti*, 24.3.1969, p. 3.

to the *Baltiska kommittén* (Baltic Committee), a joint organization for Swedish anti-communists and Baltic emigrants, which had already been founded in 1943, but it had been hibernating after the war.[21]

Following the Economic Community

Like before in the Paneuropean discussion, the economic aspect was rarely touched by the ENCEM. The exception for this was the Estonian delegation at the London conference of 1952. It also provided reasons for this neglect, as it required considerable work to produce necessary calculations, which would most likely be useless.

In the preparations for London conference, an "Economic Union" was considered the final goal. A customs union as such was inadequate. The Estonians would also have required a common currency as well as whatever administrative changes that would have been necessary. Planning should take place despite the occupation and development in the West. The East could even show an example to the West. Eventually these lines would emerge into a single European community.[22] Personally, Warma did not favour a customs union in Eastern Europe, which "does not constitute an autarkic economic whole but is a necessary component of the European economic sphere". Furthermore economic isolation could not support political unification.[23]

The largest paper in the Estonian material was the 34-page "rehabilitation plan of Estonia's economy after liberation". The document was written mostly by Johannes Sikkar with the assistance of for example, Eduard Poom, Professor of Economics from the University of Tartu. It required the focus to be put on agriculture and, first and foremost, on de-collectivization, which would strengthen Western society as well.[24] Due to Baltic cooperation, in the final resolution of the agrarian committee, de-collectivization was mentioned as the primary general policy concerning the liberated countries.[25] De-collectivization was one of the first decisions made in the

21 "Nõuame vabadust Balti riikidele!" in *Teataja*, 24.7.1955, p. 1; "Tähelepanekuid Genfi konverentsilt," in *Teataja*, 7.8.1955, pp. 1, 8; Nerman, 1969.

22 BA. Warma 10. Positions on the materials of the London conference, undated.

23 BA. Warma 20. Considerations of the Estonian Commitee, 11.10.1950.

24 BA. Warma 10. P.M. Conference on Eastern and Central Europe, 12.1.1952; BA. Warma 10. Positions on the materials of the London conference, undated; BA. Warma 10. Remarks concerning Estonia's industry; "Arvukas Eesti delegatsioon Londonis," in *Eesti Teataja*, 19.1.1952, p. 1; *Rehabilitation plan*, 1952.

25 BA. Warma 10. ENCEM Summary on London Conference, 20.2.1952; "Eesti delegatsiooni seisukohad," in *Eesti Teataja*, 19.1.1952, p. 1; "Uut lootust ikestatud rahvastele," in *Välis-Eesti*, 3.2.1952, pp. 1, 5.

independent Estonia but it was hard to implement in all cases. For example, due to long delay, legitimate owners could not be found and Estonian agriculture was also generally anticipating the EU membership, which frankly does not support small-farms.

At the London conference only a small part of Estonian papers dealt with the industrial economy. The major concern was on the Estonian special natural resource: oil shale. Gas from oil shale being transferred to Leningrad and Estonian figures already predicted an unproductive extension in oil shale mining and production. Machine-building and shipyards seemed to serve the needs of the occupying army at the expense of consumer goods and agricultural equipment. There also appeared to be a lack of skilled labour and improved vocational training. Drawing female labour into industry was also seen as needed. Due to rough handling and working pace most of the existing machinery would be scrap iron "to the extent they will survive the probable warfare" – a grim reminder that all methods were acceptable in liberating the country.[26]

During the conference the Estonians worked towards developing a common economic plan based on separate calculations, which were already supported by their own work. In his opening speech, Rei urged the delegates to "consider that the drawing up of such a plan for each country is of some practical value, though the date of realization is uncertain, and the circumstances keep changing." These individual plans would then be summed up. "An overall rehabilitation plan for the entire liberated territory can be compiled without undue delay when the need arises, only the separate National Committee concerned can closely and consistently follow developments in the home country."[27]

These calculations would be useful when the Marshall Plan continued to the East, which was "emphasized particularly" in Estonian papers: "The Western world must give generous financial and technical aid towards the economic reconstruction of these countries."[28] The request was later repeated by, among others, the Council of Europe in October 1952, and again by Warma in the Estonian press.[29] Moreover, during the second Economic Conference of the EM in 1954, the Estonian participant,

26 *Rehabilitation plan*, 1952.

27 BA. Warma 10. Conference on Eastern and Central Europe, Afternoon Session. Speech by Rei, 21.1.1952. Also BA. Warma 10. P.M. Conference on Eastern and Central Europe, 12.1.1952.

28 BA. Warma 10. P.M. Conference on Eastern and Central Europe, 12.1.1952. Also BA. Warma 27. European Movement and the Europe In-between. Presentation on the ENCEM general meeting, 11.12.1951.

29 "Selgeid sõnu raudeesriidetagustele rahvastele," in *Eesti Teataja*, 11.10.1952, p. 3.

economist, Eduard Poom, stressed the need to follow the developments in the West because Estonia would have to adjust to that after liberation. Protective measures could not be the method for reconstruction if a unified Europe abandoned mutual customs and tariffs.[30]

The ENCEM was concerned about the prospective integration of Estonia into the European economy. They drafted a blueprint for the necessary financial assistance and encouraged other exile groups to do the same. Their reluctance, however, was one of the reasons for Estonians turning away from the European Movement. Simultaneously, the ENCEM began to acknowledge the new methods introduced in the West, which would make national economies obsolete. Arvo Horm envisioned the next phase, i.e. a "Europe of pools", where the ECSC was accompanied by similar narrow unions on other fields as well. In the future, these unions would be joined together under a common constitution. The six member-states already seem to have agreed on this nucleus, which other Europeans, including Estonia, could later join.[31] In addition, during the second Economic Conference of the EM in 1954, the Estonian participant, Eduard Poom, stressed the need to follow the development in the West because Estonia would have to adjust to that after liberation. Protective measures could not be the method for reconstruction if a unified Europe abandoned mutual customs and tariffs.[32]

According to Warma, the Geneva meeting of the big four in 1955 gave a new boost and renewed energy for all plans concerning European unification.[33] Roughly a year later, he returned to the issue, when the events in Hungary and Poland had demonstrated the danger of the Communist system. This insecurity influenced on the establishment of the EEC, or like Warma expressed, "plans on a gigantic scale for a dynamic European economy and enhancing its natural development."[34]

Warma observed the development of Western European institutions and although he recognized the economic nature of the EEC, he nevertheless regarded it as one part of the "process of European consolidation" and of Europe once again becoming the decider of its own fate. In addition, he was not concerned about unification comprising only a

---

30 HAEU. ME 965. Rebattet to Rei, 22.12.1953; Rei to Rebattet, 14.1.1954; Thibault to Rei, 16.1.1954; "Uus Euroopa ilma tollipiirideta," in *Teataja*, 7.3.1954, p. 1.

31 Horm, Arvo, "Mis toimub Euroopas?" in *Eesti Teataja*, 15.11.1952, p. 6.

32 HAEU. ME 965. Rebattet to Rei, 22.12.1953; Rei to Rebattet, 14.1.1954; Thibault to Rei, 16.1.1954; "Uus Euroopa ilma tollipiirideta," in *Teataja*, 7.3.1954, p. 1.

33 Warma, Aleksander, "Välispolitilisi marginaale," in *Teataja*, 21.8.1955, p. 7; also "Uus hoog Euroopa ühendamise taotlustes," in *Teataja*, 11.12.1955, p. 1.

34 Warma, Aleksander, "Mis edasi…?" in *Teataja*, 16.2.1957, pp. 2–3.

certain part of Europe, because "the further Europe has advanced on this path, the easier it is for it to assert itself on the question of the unification of Central and Eastern Europe." He considered the expansion as an essential part of the EEC and calculations were already completed for the first enlargement. It would take a long time before the EEC would arrive in Estonia, but in the meantime, the Estonians needed to follow its development "for the interest of restoring our nation's rights and independence".[35]

Following these events was not hard. Dutch Foreign Minister, Paul van Zeeland, had provided material from the ECSC meeting in Messina to Kaarel Robert Pusta, who then conveyed it to Stockholm. Van Zeeland was confident that the meeting was a new start for unification; he hoped that experts from behind the Iron Curtain would familiarize themselves with the material and even make comments on the plan, so they could take charge after the imminent liberation.[36] In this way, van Zeeland and Warma seemed to think alike. However, according to Pusta, van Zeeland was quite strikingly and demonstrably unaware of even basic information concerning the situation behind the Iron Curtain, which did not however affect his confidence.[37]

Warma indeed closely followed the progress of the EEC. He was surprised how fast their founding was completed and it was the most promising international event of the year 1958. He later repeated his belief that Western European economic upheaval could not be separate from its increasing political weight and expansion was only a matter of time. In 1962, Europe was already the third superpower besides the Soviet Union and the U.S.[38] Horm shared Warma's optimism for constantly expanding integration by the functionalist method, which would, in the near future, be completed by the European parliament.[39]

The problems of the early 1960s, however, decreased Warma's mood. He wrote bluntly: "We do not believe that European unification materializes

---

35 *Ibid.*

36 Compare to Goddeeris, 2005, pp. 86–88.

37 BA. Warma 17. Pusta to Warma, 31.10.1955.

38 Warma, Aleksander, "Aasta vahetusel," in *Teataja*, 11.1.1958, p. 2; "Aktiivse välistegevuse aasta," in *Teataja*, 31.5.1958, p. 1; Warma, Aleksander, "Kas lavastus või majandus?" in *Teataja*, 21.5.1960, p. 2; "Euroopa majanduslik koostöö," in *Teataja*, 22.4.1961, p. 3; "Euroopa majandusunioon taotleb poliitilist ühtsust," in *Teataja*, 5.8.1961, p. 1; Warma, Aleksander, "Poliitiline pärand aastale 1962," in *Teataja*, 6.1.1962, p. 1; "Välispoliitiline töö muuttuvas maailmas," in *Teataja*, 26.5.1962, p. 2.

39 Horm, Arvo, "Teel Atlanti Uniooni," in *Teataja*, 27.1.1962, p. 2.

in the near future, during the next years."[40] The fast pace had decreased, but Warma described it as normal and not alarming. His main concern undeniably focused on hesitations and disputes. However, Warma did see advancement in lower levels. First he recognized a tendency to define the European civilization as one of the major reasons to expand economic cooperation. Secondly, he pointed out the emerging social outcomes of integration, such as employment around the EEC countries. From this practical point of view, Warma could declare: "We are not expecting any heavenly bliss from the United Europe." He was replying to a French comparison between heaven and the United Europe, where everyone hopes to enter but no one makes a hurry to get there.[41]

De Gaulle's European policy of preventing British membership in the EEC did not naturally please Warma, but he was more concerned about the concept of "Europe from Atlantic to the Urals", which first seemed to divide the Western powers and secondly invite the Soviet Union to the same table with the oppressed Central Eastern Europe.[42] But the young federalist did not let their optimism fade away even during the early 1960s. Difficulties had always existed on the path towards unification but the direction was clear. Even Gaullism was considered an essential continental counterbalance for American enthusiasm.[43]

The founding of the European Free Trade Area brought the unification process a bit closer. The Swedish decision to join EFTA instead of the EEC received naturally little appreciation from Estonians. The positive aspect was increased and intensified discussion on unification in Sweden although it was only short-lived.[44] *Välis-Eesti*, which became closer and closer with

---

40 Warma, Aleksander, "Ülevaade rahvusvahelisest olukorrast," in *Teataja*, 30.10.1964, pp. 4–5.

41 Warma, Aleksander, "Mis toimub Euroopas," in *Teataja*, 15.3.1965, p. 2.

42 Warma, Aleksander, "Spekulatsioone Prantsuse poliitika umber," in *Teataja*, 2.2.1963, p. 2; "Ohustatud sõprus," in *Teataja*, 16.2.1963, p. 2; Warma, Aleksander, "Välispoliitilised varjud ja vastuolud," in *Teataja*, 7.8.1965, p. 2; Warma, Aleksander, "Suur-Euroopa," in *Teataja*, 21.8.1965, p. 2; Warma, Aleksander, "Ta liikub siiski," in *Teataja*, 11.12.1965, p. 2.

43 Grabbi, Hellar, "Eesti rahva väljavaadetest maailmapoliitilise olukorra taustal," in *Vaba Eesti*, 1962:4/5, pp. 50–53; Taagepera, Rein, "Euroopa Ühendriikide lävel," in *Vaba Eesti*, 1962:4/5, pp. 54–55; Hunt, Heino S., "Uus Euroopa gaullistlikus hiilguses - üle Atlandi nähtuna," in *Vaba Eesti*, 1963:4, pp. 62–64.

44 Warma, Aleksander, "EEC - EFTA liitumise poolt ja vastu," in *Teataja*, 17.6.1961, p. 2; "Euroopa majandusblokid otsivad ühinemise teed," in *Teataja*, 24.6.1961, p. 3; "Rootsi valitsus otsustab mitte liitude Euroopa suurturguga," in *Teataja*, 2.9.1961, p. 2; "Euroopa ühisturu probleemid arutuse all," in *Teataja*, 14.10.1961, p. 2; "Neutraalsete kaitseks…" in *Teataja*, 14.7.1962, p. 2; Lasberg, Max, "Euroopa integratsioon ja Rootsi," in *Vaba Eesti*, 1961:6, pp. 74–75.

the Swedish right-wing parties, published articles by Swedish supporters of the EEC membership.[45] Even ten years later, when the EEC managed to expand to Denmark, the Estonians supported the idea of Swedish membership and also expected the Swedes to familiarize themselves with European problems. Swedish neglect of European unification was well-known. ENCEM was the only private organization promoting it.[46]

Warma could yet see the newly activated EEC after de Gaulle's departure.[47] He was nevertheless still concerned about the economic nature of unification. He did not share the faith of the European politicians that saw mere economic measures as the key solution for the problems. Although they undeniably were important, Warma wanted to stress European "feeling and cognition that there is legal jurisdiction, which is actually respected by all states, both big and small." This also applied to the human rights, but both of them required the restoration of national sovereignty in Eastern Europe. This would result in the "common political will of European nations."[48]

On his 80th birthday in 1970, Warma could thus look peacefully back on the process of unification. "It can be predicted that it will reach its goal within a generation." Economically, Western Europe was connected in such a way that a mutual war was unthinkable. Furthermore it supported the "general crystallization of national feelings" and represented a "strong tendency for national preservation in earnest searching to solve the current turbulences in society." The Eastern part of the continent remained the source of insecurity but it would facilitate in time, when the same process would expand there.[49]

Warma's successor as chairman of the foreign delegation of the ENC, Johannes Mihkelson, continued on Warma's thinking. On the one hand, he pessimistically viewed the Estonian possibilities within international politics: "Opportunities to bring up our situation have decreased time after time. It is inevitable: the longer we are in exile, the deeper we fall into oblivion." On the other hand, he saw positive signs in the Western European consolidation and integration. Europe was finally going to stand

45 For example, Östman, Oscar, "Euroopa majandusühiskond areneb," in *Välis-Eesti*, 30.9.1961, p. 1; Östman, Oscar, "Rootsi ja Euroopa," in *Välis-Eesti*, 24.8.1962, p. 3.

46 "Sõnavõtte Euroopa föderatsiooni, Bonni ja Euroopa julgestuskonverentsi küsimustes," in *Teataja*, 12.11.1970, p. 5; "Eesti Rahvusnõukogu tegevusest 1970.a." in *Teataja*, 28.11.1970, p. 3; Jalakas, Rudolf, "Euroopa ühisturg," in *Teataja*, 27.2.1971, p. 5.

47 Warma, Aleksander, "Muljeid Pariisist," in *Teataja*, 13.4.1968, p. 7; Warma, Aleksander, "Eurooplased omavahel," in *Teataja*, 5.7.1969, p. 2.

48 Warma, Aleksander, "Eurooplased omavahel," in *Teataja*, 5.7.1969, p. 2.

49 Warma, Aleksander, "Euroopa probleeme," in *Teataja*, 13.6.1970, p. 2.

by herself without American assistance, even though it might mean Transatlantic economic contradictions. In the future, unification would move into the political and military agenda. "Europe is thus approaching the turning point."[50]

Preparations for the Conference on Security and Cooperation in Europe naturally caught the Estonians' attention. From their point of view it definitely was not about unification but certifying the division of Europe started in Yalta.[51] Therefore, there is no need to go deeper into the discussion on the CSCE, also due to magnitude of the subject. It is worth a separate research.

---

50 Mihkelson, Johannes, "Euroopa on praegu pöördepunktil," in *Teataja*, 12.11.1970, p. 4; Mihkelson, Johannes, "Elame integratsiooni ajastul," in *Teataja*, 27.2.1971, p. 5.

51 For example, Warma, Aleksander, "Oletusi Euroopa julgeoleku konverentsi umber," in *Teataja*, 20.9.1969, p. 3; Warma, Aleksander, "Euroopa julgestuse küsimus," in *Teataja*, 15.11.1969, p. 2.

Chapter 5

Uniting the Divided Continent

The Estonian National Committee of the European Movement was established in 1949 with great enthusiasm, and with high hopes it joined the European Movement in January 1950. Immediately afterwards, the Estonians contributed a significant amount of effort to ensure the realization of the conference in London two years later, which was hailed a success. The EM membership corresponded with the Estonian aspiration for a free, democratic, secure, and prosperous Europe. Aleksander Warma envisioned a full-scale economic union where the member-state would nevertheless maintain a great deal of political independence, something that might be practically impossible. Due to their lack of power, the exiled politicians could demand more than they could be held accountable for, and promise more than they could ever deliver. On the other hand, especially for Warma, EM membership was partly bound up with the idealism from World War II – which in the Estonian perspective still continued – where a European federation was seen as an essential element of post-war planning. Continental unification and national liberation were complementary visions. As Thomas Lane has pointed out, Eastern European discussion on unification was more advanced than in the West and this also applies to the Estonians, although their discussion had also started properly only after the World War II.[1]

This European idealism faded, but did not completely disappear within the Estonian exile community. Overall, they were swimming against the current, as the European Movement had started its downfall together with the Council of Europe when Estonian National Committee was granted membership; the Schuman Declaration was just over four months away. In general, the case of ENCEM shows the wreckage of the federalist approach to unifying the continent. For the Estonians, this was not a clear prospect, and the intensified activities of the new Central and East European Commission seemed to be separate from the difficulties of the main Movement and the unification in general.

1 Lane, 2005, p. 195.

However, this was not the case. When Western unification emerged within the European Coal and Steel Community and subsequent organizations, their interest in the EM and in Central Europe diminished. At that time, Europe was not divided into two, but rather three parts. The greatest Estonian fear of creating two parallel unions in a liberal Europe was materialized. This is also when the aims of a general unification process and the national effort for re-independence collided. Therefore, the common European history of unification remains unwritten. Although the Estonians discussed the matter among themselves and took part in mutual conferences, cooperation was divided.

Other emigrant groups were also not receptive to Estonian aspirations, despite their occasional cooperation. The wish for separate economic calculations in order to complete a joint programme for reconstruction was never realized. The failure of using European unification as a tool for independence was evident, and the leaders changed their focus to American anti-communist organizations. Even before, the ENC had reacted more sensitively to Russian initiatives. The altered preferences highlight the squeezed Europe between the American and Soviet superpowers during the early Cold War.

There was only light interest in European unification within the Estonian community beyond the supporters but the change in orientation was also needed to maintain their authority throughout the refugee community. Similarly, activities in European organizations were published to support the political legitimacy of the ENC and the ENCEM. However, more generally, they must also have signified sincere efforts to keep morale and spirits among the refugees high: despite the poor political results, Estonia was not forgotten as a European nation.

I have tried to demonstrate that the ENCEM was an exceptionally active member organization in the EM. Firstly, European unification was the primary goal in their foreign policy. Estonians cherished the EM, because it allowed them to be among equals, with other Europeans. Secondly, they participated in relatively higher numbers, for example in the Central and Eastern European Conference in London in 1952. A comparison between the various national groups cannot be made, as the research on emigrant politics is only just now emerging.

Although Warma publicly denounced the EM in 1957, the ENC kept returning to its conferences and other activities, even with the EM making constant organizational changes, which discredited Eastern emigrants. Once the old actors got older and older, the younger generation adapted European unification efforts as part of their Estonian agenda. Amazingly, the period is characterized by difficulties not only for emigrants in the EM but also for the integration of the EEC, but it was filled with a persistent belief that the turn to better and more intensified integration was just around the corner, which consequently would result in the liberation of the Eastern Europe in the very near future. The crucial turn happened in the Conference of Security and Cooperation in Europe in 1975 but not in the way or speed that Estonian emigrants, or anyone else, had anticipated.

Part IV

Conclusions

Estonians for European Union?

J.M.K.E., Estonian punk rock band and one of the loudest proponents of the perestroika in the late 1980s, proclaimed at the turn of the millennium: "*See, mida Euroopa tähendas kunagi meile; sel polegi tähtsust, see oli ju kunagi eile*" (What Europe ever meant for us before; it doesn't matter, it was already yesterday).[1] The conviction behind this book has been that the past – yesterday – does matter and gives basis for the decisions of the tomorrow.

This book has presented the Estonian discussion on European unification over seven decades from the interwar period until the final stage of the Cold War; from the first years of the national independence to the restoration of the nationstate. Throughout this period, a united Europe was occasionally referred as the ideal framework for international politics. The Paneuropean idea was warmly welcomed in Estonia and it attracted prominent individuals from the Estonian elite attempting to enhance relations with the wider continent. After the loss of independence, European unification was perceived as a method to regain that status in the renewed international system. This was most evident in Aleksander Warma's plan in December 1942 and consequently in the foreign relations of the Estonian National Council in Sweden.

It is considerably difficult to estimate the success of European unification within the Estonian community as a whole, whether it was in the independent Estonia or in the exile community in Sweden. All things considered, the idea of unification touched only the political elite and even then only to a lesser degree. Membership figures for the Estonian Society of the Paneuropean Union and ENCEM exceeded roughly a hundred persons.

Opposition was the clearest indicator of the popularity of the cause, even during the limited opportunities of the exile years in Sweden; quite expectedly, Warma's plan did not meet any opposition during World War II. However, on the other hand, he seems to have been the only Estonian who referred to federations in post-war planning instead of emphasizing the restoration of full independence like had been the case before the war.

1 J.M.K.E. (lyrics by Villu Tamme), *Õhtumaa viimased tunnid* (Kaljukotkas/Stupido Twins) 2000.

It was in the interests of the unifiers to keep this topic on the agenda and opposition emerged only against sufficiently prominent issues. Furthermore, although it has been convenient to study the promoters of unification, these repeated rival stances reveal the incessant line of the opposition. For example, the claim that common political institutions may harm European culture appeared both during the interwar period and during the Cold War. Rather than unity, segregation and divisions were characteristic of Europe's past and "Europe has indeed never existed as a unity".[2] The same stance was also taken by Heinrich Laretei in 1952. For him, different nationalities comprised the main obstacle to unification. A common policy could not overcome the discord brought by differing national perspectives. "It is probable that only egoistic interests can do away with the barriers encountered on the way to the European federation."[3]

The fact that unification was both opposed and promoted for the same reasons highlights the national basis of discussion: the programme from the European core, or the context of the Estonian state, or that the discussants may have changed. However, the discussants were looking at the programme from the perspective of what was best in their idea of national identity. The promoters regarded unification as a vital method to keep contact with the progressive Europe. Their opponents considered unification practically infeasible and preferred another kind of international cooperation – be it Baltic cooperation during the interwar period or Transatlantic cooperation during the Cold War.[4]

In the longitudinal perspective, certain similar features emerged time after time. One of them is naturally the recurring faith shown towards European unification. Moreover, this idea attracted new supporters after old ones had turned away disappointed. Both the Paneuropean Union during the interwar period and the European Movement during the Cold War era had enthusiastic Estonian followers. However both movements were not willing to support their radical proposals. Thus, Estonian activities can be seen as narratives of failures rather than successes. Having said this, the context surrounding the cooperation of European nations demanded bold initiatives in order to get one's voice heard; however, these bold initiatives proved difficult for all sides to reach agreement on.

---

2 J. "E. Ü. R. – Euroopa Ühendatud Riigid," in *Päevaleht*, 20.9.1927, p. 2.

3 Laretei, Heinrich, "Idealism ja egoism välispoliitikas," in *Välis-Eesti*, 16.3.1952, p. 2; also J.K., "Quo vadis, Europa?" in *Eesti Teataja*, 10.1.1948, p. 2.

4 This is a clear difference compared to the fundamental distinction in the Finnish discussion on Paneurope, where the promoters wanted to have stimuli from abroad to enhance the Finnish national idea, whereas the opponents preferred to protect the national essence from the external influences (Heikkilä 2006, pp. 245–263).

The comparison between Baltic and European cooperation was another recurring theme. Most of the time, the limited Baltic dimension was disparaged by the Europeanists. It was only during the tranquil 1920s that the Baltic League remained an ideal model which could be seen as a first step towards Europe – the example of cooperation on a broader scale. At the same time, there was no need to take action on these miscellaneous visions and, therefore, unification sceptics cited the Baltic case as an example of the futility of practical measures in international cooperation. When editing the reply to the Briand Memorandum, the Estonian foreign ministry failed to find a positive response from their desired partners, especially from Sweden, and to a lesser extent from Finland and Latvia. When the economic depression started in the 1930s, discussion on regional as well as European cooperation intensified, but it was held back by mutual complaints. Regional unions were fundamental in Warma's plan of 1942, but they were relevant only as members of a larger European union. A similar approach continued in the European Movement. Although the Estonians supported collaboration with other emigrant groups and, therefore, also regional cooperation, it was seen as more crucial to maintain this cooperation within the European dimension.

On the other hand, European organizations have regarded regional cooperation as a sort of litmus test for the Baltic states. The EM required a joint Baltic Council as a middle-organ before their separate memberships were granted. This has continued even after the Cold War with integration in European and Transatlantic institutions. This applies less to political and economic integration than to the involvement with the NATO, where defense units are common with the three Baltic states. Estonia could advance faster in the negotiations surrounding EU membership, although membership was eventually granted to all three states at the same time. More recently Estonia has been the first Baltic state to adopt the Euro, while Latvia and Lithuania have made slower progress.[5]

The contemporary actors themselves used the tri-partition of diplomacy, culture, and economics in describing unification. According to Pusta, "When we are supporting Paneuropean Union, we are working for our own independence, economic success and the preservation of national culture."[6] His triangular justification was an answer to his opponents, who highlighted the flaws of Paneurope in three themes: a diplomatic threat to the League of Nations, an economic antagonist against outsiders, and a culturally inadequate development of the national idea.

5 Vilpišauskas, 2003; Jurkynas, 2007; Elsuwege, 2008, pp. 118–119, 231–252.

6 Pusta, 1929a.

Later, during the Cold War, the Commission on Central and Eastern Europe of the European Movement worked for the aim that these "nations should, on the basis of equality, belong to a complete European society, culturally, politically, and economically".[7] In a similar fashion, the ENCEM had three temporary committees (political, economic, and cultural) to draft Estonian considerations for the Conference on Central and Eastern Europe of the European Movement in London in January 1952. Eventually these committees joined and August Rei, in his speech during the conference, called attention to the opinion that "it would be most undesirable to establish two parallel unions, one for the West and another for East and Central Europe, as both these parts of our continent are the natural complements of each other, economically, culturally, as well as politically."[8]

Throughout the period, there was considerable confidence in the good will of politicians and decision-makers. Once they could be gathered together in one place, they could draft the guidelines and constitution for European unification. The diplomatic institution supported by a common culture would then automatically spread unification into other dimensions. More generally, the Estonian discussion on European unification and especially the failure of these plans to materialize also illustrates the fate of the federalist approach to unifying Europe. In the discussion, the nation state was usually the inherent basis for international politics and European unification; this was questioned only by the younger federalists of the 1950s. This coincidental downfall of the federalist approach and nation-states cannot be incidental.

During the early interwar period, the federalist approach was supported by the existence of the League of Nations, which was occasionally considered a nucleus of the future European federation. In general, Estonia's foreign policy relied on the League of Nations and since Briand's Memorandum meant establishing a European federation within the League of Nations, the Estonians wholeheartedly supported the idea.

The Estonian reply nevertheless highlighted the importance of actions in the economic field, because the League of Nations was considered the foundation by default. Regarding the discussion of economics, the federalist undertones were not so much about trade and the exchange of goods but rather macroeconomics. Great Britain was the largest trading partner for Estonia and, therefore there was no question as to whether it belonged

---

7 BA. Warma 27. European Movement and the Europe In-between. Presentation on the ENCEM general meeting, 11.12.1951.

8 BA. Warma 10. Conference on Eastern and Central Europe. Afternoon Session. Speech by Rei, 21.1.1952.

to Europe or not. In general, the original programmes from the European core paid little attention to economics, which is striking given the economic basis of the current European Union. The economic aspect was also only briefly discussed in the Estonian context. An improved economy was considered a consequence of unification but not the justification for it. The same setting was evident in Warma's plan during World War II. Economic calculations dominated the Estonian delegation's intentions for the EM conference in London in 1952 but they were rapidly dropped out, as the other emigrant groups were not receptive to a common plan and it constantly became more and more difficult to estimate the necessary economic requirements.

Reference to the third cultural dimension was frequently done together with economic and diplomatic unification. A common European culture was mentioned in various Estonian texts as both the ultimate beginning and the goal of unification. The unfortunate possibilities associated with this were also acknowledged and the perceived dangers of a small nation assimilating with a larger entity were expressed both during the interwar period and during the Cold War. However, promoters of unification could not stand waiting for this to happen and Jaan Tõnisson and Kaarel Robert Pusta proposed the use of governmental resources to enhance European solidarity in the League of Nations in 1931. In 1942, Warma was confident that a political union would lead to "the mentality of increased general interests".[9] Additionally, when the European Movement organized a questionnaire among its member organizations, the Estonians proposed more drastic methods so that "wide masses adopt this idea," which was a prerequisite for the final unification.[10]

Appeals like these were possible only within the federalist framework, where political decisions were considered to control economic and social development – so why not also cultural development? The current cultural policy of the European Union does rely on common symbols, such as the flag and the anthem, but it simultaneously claims to protect national cultures. One good example of this is in the realm of education, where a common curriculum remains a desperate call and the Council of Europe modestly supports the revision of history textbooks.[11]

Accordingly, proposals for European unification also contained plans for transforming international politics in general. This aspect played only a

---

9 BA. Warma 2. "Rahu konsolideerimise probleemist pärastsõjaaegses Euroopas" with Finnish and English translations; Warma, 1971, pp. 182–187.

10 HAEU. ME 2271. ENCEM to Rebattet, September 1954.

11 Stobart, 1999; Shore, 2000.

small part in Estonian discussion. The general trend relied on cordial relations between the large geopolitical entities, including the Soviet Union, even during the interwar period, which is perhaps surprising, above all, because the Paneuropean Union had both Russophobia and anti-communism at its ideological core. The Soviet Union was almost ignored by Estonians, as it was believed as building "socialism in one country".

When Jaan Tõnisson spoke at the Study Commission in September 1931, he pointed out "the full weight of a universal catastrophe", referring to World War I, was needed "before the sovereign states could accept the interference of a higher authority in their political life".[12] His words now seem prophetic, as World War II produced an even greater change in European politics. My preliminary aim was to question World War II as the point of departure in the history of European integration. This study shows that a considerable number of features remained the same in Estonian discussion over the war despite the cardinal changes.

On the other hand, Soviet occupation in 1940 and the memory of it transformed the fundamental justifications for unification and thus it became a turning point in Estonian discussion. Since Warma's plan in 1942, the threat from the East became the greatest reason for Westward integration. Estonian integrationists were pro the establishment of a United States of Europe in order to escape from the Soviet Union, which was almost named the Socialist United States of Europe in 1922 (and later used by the Trotskyist opposition).[13] Warma also continued to point out this motive in the European Movement. This turning point also concerns Europe as a whole, not only Estonia. Although the presence of the Soviet army in the heart of Europe was a decisive factor for unification, few dared to say it publicly; just like the Estonians had refrained from declaring it during the interwar period. The Estonians made several attempts to include this essential reason in the conference resolutions. However, none of them had any success.

The coexistence of national and European identities had started already during the Russian Empire. The Young Estonia movement and Gustav Suits, in particular, had declared "*Olgem eestlased, aga saagem eurooplasteks*" (Let's be Estonians, but let's also become Europeans). Additionally, activists in the European Movement occasionally referred to previous Estonian attempts at European unification, especially Tõnisson's and Pusta's appeal in 1931. This was partly to show the continuation of a state in exile, moreover the call by the ENCEM in 1954 to focus attention on

12 Commission 1931.

13 Minkkinen, 2005, pp. 10–11.

teachers was an obvious repeat of this previous attempt. Consequently, this was to create a thin tradition of European unification. This tradition was transferred to the young authors of *Vaba Eesti* but they moved gradually to other issues and neither William Muld nor Fanni Sivers alone could carry the idea further during the 1970s.

Together with the rest of the former Eastern bloc, Estonia first "returned to Europe" by regaining independence in 1991. Then the main task of the new state was to construct national structures while at the same time simultaneously create connections with the unifying Europe. A result of these partly contradicting phenomena can be seen at the Estonia-Latvia border: the modern tollbooth stations have stood abandoned for the past number of years, since both countries joined the EU and the Schengen Area in 2004. Membership was the culmination of the sole direction pursued in the new foreign policy and Estonians worked hard to meet the entrance criteria set by the EU institutions. Although the target has been more or less unanimous, the process has not been without challenges or disagreements, some domestic and some with the EU.

On surface this European orientation continued the aspirations of the Estonian emigrants. However, despite some exceptions, the Estonian foreign ministry recruited its personnel from domestic sources and additionally the European idea had long ceased to dominate emigrant discussion. Rather its strong popularity during the application phase reflected the more persistent national narrative of incorporating both Estonian and European interests. Both the cultural and economic benefits of EU membership remain common themes in the public speeches made by leading politicians.[14]

Estonians were not working for European unification, as such, but were rather improving the conditions of their own nationality. Primarily, this meant proving that Estonians are Europeans. This objective of coexistence between national and European identity was popular but it was never tested. Although the current European Union differs in many ways from the Estonian blueprints of the past, it also constitutes a major change in the international situation. At the same time, the economy has extended beyond political borders and has become global. Nevertheless, national frameworks remain a crucial factor in both citizen's lives and world politics. Hence, as waves keep pounding European shores, finding a balance between these three dimensions will remain a continuous task for the future.

---

[14] Smith, 2002, pp. 147–175; Kasekamp, 2010, pp. 188–199; for example, President Ilves during the Restoration of Independence Day, August 20, 2012. [http://www.president.ee/et/ametitegevus/koned/7832-2012-08-20-16-26-12/index.html].

List of abbreviations

ACEN	Assembly of Captive European Nations
CEEC	Central and Eastern European Commission
CIA	Central Intelligence Agency
COMECON	Council of Mutual Economic Assistance
DP	Displaced Person
EBU	European Broadcasting Union
ECSC	European Coal and Steel Community
EEC	European Economic Community
EFTA	European Free Trade Area
EM	European Movement
ENC	Eesti Rahvusnõukogu (Estonian National Council)
ENCEM	Estonian National Committee of European Movement
ERF	Eesti Rahvusfond (Estonian National Fund)
EU	European Union
NATO	North Atlantic Treaty Organization
OSCE	Organization of Security and Cooperation in Europe
OSS	Office of Strategic Services
UEFA	Union of European Football Associations
U.S.	United States of America
WOFE	World Organization of Free Estonians

Bibliography

Archives

Baltiska Arkivet (Baltic Archives at Swedish National Archives) Stockholm, Sweden (BA)

Aleksander Warma's collection

August Koern's collection

August Rei's collection

Tõnis Kint's collection

Central Archives of the Council of Europe, Strasbourg, France (COCA)
337–343 Committee on European Non-member Countries

Eduskunnan kirjasto (Library of the Finnish Parliament), Helsinki, Finland
Post World War II Foreign Policy Planning. State Department Records of Harley A. Notter, 1939–1945. Bethesda, Maryland. Congressional Information Service, 1987

Eesti kirjandusmuuseum (Estonian Literary Museum), Tartu, Estonia

Eesti ajakirjanduse analüütiline bibliograafia

Eesti rahvusraamatukogu (National Library of Estonia), Tallinn, Estonia (NLE)

Eesti ajakirjanduse analüütiline bibliograafia

Archives F. 3 Eesti Rahvusnõukogu Rootsis

Historical Archives of the European Union, Florence, Italy (HAEU)

PAN/EU International Paneuropean Union

ME Mouvement Européen

Kansallisarkisto (Finnish National Archives), Helsinki, Finland (KA)

Hjalmar J. Procopé's collection

Risto Ryti's collection

Rudolf Holsti's collection

Riigiarhiiv (Estonian State Archives), Tallinn, Estonia (ERA)

ERA 957-13-401. Information from the ministry of foreign affairs to legations

ERA 957-13-404. Correspondence between Estonian legations and foreign states concerning Briand's memorandum on European federal union

ERA 957-13-406. Monthly political review for Estonian legations

ERA 957-13-430, 431, 432. Agriculture conferences in Warsaw and Bucharest

ERA 957-13-441. Political section of the ministry

Riksarkivet (Swedish National Archives), Stockholm, Sweden (RA)

RA UD HP1255 II-IV. Briand's memorandum of the European federative union

Ulkoasiainministeriön arkisto (Archives of the Finnish Ministry for Foreign Affairs), Helsinki, Finland (UM)

UM 15 VII 35. Briand Memorandum concerning the federation of the European states

UM 5 C 12. Legation in Tallinn 1930

Российский государственный военный архив (Russian State Military Archives), Moscow, Russia (RGVA)

554-1-14-51 Correspondence between national sections and the Centre of Paneuropa Union 1927–1936

Newspapers

Austrian:

Paneuropa (Wien) 1924–1935

Estonian:

Eesti Sõna (Berlin/Tallinn) 1942

ERK. Üld-, majandus- ja kultuuripoliitiline ajakiri (Tallinn) 1934

Kaja (Tallinn) 1924–1934

Postimees (Tartu) 1924–1934, 1991–1992

Päevaleht (Tallinn) 1924–1934

Sõdur. Sõjaasjanduse ajakiri (Tallinn) 1927–1934

Vaba Maa (Tallinn) 1924–1934

Ühendus (Tallinn) 1927

Uus Eesti (Tallinn) 1939

German:

Eesti Post (Geislingen) 1948

Der Europäische Osten (München) 1954–1967

Baltisches Handbuch für das Jahr (Danzig) 1929–1931

Swedish:

Baltic Review (Stockholm) 1945–1949

Eesti Teataja (Stockholm) 1948–1953

Eesti Rahvusfondi Teated (Stockholm) 1947–1960
Stockholm-Tidning eestlastele (Stockholm) 1948–1952
Teataja (Stockholm) 1953–1988
Välis-Eesti (Stockholm) 1948–1970
Vaba Eesti (Stockholm/New York) 1952–1964

Printed primary material (including articles from publications other than newspapers listed above)

Assembly of the Captive European Nations. First Session, September 20, 1954-February 11, 1955. Organization, Resolutions, Reports, Debate. Carnegie Endowment International Center, New York, 1955.

Atlantic Charter. 14.8.1941. [http://avalon.law.yale.edu/wwii/atlantic.asp]

Boheman, Erik, *På vakt. Från attaché till sändebud. Minnesanteckningar*, Stockholm, P.A. Norstedt & Söners Förlag, 1963.

Commission of Enquiry for European Union. Minutes of the fourth Session of the Commission. Held at Geneva from September 3 to 5, 1931, Geneva, League of Nations, 1931.

Coudenhove-Kalergi, Richard, *Paneuroopa liit* (Foreword by Kaarel Robert Pusta), Tallinn, J. Zimmerman, 1929.

Coudenhove-Kalergi, Richard, *Paneuroopa ABC*, Tallinn, J. Zimmerman, 1931.

Coudenhove-Kalergi, Richard, *Totaalne riik - totaalne inimene*, (transl. H. Anto. Foreword by Joakim Puhk) Tallinn, Eesti kirjastus-ühistus, 1938.

Den Estniska boken i den fria världen. Bibliografisk översikt 1944–1970, (Ed. Bernard Kangro) Lund, Eesti kirjanike kooperativ, 1971.

Eesti entsüklopeedia, II. (Ed. R. Kleis), Tartu, Loodus, 1933.

Eesti entsüklopeedia, VI. (Ed. R. Kleis), Tartu, Loodus, 1936.

Eesti vabaduse eest II. Eesti Rahvusfond 1946–1956, (Ed. Arnold Peets) Stockholm, ERF, 1956.

Eesti Rahvusfond 1946–51, (Ed. Endel Krepp) Stockholm, ERF, 1952.

Eesti Rahvusnõukogu välispoliitilise tegevuse kroonika, Stockholm, ENC, 1965.

Eestiläinen kirja vapaassa maailmassa. Bibliografinen katsaus v. 1944–1956. (Ed. Bernard Kangro), Stockholm, ERF, 1957.

ERN 1947–1982. Välispoliitilise tegevuse kroonika II 1963–1982, Stockholm, ENC, 1982.

Estonian Information Centre Ten Years. A Refugee Group's Efforts on behalf of their Country, Stockholm, ERF, 1956.

Estonian National Council 1947–1957. Structure and Organisation – Historical Background – Activities, Stockholm, ENC, 1957.

Estonians in the Free World, Stockholm, ENC, 1960.

Baron Hervé de Gruben (Ajax), "A Plan for the International Organization of Europe," in W. Lipgens (ed.), *Documents on the History of European integration. Volume 2. Plans for European Union in Great Britain and in Exile 1939–1945*, Berlin, Walter de Gruyter, 1986 (Originally published in *Belgium* (New York), Vol. II, No. 23, 2.3.1942).

Horm, Arvo, "Kesk ja Ida Euroopa poliitiline taastamine ja selleks rakendatud rahvuslikud ja vahvusvahelised organisatsioonid," in R. Kõrgma (ed.), *Eesti probleeme maailmapoliitika taustal*, ERF, Stockholm, 1958.

Kaasik, Nikolai, *Rahvasteliit*, Tartu, Akadeemilise kooperatiivi kirjastus, Tartu, 1933.

Kant, Edgar, "Euroopa tulevikust," *Postimees* 1.12.1942, p. 4.

Keyserling, Hermann von, *Das Spektrum Europas*, Heidelberg, Kampmann, 1928.

"Käymme omaa erillistä sotaamme". Risto Rytin päiväkirjat, (Eds. Ohto Manninen and Kauko Rumpunen) Helsinki, Edita, 2006.

Laretei, Heinrich, "Iseseisvusaegsest välispoliitikast," in Richard Maasing *et al.* (eds.), *Eesti riik ja rahvas teises maailmasõjas I. Eesti nagu ta oli*, Stockholm, EMP, 1954.

Oras, Ants, *Baltic Eclipse*, London, Victor Gollanz Ltd, 1948.

Orav, Mart and Nõu, Enn (eds.), *Tõotan ustavaks jääda... Eesti vabariigi valitsus 1940–1992*, Tartu, Eesti kirjanduse selts, 2004.

Pekka Peitsi, "Pienet kansat ja Eurooppa," *Suomen Kuvalehti* 1944:6, pp. 168–169.

Piip, Ants, *Nüüdne maailmapolitika ja Eesti*, Tartu, Eesti Kirjanduse Seltsi Kirjastus, 1932.

Ponomarev, Boriss, *Euroopa rahvad Hitleri vastu*, Moscow, ENSV Riiklik Kirjastus, 1943.

Pusta, Kaarel Robert, "Paneuroopa liikumine ja selle lähemad ülesanded," in *Postimees*, 16.8.1929, p. 4 and 17.8.1929, p. 4; reprinted in Hanno Runnel (ed.), *Kontrastide aastasada*, Tartu, Ilmamaa, 2000, pp. 110–118. (Pusta 1929a)

Pusta, Kaarel Robert, "Eessõna," in *Paneuroopa Liit*, Tallinn, Paneuroopa kirjastus, 1929. (Pusta 1929b)

Pusta, Kaarel Robert, *Saadiku päevik*, 2nd edition, Tallinn, Olion, 1992.

Rehabilitation plan of Estonia's economy after liberation. Tendered to the East European Conference, London, on January 21–24, 1952, Stockholm, 1952.

Ruubel, Peeter, "Euroopa panganduse koostöö ja Pan-Euroopa," in Eldor Fählmann (ed.), *Majandusteaduslikud, eriti eramajanduslikud kirjad*, Tartu, 1929, pp. 59–86.

Röpke, Wilhelm, *Die Gesellschaftskrisis der Gegenwart*, Zürich, Erlenbach, 1942.

Tammekann, August, "Euroopa," in August Tammekann and Edgar Kant (eds.), *Maailma maad ja rahvad. Tänapäeva maailm sõnas ja pildis 13. Taga-Euroopa ja vahemeremaad*, Tartu, Loodus, 1932.

Tammekann, August, "Euroopan maantieteellinen suurjako," in *Terra* 1942:1/2, pp. 199–211.

Tõnisson, Jaan, "Euroopa föderatsiooni idee," in *Eesti Üliõpilaste Seltsi album XI*, Tartu, EÜS, 1940, pp. 64–74.

Tõnus, Peeter (ed.), *Vaba Eesti tähistel. Valimik tsensuurivaba eesti mõttelugu aastaist 1948-64*, Tallinn, Eesti Entsüklopeediakirjastus, 2000.

Voionmaa, Väinö, *Kuriiripostia 1941–1946*, Helsinki, Tammi, 1971.

Warma, Aleksander, "Liikumine Euroopa ühendamiseks ja eksiilide osa selles," in Rein Kõrgma (ed.), *Eesti probleeme maailmapoliitika taustal*, Stockholm, ERF, 1958.

Warma, Aleksander, *Diplomaadi kroonika. Ülestähendusi ja dokumente aastatest 1938–44*, Lund, Eesti Kirjanike kooperatiiv, 1971.

Secondary literature

Alenius, Kari, *Ajan ihanteiden ja historian rasitteiden ristipaineissa. Viron etniset suhteet vuosina 1918–1925*, Rovaniemi, Pohjois-Suomen historiallinen yhdistys, 2003.

Ant, Jüri, *August Rei. Eesti riigimees, poliitik, diplomaat*, Tartu, Rahvusarhiiv, 2012.

Arumäe, Heino, *At the Crossroads. The Foreign Policy of the Republic of Estonia in 1933–1939*, (transl. Gustav Liiv) Tallinn, Perioodika, 1983.

Bell, Philip M.H, "Other Contributions 1939–1941. Introduction," in Walter Lipgens (ed.), *Documents on the History of European integration. Volume 2. Plans for European Union in Great Britain and in Exile 1939–1945*, Berlin, Walter de Gruyter, 1986.

Berzins, Valdis, "The Response to the Briand Plan in Latvia," in Antoine Fleury and Lubor Jilek (eds.), *Le Plan Briand d'Union fédérale européenne*, Bern, Peter Lang, 1998.

Boyce, Robert, "Britain's first 'no' to Europe. Britain and the Briand Plan 1929–1930," in *European Studies Review* 1980(10):1, pp. 17–45.

Carlgren, Wilhelm M., *Sverige och Baltikum. Från mellankrigstid till efterkrigsår. En Översikt*, Stockholm, Publica, 1993.

Conway, Martin, "Legacies of Exile. The Exile Governments in London during the Second World War and the Politics of Post-war Europe," in Martin Conway and José Gotovich (eds.), *Europe in Exile. European Exile Communities in Britain 1940–1945*, New York, Berghahn Books, 2001.

Crols, Dirk, "Old and New Minorities on the International Chessboard. From the League to Union", in David Smith (ed.), *Baltic States and their Region. New Europe or Old*, Amsterdam, Rodopi, 2005.

Danytė, Milda, "The Baltic Evening in Parliament. How Canadian Lithuanians and Other Balts Lobbied for Their Homelands During the Cold War Period," in Dalia Kuizinienė (ed.), *Beginnings and Ends of Emigration. Life Without Borders in the Contemporary World*, Vilnius, Versus Aureus, 2005.

Davies, Norman, *Europe. A History*, Oxford, Oxford University Press, 1996.

Delanty, Gerard, *Inventing Europe. Idea, Identity, Reality*, Basingstoke, Macmillan, 1995.

Delanty, Gerard and Rumford, Chris, *Rethinking Europe. Social Theory and the Implications of Europeanization*, Abingdon, Routledge, 2005.

Duchhardt, Heinz, "Der deutsche Europa-Diskurs des 19. und frühen 20. Jahrhunderts," in Wlodzimierz Borodziej *et al.* (eds.), *Option Europa. Deutsche, polnische und ungarische Europapläne des 19. und 20. Jahrhunderts. Band 1. Essays*, Göttingen, Vandenhoeck & Ruprecht, 2005.

Dülffer, Jost, "The History of European Integration. From Integration History to the History of Integrated Europe," in Wilfried Loth (ed.), *Experiencing Europe. 50 years of European Construction 1957-2007*, Baden-Baden, Nomos, 2009.

Elsuwege, Peter van, *From Soviet Republics to EU Member States. A Legal and Political Assessment of the Baltic States' Accession to the EU*, Leiden, Martinus Nijhoff Publishers, 2008.

Fleury, Antoine and Jilek, Lubor (eds.), *Le Plan Briand d'Union fédérale européenne*, Bern, Peter Lang, 1998.

Frank, Robert, "The Meaning of Europe in French National Discourse. A French Europe or an Europeanized France?," in Mikael af Malmborg and Bo Stråth (eds.), *The Meaning of Europe. Variety and Contention Within and Among Nations*, Oxford, Berg, 2002.

Gadomski, Feliks, *Zgromadzenie Europejskich Narodów Ujarzmionych. Krótki zarys*, New York, Bicentennial Publishing Corporation, 1995.

Goddeeris, Idesbald, "Stefan Glaser. Collaborator in European umbrella organisations," in Michel Dumoulin and Idesbald Goddeeris (eds.), *Intégration ou représentation? Les exilés polonais en Belgique et la construction européenne. Integration or Représentation? Polish Exiles in Belgium and the European Construction*, Leuven, Academia Bruylant, 2005.

Gotovich, Jose, "Views of Belgian Exiles on the Postwar Order in Europe. Introduction," in Walter Lipgens (ed.), *Documents on the History of European integration. Volume 2. Plans for European Union in Great Britain and in Exile 1939–1945*, Berlin, Walter de Gruyter, 1986.

Gross, Feliks and Dziewanovski, M. Kamil, "Plans by Exiles from East European Countries. Introduction," in Walter Lipgens (ed.), *Documents on the History of European integration. Volume 2. Plans for European Union in Great Britain and in Exile 1939–1945*, Berlin, Walter de Gruyter, 1986.

Habermas, Jürgen and Derrida, Jacques, "Nach dem Krieg. Die Wiedergeburt Europas," in *Frankfurter Allgemeine Zeitung* 31.5.2003.

Halila, Aimo, *Väinö Voionmaa*, Helsinki, Tammi, 1969.

Hecker-Stampehl, Jan, "Föderationspläne in Nordeuropa im Zweiten Weltkrieg. Ein Überblick," in Imke Sturm-Martin and Jan Hecker-Stampehl (eds.), *Europa im Blick. Westeuropäische Perspektiven im 20. Jahrhundert*, Hamburg, Verlag Dr. Kovac, 2007.

Heikkilä, Pauli, "'Meillä jo nyt on kaksi isänmaata, omamme ja Europa'. Eurooppalaisuus suomalaisessa keskustelussa maailmansotien välisenä aikana," in Laura-Kristiina Moilanen and Susanna Sulkunen (eds.), *Aika ja identiteetti. Katsauksia yksilön ja yhteisön väliseen suhteeseen keskiajalta 2000-luvulle*, Helsinki, SKS, 2006.

Heikkilä, Pauli, "Baltic Council of the European Movement (1948–1950). Regional Exception in Early European Unification", in Olaf Mertelsmann and Kaarel Piirimäe (eds.), *Baltic Sea Region and the Cold War*, Frankfurt am Main, P.I.E. Peter Lang, 2012.

Hick, Alan, "The 'European Movement,'" in Walter Lipgens and Wilfried Loth (eds.), *Documents on the History of European Integration. Volume 4.*

Transnational Organisations of Political Parties and Pressure Groups in the Struggle for European Union, 1945–1950, Berlin, Walter de Gruyter, Berlin, 1990.

Hiden, John and Salmon, Patrick, *The Baltic Nations and Europe. Estonia, Latvia and Lithuania in the Twentieth Century*, London, Longman, 1991.

Hiden, John, *Defender of Minorities. Paul Schiemann, 1876–1944.* London, Hurst & Co, 2004.

Hough, William, "The Annexation of the Baltic States and its Effect on the Development of Law Prohibiting Forcible Seizure of Territory," in *New York Law School Journal of International and Comparative Law* 1985(6):2, pp. 303–533.

Hoyer, Svennik, Lauk, Epp and Vihalemm, Peeter, *Towards a Civic Society. The Baltic Media's Long Road to Freedom. Perspectives on History, Ethnicity, and Journalism*, Tartu, Baltic Association for Media research, 1993.

Janauskas, Giedrius, *Kongresinė aksija. JAV ir Kanados lietuvių politinus lobizmas.* Vilnius, Versus Aureus, 2008.

Jurkynas, Mindaugas, *How Deep is Your Love? The Baltic Brotherhood Re-examined*, Vilnius, Vilnaus universiteto leidykla, 2007.

Kaiser, Wolfram, *Christian Democracy and the Origins of the European Union*, Cambridge, Cambridge University Press, 2007.

Kaiser, Wolfram and Varsori, Antonio (eds.), *European Union History. Themes and Debates*, Basingstoke, Palgrave Macmillan, 2010.

Karjahärm, Toomas, *Unistus Euroopast*, Tallinn, Argo, 2003.

Karlsson, Klas-Göran, "Europe's Eastern Outpost? The Meaning of 'Europe' in Baltic Discourses," in Mikael af Malmborg and Bo Stråth (eds.), *The Meaning of Europe. Variety and Contention Within and Among Nations*, Oxford, Berg, 2002.

Kasekamp, Andres, *The Radical Right in Interwar Estonia*, Basingstoke, Macmillan, 2000.

Kasekamp, Andres, *A History of the Baltic States*, Basingstoke, Palgrave Macmillan, 2010.

Klesment, Johannes, "Kolm aastat iseseisvuse võitlust võõra okupatsiooni all," in Richard Maasing *et al.* (eds.), *Eesti riik ja rahvas II maailmasõjas. Heitluses kahe suurvõimuga*, Stockholm, EMP, 1959.

Kletzin, Birgit, *Europa aus Rasse und Raum. Die nationalsozialistische Idee der Neuen Ordnung*, Münster, LIT, 2000.

Lane, Thomas, *Victims of Stalin and Hitler. The Exodus of Poles and Balts to Britain*, Basingstoke, Palgrave Macmillan, 2004.

Lane, Thomas, "An Historical Epilogue. East Europeans and the European Movement," in Thomas Lane and Elzbieta Stadtmüller (eds.), *Europe on the Move. The Impact of Eastern Enlargement on the European Union*, Münster, LIT, 2005.

Lane, Thomas, "East European Exiles and their Interpretations of the Meaning of Europe," in José Faraldo, Paulina Gulinska-Jurgiel and Christian Domnitz (eds.), *Europa im Ostblock. Vorstellungen und Diskurse (1945–1991)/Europe in the Eastern Bloc. Imaginations and Discourses (1945–1991)*, Köln, Böhlau, 2008.

Łaptos, Jósef and Misztal, Mariusz, *American Debates on Central European Union, 1942–1944. Documents of the American State Department*, Brussels, P.I.E.-Peter Lang, 2002.

Łaptos, Józef, "Visionen des gemeinsamen Europas. Díe ostmitteleuropäische Emigration zu Beginn des Kalten Krieges," in José Faraldo, Paulina Gulinska-Jurgiel and Christian Domnitz (eds.), *Europa im Ostblock. Vorstellungen und Diskurse (1945–1991) Europe in the Eastern Bloc. Imaginations and Discourses (1945–1991)*, Köln, Böhlau, 2008.

Lauk, Epp, "A Sombre Interlude. The Two Occupations from the Summer of 1940 to the Autumn 1944," in Svennik Hoyer, Epp Lauk and Peeter Vihalemm (eds.), *Towards a Civic Society. The Baltic Media's Long Road to Freedom. Perspectives on History, Ethnicity, and Journalism*, Tartu, Baltic Association for Media research, 1993.

Lehti, Marko, *A Baltic League as a Construct of the New Europe. Envisioning a Baltic Region and Small State Sovereignty in the Aftermath of the First World War*, Bern, P.I.E.-Peter Lang, 1999.

Lévy, Marie-Francoise and Sicard, Marie-Noële, "Culture in the Public Sphere as an Issue of European Construction. Missions and Experiences," in Wilfried Loth (ed.), *Experiencing Europe. 50 years of European Construction 1957–2007*, Baden-Baden, Nomos, 2009.

Lilja, Pekka and Raig, Kulle, *Urho Kekkonen ja Viro*, Hämeenlinna, Minerva, 2006.

Lipgens, Walter, "Europäische Einigungsidee 1923–1930 und Briands Europaplan im Urteil der deutschen Akten (2. Teil)," in *Historische Zeitschrift* 1966(203):2, 316–363.

Lipgens, Walter, "Plans of the Other Transnational Groups for European Union. Introduction," in Walter Lipgens (ed.), *Documents on the History of European integration. Volume 2. Plans for European Union in Great Britain and in Exile 1939–1945*, Berlin, Walter de Gruyter, 1986.

Loth, Wilfried, "Europäische Identität und europäisches Bewusstsein," in Reiner Marcowitz (ed.), *Nationale Identität und transnationale Einflüsse. Amerikanisierung, Europäisierung und Globalisierung in Frankreich nach dem Zweiten Weltkrieg*, München, Oldenburg, 2007.

Lukasiewicz, Slawomir, *Trzecia Europa*, Cracow, IPN, 2010.

Macher, Anikó, "Une institution pour promouvoir l'idée de l'unité européenne. La Commission de l'Europe centrale et orientale du Mouvement Européen (1948–1953)," in Jean-Michel Guieu, Christophe Le Dréau (eds.), *Publication des Actes du Colloque sur le Congrès de La Haye (1948-2008) - Proceedings of the Symposium on The Hague Congress (1948-2008)*, Brussels, P.I.E.-Peter Lang, 2009.

Made, Vahur, *Külalisena maailmapoliitikas. Eesti ja Rahvasteliit 1919-1946*, Tartu, Tartu ülikooli kirjastus, 1999.

Made, Vahur, "*Estonian Government-in-Exile. A Controversial Project of State Continuation*," in John Hiden, Vahur Made, David Smith (eds.), *Baltic Question during the Cold War*. Abingdon, Routledge, 2008.

Mans, G.M.V., "Ideas of Netherlands Exiles on the Postwar International Order. Introduction," in Walter Lipgens (ed.), *Documents on the History of European integration. Volume 2. Plans for European Union in Great Britain and in Exile 1939–1945*, Berlin, Walter de Gruyter, 1986.

Mark, Eduard, "History and Significance of the Records of Harley A. Notter, 1939–1945," in *Post World War II Foreign Policy Planning, 1939–1945*, Bethesda (MD), Congressional Information Service, 1987.

Mazover, Mark, *Dark Continent. Europe's Twentieth Century*, St. Ives, Penguin Books, 1999.

Mazurkiewicz, Anna, "The Voice of the Silenced Peoples. The Assembly of Captive European Nations," in Ieva Zaķe (ed.), *Anti-Communist Minorities in the U.S. Political Activism of Ethnic Refugees*, New York, Palgrave Macmillan, 2009.

Medijainen, Eero, "Eesti Pan-Euroopa ühingu ajaloost," in *Postimees*, 14.9.1991.

Medijainen, Eero, *Saadiku saatus. Välisministeerium ja saatkonnad 1918–1940*, Tallinn, Eesti Entsüklopeedia-kirjastus, 1997.

Messenger, David A., "Dividing Europe. The Cold War and European Integration," in Desmond Dinan (ed.), *Origins and Evolution of the European Union*, Oxford, Oxford University Press, 2006.

Milward, Alan, *The reconstruction of Western Europe 1945–51*, London, Methuen, 1984.

Milward, Alan, "Conclusions. The Value of History," in Alan Milward *et al.* (eds.), *The Frontier of National Sovereignty. History and Theory 1945–1992*, Padstow, Routledge, 1994.

Mikkeli, Heikki, *Europe as an Idea and an Identity*, Basingstoke, Macmillan, 1998.

Minkkinen, Aimo, "Leninin ja Stalinin riita Neuvostoliiton perustamisesta," in *Idäntutkimus* 2005:2, pp. 3–14.

Misiunas, Romuald J. and Taagepera, Rein, *The Baltic States. Years of Dependence, 1940–1980*, London, Hurst, 1983.

Charles-Louis de Sedondat de Montesquieu, *Oeuvres Complétes I*. Paris, Bibliothèque de la Pléiade, 1949.

Mulla, Triin *et al.* (eds.), *Eesti välisteenistus. Biograafiline leksikon 1918–1991*, Tallinn, Estonian Ministry of Foreign Affairs, 2006.

Myllyniemi, Seppo, *Die Neuordnung der Baltischen Länder 1941–1944. Zum nationalsozialistischen Inhalt der deutschen Besatzungspolitik*, Helsinki, SHS, 1973.

Mälksoo, Lauri, "The Government of Otto Tief and the Attempt to Restore the Independence of Estonia in 1944. A Legal Appraisal," in Toomas Hiio, Meelis Maripuu and Indrek Paavle (eds.), *Estonia 1940–1945. Reports of the Estonian International Commission for the Investigation of Crimes Against Humanity*, Tallinn, EICICAH, 2006.

Mälksoo, Lauri, *Rahvusvaheline õigus Eestis. Ajalugu ja poliitika*, Tallinn, Juura, 2008.

Nerman, Birger, *För Balticums frihet. Baltiska kommittén 1943–1968*, Stockholm, Baltiska kommittén, 1969.

Neumann, Iver B., *Uses of the Other. "The East" in European Identity Formation*, Manchester, Manchester University Press, 1999.

Nielsen, Henning, "Views of Danish Exiles on the Future of Europe. Introduction, "in Walter Lipgens (ed.), *Documents on the History of European integration. Volume 2. Plans for European Union in Great Britain and in Exile 1939–1945*, Berlin, Walter de Gruyter, 1986.

Paavle, Indrek, "Repressions by Soviet Security Agencies Against Underground Estonian National Opposition Operating during German Occupation," in Toomas Hiio, Meelis Maripuu, Indrek Paavle (eds.), *Estonia since 1944. Reports of the Estonian International Commission for the Investigation of Crimes Against Humanity*, Tallinn, EICICAH, 2010.

Pagden, Anthony, "Introduction," in Anthony Padgen (ed.), *The Idea of Europe. From Antiquity to the European Union*, Washington, DC &

New York, Woodrow Wilson Center & Cambridge University Press, 2002.

Pagden, Anthony (ed.), *The Idea of Europe. From Antiquity to the European Union*, Washington, DC & New York, Woodrow Wilson Center & Cambridge University Press, 2002.

Palayret, Jean Marie, "Eduquer les jeunes à l'union. La Campagne européenne de la jeunesse 1951–1958," in *Journal of European Integration History* 1995(1):2, pp. 47–60.

Palk, Paavo, *Euroopa ühendamise lugu*, Tallinn, Tuum, 1999.

Passerini, Luisa, "The Last Identification. Why Some of Us Would Like to Call Ourselves Europeans and What We Mean by This," in Bo Stråth (ed.), *Europe and the Other and Europe as the Other*, Brussels, P.I.E.-Peter Lang, 2004.

Paul, Ina Ulrike, "Einigung für einen Kontinent von Feinden? R.N. Coudenhove-Kalergis "Paneuropa" und K.A. Rohans Reich über Nationen als konkurrierende Europaprojekte der Zwischenkriegszeit," in Heinz Duchhardt and István Németh (eds.), *Der Europa-Gedanke in Ungarn und Deutschland in der Zwischenkriegszeit*, Mainz, Institut für Europäische Geschichte, 2005.

Pegg, Carl H., *Evolution of the European Idea, 1914–1932*, Chapel Hill, The University North Carolina Press, 1983.

Pihlamägi, Maie, *Väikeriik maailmaturul. Eesti väliskaubandus 1918–1940*, Tallinn, Argo, 2004.

Pihlau, Jaak, "Lisandusi ja täpsustusi Tõnis Ritsoni artiklile 'Toomas Hellat ja KGB'," in *Tuna* 2001:1, pp. 136–142.

Raig, Ivar, *Eesti tee Euroopa Liitu. Unistus paremast Euroopast*, Tallinn, Audentes University, 2008.

Raik, Kristi, *Democratic Politics or the Implementation of Inevitabilities? Estonia's Democracy and Integration into the European Union*, Tartu, Tartu University Press, 2003.

Raun, Toivo, *Estonia and the Estonians*, 2nd edition, Palo Alto, Hoover Institution Press, 1991.

Rebattet, F.X., *The "European Movement" 1945–1953. A Study in National and International Non-Governmental Organisations Working for European Unity*, Oxford, St. Anthony's College, 1962.

Renouvin, Pierre and Duroselle, Jean-Baptiste, *Introduction to the History of International Relations*, (transl. Mary Ilford) Oxford, Pall Mall Press, 1967.

Ristikivi, Karl, *Inimese teekond*, Lund, Eesti kirjanike kooperatiiv, 1972.

Ruutsoo, Rein, "Rahvusriik, identiteet ja Euroopa Liit", in *Eesti ja Euroopa Liit* 16 (October 2000).

Schmale, Wolfgang, *Geschiche Europas*, Wien, Böhlau, 2001.

Shore, Cris, *Building Europe. The Cultural Politics of European Integration*, Abingdon, Routledge, 2000.

Smith, Anthony D., "National Identity and the Idea of European Unity," in *International Affairs* 1992(68):1, pp. 55–76.

Smith, Bradley F., *The Shadow Warriors. O.S.S. and the Origins of the CIA*, New York, Basic Books, 1983.

Smith, David, "Retracing Estonia's Russians. Mikhail Kurchinskii and Interwar Cultural Autonomy," in *Nationalities Papers* 1999(27):3, pp. 455–474.

Smith, David, *Estonia. Independence and European integration*, Abingdon, Routledge, 2002.

Spiering, Manno, "Engineering Europe. The European Idea in Interbellum Literature. The Case of Paneuropa," in Manno Spiering and Michael Wintle (eds.), *Ideas of Europe since 1914. The Legacy of the First World War*, Basingstoke, Palgrave Macmillan, 2002.

Stobart, Maitland, "Fifty Years of European Cooperation on History Textbooks. The Role and Contribution of the Council of Europe," in *Internationale Schulbuchforschung/International Textbook Research* 1999(21), pp. 147–161.

Streikus, Arūnas, *Diplomatas Stasys Antanas Bačkis*, Vilnius, The Genocide and Resistance Research Centre of Lithuania, 2007.

Stråth, Bo, "Multiple Europes. Integration, Identity and Demarcation to the Other," in Bo Stråth (ed.), *Europe and the Other and Europe as the Other*, Brussels, P.I.E.-Peter Lang, 2000.

Tamm, Marek, "Pariis – Iowa City. Aleksander Aspeli võõrsiloleku aastad (1938–1975)," in *Keel ja Kirjandus* 1998:7, pp. 467–477.

Tamman, Tiina, *The Last Ambassador. August Torma, Soldier, Diplomat, Spy*, Amsterdam, Rodopi, 2011.

Tammaru, Tiit, Kumer-Haukanõmm, Kaja and Anniste, Kristi, "The Formation and Development of the Estonian Diaspora," in *Journal of Ethnic and Migration Studies* 2010(36):7, pp. 1157–1174.

Trunk, Achim, *Europa, ein Ausweg. Politische Eliten und europäische Identität in den 1950er Jahren*, München, Oldenburg, 2007.

Tully, James, "The Kantian idea of Europe. Critical and Cosmopolitan Perspectives," in Anthony Padgen (ed.), *The Idea of Europe. From*

Antiquity to the European Union, Washington, DC & New York, Woodrow Wilson Center & Cambridge University Press, 2002.

Undusk, Jaan, "Eesti kui Belgia. Viimne baltlane Hermann Keyserling," in *Tuna* 2003:2, pp. 48–71.

Valenta, Jaroslav, "Mitteleuropäische Föderationspläne in der Kriegszeit 1939–1945. Der Versuch einer polnish-tschechoslovakischen (Kon-)Föderation," in Richard Plaschka *et al.* (eds.), *Mitteleuropa-Konzeptionen in der ersten Hälfte des 20. Jahrhunderts*, Wien, Verlag der Österreichischen Akademie der Wissenschaften, 1995.

Valmas, Anne, *Eestlaste kirjastustegevus välismaal 1944–2000. I osa.* Tallinn, Tallinna Pedagoogikaülikooli kirjastus, 2003.

Viivik, Allar, "Euroopa Liidu hümn sai eestikeelse tõlke juba sügaval nõukogude ajal," in *Õhtuleht* 11.2.2008 [http://www.ohtuleht.ee/266182].

Vilpišauskas, Ramūnas, "Regional Integration in Europe. Analysing Intra-Baltic Economic Cooperation in the Context of European Integration," in Vello Pettai and Jan Zielonka (eds.), *The Road to the European Union. Volume 2. Estonia, Latvia and Lithuania*, Manchester, Manchester University Press, 2003.

Voigt, Klaus, "Ideas of German exiles on the Postwar Order in Europe. Introduction," in Walter Lipgens (ed.), *Documents on the History of European integration. Volume 2. Plans for European Union in Great Britain and in Exile 1939–1945*, Berlin, Walter de Gruyter, 1986.

Wilford, Hugh, *The CIA, the British Left and the Cold War. Calling the Tune?* London, Frank Cass, 2003.

Woolf, Stuart, "Europe and its Historians," in *Contemporary European History* 2003(12):3, pp. 323–337.

Ziegerhofer-Prettenthaler, Anita, *Botschafter Europas. Richard Nicolaus Coudenhove-Kalergi und die Paneuropa-Bewegung in den zwanziger- und dreissiger Jahren*, Wien, Böhlau, 2004.

Zgorniak, Marian, "Föderativa Konzeptionen der polnischen Emigrationregierung in London während des Zweiten Weltkrieges," in Richard Plaschka *et al.* (eds.), *Mitteleuropa-Konzeptionen in der ersten Hälfte des 20. Jahrhunderts*, Wien, Verlag der Österreichischen Akademie der Wissenschaften, Wien 1995.

Location (town) index

A
Athens 51
Augustdorf 119

B
Basel 77
Berlin 40, 78n, 149, 163
Bonn 163
Bruges 146
Brussels 159, 161
Bucharest 51
Budapest 158
Bulduri 67–69

C
Caen 158
Copenhagen 65, 143, 163

D
Darmstadt 21

F
Florence 14, 99

G
Geneva 34, 41, 75, 76, 83, 170, 173

H
Haapsalu 27
Hamburg 111, 134, 136
Helsinki 38, 41, 97, 101, 105, 107, 113, 119

I
Interlaken 124

K
Karlsruhe 79
Kaunas 50, 69, 72, 81
Kehl 79
Kiel 79

L
Lausanne 129
Leningrad 97, 172
Linköping 165
Locarno 34, 50
London 27, 39, 54, 101–102, 114, 120, 126–128, 131, 134–139, 142, 145, 150–154, 158, 171–172, 179–180, 188–189
Lund 150

M
Madrid 148
Messina 174
Moscow 14, 42, 91, 105, 109–110, 149
Munich 159
New York, NY 78, 101, 110, 148

O
Oslo 57, 119

P
Paris 21, 26, 33, 40, 42, 47, 54, 56, 76, 79, 122, 127, 130, 135, 139, 142, 156, 165
Prague 151
Potsdam 136

R
Riga 28, 37, 50, 56, 67, 69
Rio de Janeiro 147
Rome 134, 149, 158, 163–164

S
Stockholm 17, 26, 39, 76, 79, 81, 97, 101, 107, 117, 121, 123, 125–128, 130, 134–136, 142, 154, 164, 167, 170, 174
Strasbourg 19, 79, 128, 137, 142, 154, 167–169, 183

T
Tallinn 15, 17, 26–28, 35, 69, 71, 77, 79, 92–93, 101, 125
Tartu 15, 26, 50, 64, 80, 121, 171
The Hague 18, 52, 120-123, 134, 154, 159

V
Vienna 27, 46, 52, 67, 77–78
Vilnius 69, 81

W
Warsaw 26, 51, 69, 81
Washington, DC 106, 108–109, 113–114

Y
Yalta 136, 161, 177

Personal index

(years of living; nationality if not Estonian)

A

Alver, Hans (1887–1942), 27

Aspel, Aleksander (1908–1975), 135, 156

Ast, Karl (1886–1971), 27, 92, 147, 157

Auer, Pál (Paul) (1885–1978; Hungarian), 138, 154

B

Bačkis, Stasys (1906–1999; Lithuanian), 130, 135, 154–155

Beethoven, Ludwig van (1770–1827; German), 156

Berģis, Pēteris (1863–?; Latvian), 28, 69, 73

Bērziņš, Valdis (1935–; Latvian), 37

Blum, Léon (1872–1950; French), 120

Bonaparte, Napoleon (1769–1821; French), 62, 63

Briand, Aristide (1862–1932; French), 16, 17, 33–36, 38–43, 47, 50, 52–53, 56, 65, 77

Brugmans, Hendrik (1906–1997; Dutch), 146

Bukss, Mikelis (1912–1977; Latvian), 126, 128

Burlandt, Louis (1881–?; Baltic German), 28

Bøgholm, Karl (1898–1976; Danish), 125

C

Caillaux, Joseph (1863–1944; French), 82

Churchill, Winston (1874–1965; British), 120, 122, 149

Cicconardi, Vincenzo (1889–?; Italian), 98

Cosme, Henry (1885–1952; French), 35, 40

Coudenhove-Kalergi, Richard (1894–1972; Austrian), 14–16, 26, 28, 32–36, 42–43, 45, 48–50, 59–62, 62, 65–66, 71, 77–79, 86, 110–111, 124

Curtius, Julius (1877–1948; German), 52

Čakste, Mintauts (1893–1962; Latvian), 126, 128–129

D

Dautry, Raoul (1880–1951; French), 124–125

Davies, Norman (1939–; British), 14, 27n

De Gasperi, Alcide (1881–1954; Italian), 120

de Gaulle, Charles (1890–1970; French), 170, 175–176

de Gruben, Hervé (1894–1967; Belgian), 99, 101–102, 104, 114

de Rougemont, Denis (1906–1985; Swiss), 143

Derrida, Jacques (1930–2004; French), 87
Deutsch, Otto (Dutch, Oswald) (1894–1983; Austrian), 26, 71, 85
Dickson, James (1899–1980; Swedish), 123
Dostoevsky, Fyodor (1821–1881; Russian), 61
Drummond, Eric (1876–1951; British), 41
Dülffer, Jost (1943–; German), 12, 19n

F
Fisher, Herbert A.L. (1865–1940; British), 99

G
Gafencu, Grigore (1892–1958; Romanian), 122, 154
Gensher, Hans Dietrich (1927–; German), 166
Girault, René (1929–1999; French), 19
Grosvalds, Olgerds (1884–1962; Latvian), 128

H
Habermas, Jürgen (1929–; German), 87
Habsburg, Otto von (1912–2011; Austrian), 14, 79–80, 165
Hallstein, Walter (1901–1982; German), 165
Haman, Artur (1897–1942), 27
Hellat, Alexander (1881–1943), 38, 41
Herder, Johann Gottfried (1744–1803; German), 20
Helbemäe, Gert (1913–1974), 134n
Hindrey, Karl August (1875–1947), 33, 70
Hitler, Adolf (1889–1945; German), 80, 82, 91, 109
Holsti, Rudolf (1881–1945; Finn), 110–111
Hopper, Bruce (1893–1973; American), 107
Horm, Arvo (1913–1996), 18, 79, 119, 121–123, 133–134, 144, 149, 159–160, 162–165, 169, 173–174
Hull, Cordell (1871–1955; American), 97
Hynninen, Paavo Juhani (1883–1960; Finn), 37

I
Inglist, Endel (1906–1945), 94
Ilves, Toomas Hendrik (1953–), 191n

J
Jakobson, Evald (1903–1973), 131, 134n
Johanson, Voldemar (1900–1942), 78
Princess Juliana (1909–2004; Dutch), 122

K
Kaasik, Nikolai (1900–1950), 33, 43, 93, 131–132
Kaiv, Johannes (1897–1965), 111
Kaljot, Philipp (1891–1942), 65
Kallas, Oskar (1868–1946), 27, 39
Kalniņš, Brūno (1899–1990; Latvian), 128
Kangro, Bernard (1910–1994), 145
Kann, Peeter (1883–1943), 27, 66
Kant, Immanuel (1724–1804; German), 20

Kant, Edgar (1902–1978), 81, 93, 95, 113
Karjahärm, Toomas (1944–), 15–16, 33
Kasekamp, Andres (1966–), 92
Kekkonen, Urho (1900–1986; Finn), 106–107
Kerem, August (1889–1942), 27, 51
Kerstens, Pieter (Piet) (1896–1958; Dutch), 122
Keyserling, Hermann von (1880–1946; Baltic German), 21
Kint, Tõnis (1896–1991), 119, 157–158, 171, 165
Kirk, Peter (1928–1977; British), 141
Klesment, Johannes (1896–1967), 107
Knatchbull-Hugessen, Hughe (1886–1971; British), 125
Koern, August (1900–1989), 163–164
Kotsar, Valter (1903–1977), 160
Krivickas, Jean (1914–; Lithuanian), 128
Kristelstein, Jakob (1889–1969), 27, 92
Kurchinskii, Mikhail (1876–1939; Russian, Estonian), 49–50

L

Laaman, Eduard (1888–1941), 76
la Vallée-Poussin, Étienne de (1903–1996; Belgian), 139–140, 143
Laid, Eerik (1904–1961), 95
Laidoner, Johan (1884–1953), 27, 32, 49, 60, 62, 70, 87
Lanskoronskis, Juozas (1893–1980; Lithuanian), 18, 122–123
Laretei, Heinrich (1892–1973), 19, 84, 97, 151, 162, 167–170, 186
Lattik, Aldo (1912–1983), 153–154
Lattik, Jaan (1878–1967), 40–41
Law, Richard (1901–1980; British), 139
Léger, Alexis (1887–1975; French), 47–48
Lemberg, Adelaida (1904–1986), 134n
Lilienfeld-Toal, Hans-Paul (1897–?; Baltic German), 15
Lindhagen, Carl (1860–1946; Swedish), 81
Linnuste, Vahur (1925–), 146, 156, 168
Lipgens, Walter (1925–1984; German), 50
Lozoraitis, Stasys (1898–1983; Lithuanian), 141
Luikmil (Luikmel), Johannes (1895–1974), 27, 92

M

MacMillan, Harold (1894–1986; British), 135–136, 139
Madariaga, Salvador de (1886–1978; Spanish), 147
Mark, Aksel (1913–), 149
Mark, Heinrich (1911–2004), 79
Maurer, Alfred (1888–1954), 93, 119
McClintock, Robert (1909–1976; American), 97–99, 107
Michelson, Philip (Mihelsons, Filips) (1878–1938; Latvian), 15, 28, 69, 73
Mihkelson, Johannes (1907–1992), 128, 140, 151, 158, 165, 176–177

Mikiver, Ilmar (1920–2010), 134n
Milward, Alan (1935–2010; British), 13, 19, 117
Montesquieu, Charles-Louis de Secondat (1689–1755; French), 87
Muld, William (1914–1984), 160, 162–163, 191
Mäe, Hjalmar (1901–1978), 92–93
Mäll, Linnart (1938–2010), 80

N
Naumann, Friedrich (1860–1919; German), 63

O
Oiderman, Hans (1891–1941), 81
Oras, Ants (1900–1982), 93, 95
Ots, Jaan (1908–1982), 95

P
Paasikivi, Juho Kusti (1870–1956; Finn), 105
Pakštas, Kazys (1893–1960; Lithuanian), 17, 102
Pegg, Carl H. (1905–1995; British), 14
Perlitz, Harald (1889–1973), 124, 134n
Piip, Ants (1884–1942), 26–28, 41, 43, 46, 60–62, 69, 70, 76, 80–81
Pitka, Johan (1872–1944?), 93–94
Plato (424BC–348BC; Greek), 98
Poom, Eduard (1902–1986), 134, 154, 171–173
Procopé, Hjalmar (1889–1954; Finn), 38, 125–126, 128
Proudhon, Pierre-Joseph (1809–1865; French), 146, 151
Puhk, Joakim (Joachim) (1888–1942), 27, 49, 72, 78
Purre, Helene (1906–1977), 134n
Pusta, Kaarel Robert (1883–1964), 14, 26–27, 29, 31, 34–35, 42, 45–50, 56, 60–62, 64–66, 68–69, 71–72, 76–79, 85, 92, 103, 111, 131, 137, 148, 156–157, 161–162, 168, 174, 187, 189–190
Päts, Konstantin (1874–1956), 28, 82, 94, 100

R
Ramadier, Paul (1888–1961; French), 122
Ramel, Fredrik (1872–1947; Swedish), 39
Raud, Märt (1878–1952), 27, 61
Raud, Villibald (1898–1982), 127, 150
Rebane, Hans (1881–1961), 33, 46, 48, 125
Rebattet, Georges (1907–1976; French), 128, 130
Retinger, Joseph (Józef) (1888–1960; Polish), 125–129, 135, 150
Rei, August (1886–1963), 97, 119, 123, 125–131, 133–136, 141, 147–150, 152, 154–159, 169, 172, 188
Reigo, Juhan (1906–1945), 94
Renouvin, Pierre (1893–1974; French), 19
Reutersvärd, Carl (1885–1963; Swedish), 37
Ridala, Esmo (1923–1988), 161
Ristikivi, Karl (1912–1977), 11
Rohan, Karl Anton (1898–1975; German), 25
Rosenberg, Alfred (1893–1946; German), 92

Roosevelt, Franklin D. (1882–1945; American), 107
Ruubel, Peeter (1885–1957), 48
Ryti, Risto (1889–1956; Finn), 94, 106, 109
Ränk, Gustav (1902–1998), 160
Röpke, Wilhelm (1899–1966; German), 99–100

S
Saareste, Andrus (1892–1964), 146
Sandys, Duncan (1908–1987; British), 120, 122, 126–128, 131
Schendel, Robert van (?–2001; Belgian), 161
Schiller, Friedrich (1759–1805; German), 156
Schmidt, August (1895–1971), 35, 37–41, 76–77 (see also Torma, August)
Schnitker, Paul (1927–; German), 165
Schoenfeld, H. F. Arthur (1889–1952; American), 97–98, 107
Selter, Karl (1898–1958), 129
Shakespeare, William (1564–1616; British), 99
Sidzikauskas, Vaclovas (1893–1973; Lithuanian), 128–129
Sikkar, Johannes (1897–1960), 119, 128, 171
Sirk, Väino (1942–), 16
Sivers, Fanny (de) (1920–2011), 165, 191
Skrzyński, Aleksander (1882–1931; Polish), 69
Spaak, Paul-Henri (1899–1972; Belgian), 120, 149, 170
Stalin, Josef (1878–1953; Georgian), 105, 109–110, 154
Strandman, Otto (1875–1941), 69
Suits, Gustav (1883–1956), 28, 144, 149, 190
Sörgel, Herman (1885–1952; German), 26

T
Tammekann, August (1894–1959), 11, 61, 64, 161
Tammer, Harald (1899–1942), 33, 36, 43, 46, 48–49, 53–55, 61–66, 70, 78, 82
Tarto, Enn (1938–), 80
Terras, Aleksander (1920–2006), 163–165
Tofer, Karl (1885–1942), 51
Torma, August (1895–1971), 120–121, 123–125, 134–135, 139, 154–157 (see also Schmidt, August)
Tubin, Eino (1942–), 146–147, 153
Tõnisson, Heldur (1912–), 125
Tõnisson, Jaan (1868–1941?), 14, 27, 31–32, 35–36, 46, 49, 60–62, 65, 75–77, 85, 91, 103, 113, 125, 189–190
Tõrvand, Juhan (1883–1942), 27

U
Uluots, Jüri (1890–1945), 93
Uustalu, Evald (1912–1982), 131, 134n

V
Vahter, Leonhard (1896–1983), 91
Valk, Heinz (1936–), 80n
Virgo, Eduard (1878–1938), 37

Viirlaid, Arved (1922–), 134n
Viirsoo, Osvald (1901–1989), 150
Voionmaa, Väinö (1869–1947; Finn), 102, 105–106

W

Warma, Aleksander (1890–1970), 17, 19, 97–109, 111, 113–114, 117, 119, 121, 125–126, 128, 133–139, 141–142, 144–148, 150–152, 155–163, 168–176, 179–180, 185, 187, 189–190
Wistrand, Karl (1889–1974; Swede), 140
Wuorimaa, Aarne (1892–1975; Finn), 37, 39–40

Z

Zeeland, Paul van (1893–1973; Dutch), 174
Ziegerhofer-Prettenthaler, Anita (1965–; Austrian), 14
Žilinskas, Vladas (1912–; Lithuanian), 126
Žymantas, Stasys (1908–1973; Lithuanian), 126

'Multiple Europes'

The series 'Multiple Europes' is multiple in two ways: it understands Europe in an interdisciplinary manner with a strong historical perspective, and it understands Europe as being inserted in transnational and global contexts. On both levels, the perspectives on Europe and the very role and understanding of Europe is multiple. The special emphasis of the series thus lies in understanding the pasts of Europe as well as its complex present.

The history of Europe and the history of European integration have influenced each other in the past and will continue to do so in the future. There is an inbuilt tension in the relation between European history and the history of European integration. Europe signifies a space and semantics much broader and more complex than the EU. The relations between ideas of Europe, European history, global history and European integration need to be faced more openly. In order to do this, an open dialogue between academic disciplines is just as necessary as critical self-reflection within each discipline. Furthermore, European history was preoccupied with looking at itself and needs to be connected to global relations.

Series Editor: **Hagen Schulz-Forberg**,
Associate Professor for Global and European History

Series Titles

Estonians for Europe. National Activism for European Unification since the 1920s until the End of the Cold War, Pauli Heikkilä, No.54, 2014

Zero Hours. Conceptual Insecurities and New Beginnings in the Interwar Period, Hagen SCHULZ-FORBERG (ed.), No.53, 2013

Globalisation vs Europeanisation. A Human-centric Interaction, Léonce BEKEMANS, No. 52, 2013

The Space of Crisis. Images and Ideas of Europe in the Age of Crisis: 1914–1945, Vittorio DINI & Matthew D'AURIA (eds.), No.51, 2013

EU Enlargement. Current Challenges and Strategic Choices, Finn LAURSEN (ed.), No.50, 2013

Cosmopolitanisms in Enlightenment Europe and Beyond, Mónica GARCÍA-SALMONES and Pamela SLOTTE (eds.), No.49, 2013

The European Public Sphere. From Critical Thinking to Responsible Action, Luciano MORGANTI & Léonce BEKEMANS (eds.), No.48, 2012

Intercultural Dialogue and Multi-level Governance in Europe. A Human Rights Based Approach, Léonce BEKEMANS (ed.), No.47, 2012

Imagining Europe as a Global Player. The Ideological Construction of a New European Identity within the EU, Christoffer KØLVRAA, No.46, 2012

Capital City Cultures. Reconstructing Contemporary Europe in Vienna and Berlin, Monika DE FRANTZ, No.45, 2011

Building a European Public Sphere. From the 1950s to the Present/Un espace public européen en construction. Des années 1950 à nos jours, Robert FRANK, Hartmut KAELBLE, Marie-Françoise LÉVY & Luisa PASSERINI (eds./dir.), No.44, 2010

'We belong to them'. Narratives of Belonging, Homeland and Nationhood in Territorial and Non-territorial Minority Settings, Tünde PUSKÁS, No.43, 2008

Imagining Europe. Europe and European Civilisation as Seen from its Margins and by the Rest of the World, in the Nineteenth and Twentieth Centuries, Michael WINTLE (ed.), No.42, 2008

Figures of Authority. Contributions towards a Cultural History of Governance from the Seventeenth to the Twentieth Century, Peter BECKER & Rüdiger VON KROSIGK (eds.), No.41, 2008

Europe and the Historical Legacies in the Balkans, Raymond DETREZ & Barbara SEGAERT (eds.), No.40, 2008

Histoire économique et sociale de la construction européenne, René LEBOUTTE, n° 39, 2008

Collective Traumas. Memories of War and Conflict in 20th-Century Europe, Conny MITHANDER, John SUNDHOLM & Maria HOLMGREN TROY (eds.), No.38, 2007

Reflections on Europe. Defining a Political Order in Time and Space, Hans-Åke PERSSON & Bo STRÅTH (eds.), No.37, 2007

London – Berlin. Authenticity, Modernity, and the Metropolis in Urban Travel Writing from 1851 to 1939, Hagen SCHULZ-FORBERG, No.36, 2006

(Un)Doing Europe. Discourses and Practices of Negotiating the EU Constitution, Michał KRZYŻANOWSKI & Florian OBERHUBER, No.35, 2007

Developing Cultural Identity in the Balkans. Convergence vs Divergence, Raymond DETREZ & Pieter PLAS (eds.), No.34, 2005

Statehood Before and Beyond Ethnicity. Minor States in Northern and Eastern Europe, 1600–2000, Linas ERIKSONAS & Leos MÜLLER (eds.), No.33, 2005